To Will

The Good, The Bad and The Multiplex

The glasses are classic
Rayban Wayfarers
with the sunglasses lenses
knocked out –

MARK KERMODE

THE GOOD, THE BAD AND THE MULTIPLEX

WHAT'S WRONG WITH MODERN MOVIES?

BOOKS

Published by Random House Books 2011
8 10 9 7

Copyright © Mark Kermode 2011

Mark Kermode has asserted his right under the Copyright, Designs and Patents Act, 1988,
to be identified as the author of this work

Lyrics from 'Waiting for the Great Leap Forwards' reproduced by kind permission of Billy Bragg

First published in Great Britain in 2011 by
Random House Books
Random House, 20 Vauxhall Bridge Road,
London SW1V 2SA

www.randomhouse.co.uk

Addresses for companies within The Random House Group Limited can be found at:
www.randomhouse.co.uk/offices.htm

The Random House Group Limited Reg. No. 954009

A CIP catalogue record for this book
is available from the British Library

ISBN 9781847946034

The Random House Group Limited supports The Forest Stewardship Council (FSC®), the
leading international forest certification organisation. Our books carrying the FSC label are printed
on FSC® certified paper. FSC is the only forest certification scheme endorsed by the leading
environmental organisations, including Greenpeace. Our paper procurement policy can be found at
www.randomhouse.co.uk/environment

MIX
Paper from
responsible sources
FSC
www.fsc.org   FSC® C016897

Set in Perpetua 13/16.75 pt
Typeset by Palimpsest Book Production Limited, Falkirk, Stirlingshire
Printed and bound by CPI Group
(UK) Ltd, Croydon, CR0 4YY

CONTENTS

'Everyone gets armbands and 3-D glasses'
Elvis Costello, 'Night Rally'

Prologue

'WOULD THE LAST PROJECTIONIST PLEASE TURN OFF THE LIGHTS . . .'

A long time ago in a galaxy far, far away, the most important person in a cinema was the projectionist . . .

Back then, it was the projectionist who conjured the magic of cinema, producing dazzling lights and wondrous apparitions from reels of celluloid and complex machines built from dizzying, spinning wheels and whirring cogs. It was a job that required skill and precision, and it involved no small degree of expertise, not only because to many the cinema was a sacred place, as hallowed as a church, but also because in its earliest days film was dangerous, incendiary, explosive.

Literally.

Listen . . .

When moving pictures were first exhibited in the 1890s – initially through the end-of-the-pier peep-show Kinetoscopes and later via the miracle of public projection – the greatest risk they presented was as a fire hazard. Early film was made by dissolving cotton waste in nitric acid (and a bit of sulphuric acid) to which was added a plasticiser like alcohol or camphor. This created a thin strip of highly combustible material which would then be placed dangerously close to an extremely hot lamp, usually in a confined dark space that was stuffed to bursting with men, women and children. An infernal cocktail indeed.

Today when people talk about movies being 'dangerous', they're usually referring to the medium's alleged power to deprave and corrupt viewers – most commonly young viewers. But when the Cinematograph Act was first introduced in 1909, giving local councils more power to regulate cinema than any other art form, it was public safety rather than censorious control that was the prevailing issue, with the Home Secretary acting to control firetraps rather than moral mazes. And in those heady days when film needed to be handled with extreme care, the art of projection was seen as a craft, a bona fide trade carried out by skilled operatives whose talents were as essential to the smooth running of a movie show as those of stage managers were to the proficient production of a play.

For most of the 20th century, cinema screenings were referred to as 'performances', a word that acknowledged the medium's oft-forgotten roots in the theatrical tradition. Although we may foolishly imagine that the visual thrills of films like *Titanic* are somehow unique to cinema, they were in fact prefigured by live productions that allowed audiences to witness spectacular shipwrecks and historical disasters from the comparative comfort of the 19th-century theatre stall. In 1899, a full 60 years before Charlton Heston's widescreen Technicolor outing, audiences for the first Broadway production of *Ben-Hur* watched in jaw-dropped amazement as eight specially trained horses pulling two full-sized chariots galloped at full pelt on floor-mounted treadmills, while a cyclorama allowed the background to fly past at an equivalent whack, creating a thunderous edge-of-your-seat illusion of death-defying motion. Just imagine that! Think of the noise. Think of the *smell*! Sensurround, Odorama and Dolby Digital 3-D combined would be hard-pressed to match the immersive thrill of that 19th-century play, as 32 pounding hooves kicked splinters into the air while the actors' cracking whips arced out into the auditorium above the terrified audience's heads. The stagehands working the production were run off their feet and were required to be vigilant at all times. The same was true of the projectionists who followed in their wake; they had umpteen tasks to perform and would never dream of leaving their posts. In its early incarnation, cinema – like theatre – was very much a 'live' production.

Owing to the volatile nature of plasticised nitrocellulose (or 'nitrate stock', as it was commonly known) early projection rooms had to be sealed and their walls lined with thick asbestos. If a fire broke out in such a room, containment was the only option; an early instruction film made by the Admiralty for budding projectionists entitled *This Film Is Dangerous*, showed reels of nitrate film continuing to burn even when fully immersed in water, with no need of air to continue their spectacular conflagration. In 1926, a converted barn in Dromcolliher went up in flames after a reel of nitrate film somehow came into contact with the unguarded flame of a candle, killing 48 people – for decades the worst fire disaster in Irish history. On 31st December 1929 at the Glen Cinema in Paisley, Scotland, a can of nitrate film that had just been projected as part of a children's matinee was placed into a metal box, which began to issue bilious clouds of black smoke. As the smoke seeped into the auditorium, the young audience panicked and ran to an escape door, which was padlocked and opened inwards, and in the ensuing crush 69 children were killed. An enquiry later concluded that the fire had been started when the metal box was accidentally placed on the unguarded terminals of a battery in the projection booth which then short-circuited, causing the nitrate film inside to burst into flames.

The Cinematograph Act was subsequently amended to beef up fire-prevention measures and to ensure that cinema doors were fitted with push-bars and opened *outwards*. As for projectionists, the sense that their trade was potentially lethal and needed to be carried out by highly skilled operatives was heightened as never before. Indeed, nitrate film was generally regarded with such alarm that it was not allowed to be transported on the London Underground (although smoking cigarettes on the Tube was fine!) or sent through Her Majesty's post without appropriate anti-fire precautions. And, as film archivists subsequently discovered to their cost, if you leave nitrate film in an unopened canister for a period of years it will decompose, releasing noxious gas and turning first to a honey-like goo and then to dust which has the capacity to spontaneously combust.

Eventually, nitrate gave way to 'safety film' and 'triacetate', which may not have been as explosive as nitrate stock but was still flammable (it would burn as merrily as paper under the right circumstances) and, if left unattended, would produce the distinctive vinegar whiff that signalled a descent into brittle instability. Long after the age of nitrate had passed, projectionists still had to use their noses like police sniffer dogs when opening a canister of film, a precaution which ensured that the image of a highly combustible element cloaked in a sulphurous cloud remained hard-wired into the popular imagination.

As well as being a dangerous procedure, projecting a movie was a very physical, hands-on enterprise, thanks to the need for regular reel changes, which occurred roughly once every 20 minutes. Generally, cinema screens would have two projectors, enabling the first reel of a film to be projected from one machine whilst the second reel was laced in readiness to take over from its partner. As the first reel was drawing to a close, a series of cue marks (usually dots or circles) would appear in the upper right corner of the picture. If you've been going to the pictures as long as I have, you will probably have noticed these symbols, the first of which would appear eight seconds before the end of the reel, telling the projectionist to start the second machine rolling and wait for the 'changeover cue'. Once this appeared, the projectionist had around one-and-a-half feet of film – that's about one second – to make the smooth transition from one reel to the next. In older movie theatres, this may have involved sliding manually operated covers back and forth to open or close projection booth windows. More modern systems used interconnected 'dowsers', the metal or asbestos plates which come between the lamp and the film to stop the image from projecting, or the film from burning. Either way, the projectionist needed to be on the ball or everyone would wind up watching a load of scratchy 'tail leader' being beamed onto the screen where an exciting motion picture should be.

The fact that few audiences were even aware of reel changes tells you something about how dexterously this operation could be performed. And the work was not over once a reel of film had been projected: having been duly unwound, each reel would then need to be reverse-spooled before being projected again, otherwise the film would play upside down and back to front. Sometimes an overworked projectionist might forget to reverse-spool a reel, meaning that the next projectionist would diligently have to check the print and carry out any necessary corrections, to avoid screwing up the Wednesday matinee of *The Poseidon Adventure* by having the ship mysteriously roll upright in the middle of reel five (and leaving the audience demanding their money back). The fact that such major screw-ups were not only possible but probable ensured that projectionists kept watch on the print at all times, and whilst doing so they would regularly check the framing and focus of the image in the auditorium, taking great pride in ensuring that they had used the right aperture, affixed the correct lens, properly checked the tension, and that the performance of the movie was of the highest possible standard.

This huge amount of responsibility – the fire hazard, the need for constant focus, the reel changes – was all part of the traditional projectionist's lot, and it encouraged many in the profession to see their craft as a creative and collaborative part of the cinema-going experience. In front of me, I have a copy of a letter from that great auteur Stanley Kubrick which reads: 'Dear Projectionist, An infinite amount of care was given to the look of "Barry Lyndon"; the photography, the sets, the costumes; and in the careful colour grading and overall lab quality of the prints, and the soundtrack – all of this work is now in your hands, and your attention to sharp focus, good sound, and the careful handling of the film will make this effort worthwhile.' Similarly, in 1969 writer/producer Larry Kramer gave an interview to *Today's Cinema* magazine in which he talked passionately about the projectionist's key role in the release of his controversial new movie *Women in Love*, directed by Ken Russell and adapted from D.H. Lawrence's classic novel. The film was playing at the Prince Charles Theatre in Leicester Square and, according to Kramer, the cinema had been so keen to do it justice that they had installed a new projector and 'softened some clocks' in the auditorium that the producer had felt 'were ticking too loudly'. As for the projectionist, he insisted on reading Lawrence's novel before handling the print, to ensure that he understood both the nature and the history of the work prior to running the celluloid through his magic lantern.

Such attention to detail is almost inconceivable today, for even as I write the great profession of projection (in the traditional sense of the craft) is in the process of becoming obsolete. The rot started to set in with the introduction of 'towers' and 'platters' (or 'cake-stands'), which effectively did away with the need for multiple reel changes, thereby fundamentally changing the nature of projection as a profession. With towers, the 20-minute reels are all spliced together by the projectionist on to one giant vertical reel, which then runs uninterrupted through the projector on to an equally giant take-up reel (which is then reverse-spooled at the end of the performance). With platters, in which the horizontally laid film is spooled from the centre of the reel, the movie passes through the projector and then back on to another horizontal take-up platter *the right way round* – thereby eliminating the need even for reverse spooling. There are even systems that allow the same film to run through two projectors at the same time, enabling one print to be shown in two (or more?) different screens simultaneously.

As David Norris (the West End's longest serving projectionist) told me, these operations still required great skill, with a 'good' projectionist taking care to splice the 20-minute reels correctly in the first place, and to ensure that when 'broken down' after the film's run, those reels were left in good order so that 'the next poor sod didn't end up with a six or seven-piece jigsaw puzzle to work out . . . it's happened to me, and trust me it's not funny!' Once the reels were assembled, however, these technical advancements should have freed up more time for the projectionist to spend checking the framing and focus of the picture, and correcting any imperfections through tiny tweaks of the lenses and the rack. But, in fact, in the emergent world of the multiplex it just gave them more time to go and start up *other* projectors in *other* screens, doing the job of six people for half the money and none of the thanks. So whereas in the past a good projectionist would regularly look out from their box to check that all was well in the auditorium, the more modern projectionist would be on to the next movie in the next screen before you could say, 'Oi, it's out of focus!'

Things got worse with the advent of digital projection, which, in theory, simply requires someone to turn a machine on, thereby in effect making projectionists redundant. By the time you read this book, the Odeon and Cineworld chains in the UK will have all but done away with celluloid, replacing the reels and pulleys of their old machines with the hard drives of newly installed digital projectors. As Phil Clapp of the Cinema Exhibitors' Association recently told London's *Time Out* magazine, 'while a 35mm projector is a mechanical device with moving parts, a digital projector – aside from the lamp – is very much a piece of IT. Projectionists who have been able to strip down and reassemble a 35mm projector with their eyes closed are suddenly being presented with a box with an on–off switch.'

As a result, projectionists up and down the country are losing, or stepping down from, jobs which they once loved. Projectionists like 80-year-old Ray Mascord, who was profiled in the *Guardian* in February 2011 on the eve of his retirement from Scott Cinemas in Bridgwater, Somerset (which, like everywhere else, was 'going digital'). When Ray started projecting movies back in the forties he was one of a team of five who worked two projectors, with reel changes every 20 minutes. In the fifties, he projected musicals like *Carousel* and *Oklahoma!* and fell in love with an usherette, Eileen, who became his third projectionist. In between reel changes Ray would keep a watchful eye not only on the picture but on couples canoodling in the back row. 'I used to say, "Aye-aye, where are you putting your hands!"' he told reporter Patrick Barkham, whose wonderfully nostalgic interview also records the arrival of the 'towers holding 12,000ft of film' which 'turned the cinema projectionist's job into a solitary one . . .'

Barkham's feature coincided with a number of articles documenting the end of a cinematic era. In *Time Out*'s similarly themed piece, David Jenkins found that 'a lot of veteran projectionists have taken this revolution as a cue to retire', to the extent that 'projectionists as we imagine them are on the verge of extinction'. Tracing the changeover in the UK back to 2005, when the UK Film Council's Digital Screen Network initiative put 240 digital projectors into UK cinemas, Jenkins notes that the initial take-up on the format was sluggish. It wasn't until 2009 and the advent of digital 3-D that celluloid projection really started to be eclipsed, with figures leaping from 650 digital screens to 1,400 in the space of a single year. According to *Screen Digest*'s David Hancock, 80 per cent of the movies released in 2010 in the UK were issued wholly or partly in digital format, compared to 25 per cent in France and 35 per cent in the Netherlands. Soon, that figure will be closer to 90 per cent.

The problem is not digital projection per se, but the lack of human accountability that the rise of digital has facilitated. In the past year I have sat in a UK multiplex in which a digital image simply froze – something which we are assured *cannot* happen, but an error with which many multiplex patrons will be familiar, and which no one was on hand to correct. It put me in mind of the trailer for *Westworld*, the futuristic Michael Crichton thriller from the mid-seventies about an amusement park in which the rides start to eat the customers – you know, just like *Jurassic Park*. The film was an AA-certificate outing (over-14s only), and so I didn't get to see it until it was re-released alongside its lesser sequel *Futureworld* a few years later. But that trailer remains with me to this day, with its tantalising description of an automated fantasy world in which day trippers can live out their wildest dreams ('Where robot men and women are programmed to serve you for . . . Romance . . . Violence . . . Anything!') and in which 'nothing can possibly go wrong . . . go wrong . . . go wrong . . . go wrong . . .'

Today, that *Westworld* trailer has become more prescient than ever. In fact it seems to me that 'Westworld' is a terrific name for a multiplex cinema chain: a name which combines a cineaste's sense of modern movie history with a refreshing honesty about what to expect from a trip to your local ten-screener. Think about it: in *Westworld* the customers cough up huge amounts of money in order to escape from the humdrum reality of their everyday lives and to experience excitement, adventure and really wild things, all without the attendant risks to their person of doing any of those things for real. Their safety and enjoyment are guaranteed by the high-tech nature of this futuristic amusement park, in which everything is controlled by machines and computers that are activated from a distance by the management, who are notably unable to come to anyone's assistance when everything goes pear-shaped and Yul Brynner's electronic gunslinger starts putting holes in the park's visitors. Next thing you know the fun's over, the pain's kicked in, everyone's screaming and someone's missing the top of their head. As a metaphor for the state of the 21st-century multiplex experience, I'd say that's pretty damned hard to beat.

Of course, ever since Fritz Lang's 1927 masterpiece *Metropolis* warned us all that the mediator between the hand and the brain must be the heart rather than a machine, the history of movies has been littered with rebellious or revolting circuitry that serves as a warning against exactly this kind of thing. And yet cinema, the one medium that should be especially aware of the problem of taking humans out of the equation, has been guilty of the most egregious abnegation of accountability when it comes to surrendering the controls to autopilot.

Over the past few years, the radio show that I co-host with Simon Mayo on BBC 5 Live has been receiving a steady stream of correspondence from projectionists thanking us for our very vocal support of their craft, but sadly assuring us that the battle for their future is lost. Time and again these texts, emails and letters have ended with the projectionist bidding a fond farewell to their vocation and envisaging a future in which everything is controlled from a central computer, over which even individual cinema managers will have no control.

It is this idea – that you can take the human touch out of cinema and no one will notice – which grieves me the most, and it is a central subject of this book. The questions I raise are fairly simple: Why do we pay to watch movies that we know are really terrible? How can 3-D be the future when it's failed so many times in the past? Who wants to watch a movie in a cinema that doesn't have a projectionist but *does* have a fast-food stand? For me, the sad fate of projectionists is symptomatic of a greater malaise within modern movies, an indication that something of value has been casually cast aside in the rush to maximise profit at the expense of the audience. Yes, movies have always been there to make money, but today, as we shall see, films are financed on the basis of computer-generated spreadsheets, distributed according to first-weekend box-office figures, and projected by robots. The element of danger once so integral to the cinematic experience – necessitating the constant vigilance of living, breathing people – has been replaced by an automated drone of electronic information that requires no supervision, since it is never going to set anything alight. Somehow, while we were all looking the other way, the thing which made us fall in love with movies in the first place got *lost*: the strange alchemical miracle of celluloid passing through a projector that was the heart of cinema itself. We turned our living rooms into cinemas and our cinemas into living rooms, and now there's no one left to ask, 'What's wrong with this picture?'

Do *you* believe in the Westworld?

Chapter One

LET'S GO TO THE PICTURES

'The cinema will be a pit . . .'
Wreckless Eric

It was a wet Saturday afternoon in October 2010. The sky was the colour of Morrissey's greasy tea, the climate was somewhere between mizzling and hissing down, and the economic forecast for the foreseeable future was as grim as the last two reels of the French existential torture-porn horror show *Martyrs*. Even the dogs didn't seem overly enthusiastic about the prospect of venturing outside, preferring instead to curl up in front of the television and methodically chew their way through my once collectable stash of VHS video nasties. (My partner Linda had sensibly removed the skull-splitting cover of *The Driller Killer* which I got the director to sign for her – 'To Linda, from the Driller Killer!' – so the dogs had started work on a copy of *Evilspeak* which frankly we weren't going to miss.) In the kitchen, I was struggling to get my fantastically stroppy Acer laptop to speak to my local multiplex's automated ticket booking service in order to purchase a couple of tickets for a forth-coming performance, by comparison with which it would have been fairly easy for an entire herd of camels to gallop merrily through the eye of a needle without ever dislodging Omar Sharif. The problem was partly due to the service itself, which was insistent not only upon charging me an exorbitant price to view a film which I had already seen (and knew full well that few others would be interested in seeing) but also upon stinging me for an additional 'booking fee' for the privilege of paying through the nose online. Matters were not helped by the fact that my laptop had clearly decided that it did not want me to see said film again (perhaps it thought my time could be better spent uploading Windows 7, which it kept on bloody telling me was 'waiting to install' despite the fact that I kept telling it to leave me with the version I'd got and which I understand . . . sort of) and was doing everything it could to come between me and the cinema in a 'limited connectivity' sort of way.

A few weeks later, I would finally lose all patience with this piece of hi-tech machinery and conclude that it was actually possessed by the Assyrian demon of the south-west wind whose name I had once typed into a document thereby allowing it entry to the accursed wiring. In an attempt to cleanse its foul electronic soul, I took it out into the yard, laid it down on the cold, hard ground, and then worked through our theological differences with the help of a large wooden stake that I drove through its inexorably blackened heart. The computer screamed and shattered and quaked like a soul in torment, levitating and spider-walking as the evil spirits fled from its head-spinning ruptured hard drive. And I was left with a profound feeling of calm and wellbeing, free at last from its hideous Hadean taunts . . .

But all that was in the future. For the moment I was left wrestling with the pure evil of the computer (which right now lies crucified upon my office floor) and the faceless malice of the multiplex's 'Computer Says No' automated ticket service, wondering whether this was the start of the kind of story which generally ends *really badly* in countries where firearms are legal . . .

Thank God for gun laws, I say.

Anyway, after what seemed like an eternity of swearing, booking, more swearing, rebooting, rebooking, yet more swearing, stamping, and finally *re*-rebooking (for the *third time*), I appeared to have purchased two tickets for the same price as a small house in Liverpool, and announced triumphantly to my daughter, Georgia, 'We're going to see the new Zac Efron movie!' This was a good thing, because both my daughter and I absolutely love Zac Efron. He's young, he's talented, he can sing, dance *and* act, and when I met him once (briefly) he was sweet, gracious, charming and generally lovely to be around. Even if it was only for a few minutes. Honestly, if all movie stars were as gracious and talented as Zac Efron, I'd have nothing to piss and moan about for the rest of my career. You can smirk all you want, but to my mind Efron is a reminder of the kind of fully rounded star appeal which was required of screen actors before Marlon Brando somehow managed to bamboozle everyone into believing that true talent meant mumbling and snorting like you've got a mouthful of cake, turning up late to work because you've been 'researching' your role in the cafeteria, and refusing to accept Oscars because you don't like Cowboys and Indians movies. For the record, Marlon Brando was a fool whose growing contempt for his audience caused them to stay away from his later pictures in droves. Which was probably a good thing, because the fewer people who saw his godawful later movies the better. The decline began when Hollywood studios started paying him staggering amounts of money to be really rubbish for a really short amount of time in films like *The Formula* and *Superman* – in both of which he makes what can only be reasonably described as top-billed 'cameo' appearances. Things hit rock bottom, however, with his ill-fated nineties remake of *The Island of Doctor Moreau*, which remains arguably the stupidest film of that decade. That film was the brainchild of South African-born director Richard Stanley, who had made a splash with his low-tech future-shocker *Hardware* and who had somehow persuaded Marlon to stop eating pies long enough to play the eponymous Dr Moreau in his long-gestated dream project. Apparently Marlon liked Richard, but when co-star Val 'Boring' Kilmer got him fired for being weird, Brando carried on picking up the pay cheques and enjoying the catering whilst wearing an ice bucket on his head. (Don't take my word for it; watch the film. No, on second thoughts, just take my word for it.) Too lazy to learn his lines, Brando insisted on wearing (along with the ice bucket) an earpiece through which a script assistant could prompt his slurred speech, a trick he'd learned on *The Formula*. Unfortunately, according to co-star David Thewlis, Brando's earpiece also picked up police radio transmissions, which caused Dr Moreau to observe thoughtfully that a robbery was taking place at Woolworths in the middle of a meaningful soliloquy.

Rather than being the greatest actor of his generation, Brando was actually Ron Burgundy.

None of that nonsense would have stuck back in the thirties, when stars were under contracts which demanded that they behaved their raggedy-arsed selves, and slackers swiftly found out what life looked like on the wrong end of a waiter's pad. Journalists drone on endlessly about how terrific it is that actors now get to control the products in which they star, but anyone who has actually sat through a movie in which actors get producer credits knows that modern thespians know much more about what they need than what audiences actually want. Frankly, if I want to watch someone jerking off in public then there are plenty of public toilets in the Soho area of London where I can get that pleasure for free. But when I pay a large amount of money to see a movie in a theatre which charges me for having the effrontery to attempt to buy a ticket in the first place, then forgive me for thinking that the players in that movie should look, frankly my dear, like they actually give a damn . . .

Which Zac Efron most definitely does. I was first won over to his charms by his staggeringly athletic turns in the *High School Musical* franchise, which started life as direct-to-video fodder but wound up punching above its weight in impressively packed cinemas around the world. From here he graduated to a stand-out turn in *Me and Orson Welles*, in which he played a young wannabe actor who lands himself a bit part in Welles's now infamously political reading of *Julius Caesar* in the thirties. The film was shot in large part at the restored Gaiety Theatre on the Douglas promenade in the Isle of Man, one of the last remaining theatres in the world to house a fully working 'Corsican Trap' (specially designed for the ghostly play *The Corsican Brothers*) which lent a suitably woody, mechanical period look to the understage scenes in the movie. In my role as film critic for BBC2's *The Culture Show*, I had been despatched to the island to shoot a piece about the film's Douglas premiere, to which I took my mum. We stayed at the Sefton Hotel, of which my grand-father, James Stanley Kermode, used to be the Chairman of the Directors – a great thrill for both mum and me, and one that rekindled my unfulfilled desire to move 'back' to the island (on which I had never lived in the first place) as soon as humanly possible. Mum had never heard of Zac Efron, and was genuinely bemused when a crowd of screaming teenagers almost prevented him from making his way from the pavement to the front doors of the Gaiety, his presence sparking ear-bashing displays of the kind of pant-wetting hysteria not seen since Donny Osmond topped the charts. Honestly, if the kids could have torn the shirt from his back they would happily have done so. I was nearly knocked down by an incandescent youth who barrelled past me, a look of ecstatic rapture in her eyes, screaming 'I touched his bum! I touched his bum! He squeezed past me and I *got a feel of his bum!!!*'

Mum, meanwhile, stood quietly to one side, smiling at the carnage and occasionally asking 'Who is he again?' A few moments later, I got to 'interview' Mr Efron — by which I mean that I held a microphone in front of his face for a couple of minutes and attempted to look like it was no big deal, whilst all the time resisting the overwhelming and terrifying temptation to reach out and goose him while I had the chance. After all, it seemed to have done wonders for that teenager, like taking the healing waters at Lourdes or being graced by a hands-on blessing from the Pope. Surely it could do the same for my weary aching bones? I hadn't been so excited since I unconsciously prodded Liza Minnelli to see if she was real (see previous book) and there was every chance that I was going to disgrace myself again. If Zac clocked this, then he did his consummately professional best to ignore it, answering my questions with self-deprecating wit and charm and generally being every bit as fabulous as (if a little bit smaller than) I hoped he would be. He even signed an autograph for my daughter, which earned me about a billion brownie points and made me briefly the coolest person in the world.

Briefly.

All of which brings us back to the local multiplex and my pathetic attempts to curry ongoing favour with my 11-year-old by taking her to see the new Zac Efron movie on the pretence of it being a treat for her when, in reality, it was every bit as much of a treat for me. The movie in question was *The Death and Life of Charlie St. Cloud*, which I had actually seen at a national press show in London's Leicester Square only a few days previously. At that screening there had been the usual snorting derision from some of the wizened old farts who constitute the old guard of the British film press (I speak as a wizened old fart myself), many of whom appear to have been clinically inoculated against the charms of any movie which will appeal to teenage girls. Look at the near universal critical derision which has greeted the *Twilight* movies, a series of films that resonate richly and profoundly with their target audience but that are regularly dismissed as infantile trash by men old enough to be the heroine's great-grandfather. One of the proudest moments of my life was being mentioned on a *Twilight* fan website as 'a rare example of a grey-haired weird bloke who actually *gets* our movie', a compliment which is about as barbed as it is possible to get. I'd tell you the name of the website, but it was shown to me by a computer-literate teenager who found it on their iPhone and (Luddite that I am) I now can't bloody find it myself. In fact, I can't get on to the internet without asking a 12-year-old to do it for me. You know all those 'parental locks' that are installed on internet browsers in order to give grown-ups a false sense of security about what their kids are accessing online? They are actually designed by teenagers so that they can lock their parents out, thereby allowing them to go about their daily high-speed business unencumbered by the slow-lane traffic of old people trying to buy cinema tickets online.

Anyway, after much internet irritation and the making of a solemn vow *never* to meddle with computer technology again, I got my daughter into our clapped-out old car, stuck

Nick Lowe's *Jesus of Cool* on the CD player (she's no fan but, dammit, it's time she learned) and headed off in the direction of the multiplex – one of several within striking distance from home. The journey was typically stressful and elongated, involving several diversions through various villages and town centres, and even out to a trading park and back. Eventually, we arrived at the cinema where (surprise, surprise) the automated ticket machine denied any knowledge either of my existence or (more importantly) of my pre-allocated ticket purchase. This eventuality meant that we had to queue to buy our tickets from a real-life person – or at least from a person who appeared to be breathing and partially conscious, which is as near as they got to 'real-life'. I can't blame them – clearly they had been stunned into a semi-comatose state by the decision of the management to fold the selling of tickets and / or fast food into one staggeringly inefficient (but clearly very cheap) vending process. The line to buy tickets, therefore, snaked out into the foyer, with each transaction lasting about five minutes as every ticket purchase was supplemented by an endless discussion about sweet or salty popcorn, small, medium or large-sized Cokes, and 'Do you want special sauce with your nachos?' ephemera. Never mind the fact that some of us find the entire practice of eating in cinemas an abominable curse which should be outlawed forthwith – if you wanted to get into the cinema at all you had to go through the fast-food stand *first*, and the chances were you were going to leave with a barrel-load of noisy, sickening crap whether you wanted it or not.

Finally, a good five minutes after the movie was due to start (I hate arriving late, but I assumed there'd be half an hour of terrible trailers, annoying adverts and staggeringly irritating 'thank you for not pirating this movie' notices – which always make me want to go home and download it on principle) we got to the front of the line and began the exciting process of buying a ticket all over again.

'Hello,' I said to the floppy-haired child behind the counter who was even less pleased to see me than I was to see him. 'I've booked two tickets online, for the two forty p.m. performance of *Charlie St. Cloud*, seats F8 and 9, but the machine doesn't recognise my card, so apparently I now need to pick them up here. From you. Manually. I have a copy of my computer print-out receipt if that helps.'

'Waaah?' said the child, with the tone of one who had just taken a massive hit on Ralph Brown's Camberwell Carrot and was now wondering whether to let go of, or hang on to, the balloon.

'The ticket machine doesn't recognise my card so I need to collect my tickets from you. *Manually*. Meaning, you hand them to me . . .'

'No,' he said vaguely.

'What?'

'No, you're in the wrong queue. You need the automatic ticket machines. They're back out there. In the foyer.'

He gazed at me, past me, *through me*, toward the next person in the ever-expanding queue.

'Next!' he drawled, with a surprising sense of urgency, if it is indeed possible to drawl urgently.

'No, hang on,' I said, moving my entire body to block the vending window in an attempt to regain control of the situation. 'I *know* the machine is in the foyer because that's where I went to with my card, which the machine doesn't recognise, which is why I am here now, and why I have been standing in a queue for the past twenty minutes.'

The attendant looked at me as if I was the very stupidest life form on the planet, his gaze a mixture of patronising condescension, stultified lack of interest and utter 'I'm-not-being-paid-enough-to-have-this-discussion' irritation.

'Well, you've wasted your time because you're in the wrong queue. You need the automatic ticket machine which is . . .'

'OUT IN THE FOYER! I *know!*' I almost screamed. 'But the machine *does not recognise my card* and so apparently I have to come here and get you to . . .'

I stopped dead in my tracks. I was suddenly filled with a vision of a great gaping void: an infinite chasm of despair and hopelessness into which a mere mortal may stumble and find themselves falling forever. This was presumably the void of which Nietzsche was thinking when he warned us that 'when you look long into an abyss, the abyss also looks back into you'. Right now, the abyss was indeed looking back into me, apparently eager for me to get out of the way so that it could look long into the person standing behind me in the queue who probably wanted two tickets and an industrial-sized vat of popcorn. I thought of Sisyphus heaving his boulder up a hill for all eternity; of Brutus, Cassius and Judas being endlessly devoured by a three-mouthed devil in the innermost ring of

Dante's Inferno; and of Marvin the Paranoid Android parking cars on Frogstar World B after being abandoned for ten million years by Arthur and Zaphod and Ford, left to wait while civilisations waxed and waned around him. (The first interview I ever did was with Douglas Adams and the star-struck experience has stayed with me ever since.) And, most importantly, I thought of the need to get this conversation over and done with as quickly as possible and without resorting to unpleasantness. I took a deep breath and started afresh.

'OK,' I said. 'Let's start again. I'd like two tickets, one adult, one child, to see the two forty p.m. performance of *The Death and Life of Charlie St. Cloud*, please.'

The attendant looked at me with the expression of one who has just voided his diarrhetic soul into the pre-distressed pants which he had somehow failed to raise above the level of his thighs. Then, with the sloth-like movement of a massive oil tanker lumbering its way round in a circle in the middle of the North Atlantic, he turned his head to look at the clock on the wall behind him, which now said 2.46, and then back toward me.

'It's started,' he said, like the fourth horseman quietly announcing the arrival of the apocalypse.

'What's started?'

'The programme. The two forty programme. It's started. Six minutes ago. It's two forty-six . . .'

He turned, slug-like, to look at the clock once more.

'Two forty-*seven*. The programme started seven minutes ago. The two *forty* programme. It's two forty-*seven* now. So the programme's . . .'

'Yes, yes, I know, the programme's started, but the *film* won't be on yet, will it? You'll have half an hour of trailers and adverts and annoying anti-piracy notices first, won't you. What time does the actual film start?'

Zombie boy said nothing. Instead, he looked down at his hands, seeming momentarily surprised to discover that he had opposable thumbs. Frankly, I was surprised too; from his general appearance he didn't appear to be able to hold anything as fiddly as a comb, or indeed to be able to pull up his own trousers. In evolutionary terms, he was conclusive proof that Darwin had been full of shit, and we were all heading back toward the primordial soup.

He looked at me again.

'The programme started seven minutes ago,' he repeated without a trace of irony. 'Eight, now.'

I contemplated strangling him, but decided against it – there were minors present, and the sight of extreme violence can scar the young.

Apparently.

'Right, I don't care about missing the start of the programme,' I said.

'Just so long as you know.'

'Know what?'

'That it's started. The programme.'

'Yes, I know. I understand. But I still want to buy two tickets.'

'Even though it's started?'

'Yes, even though it's started.'

'Right, how many tickets do you want for the programme . . . that's already started.'

'Two. One adult, one child.'

'How old is the child?'

'Well, she was eleven when I started queuing but she's probably sixteen by now,' I quipped.

Big mistake.

'Sixteen is "adult". So that's two adults for the programme that's already started . . .'

'No, she's not sixteen, she's eleven. It was a joke . . .'

'You said she was sixteen.'

'No, I said she was eleven but we've been waiting so long she might as well be sixteen . . .'

'Sixteen is "adult".'

'But she's not sixteen, she's *eleven.*'

'Then why did you say she was sixteen?'

Why indeed? Why oh why oh why oh why oh why oh why oh why?

'I don't know. I'm sorry.'

And that was it. He'd won. I had apologised. It was all over. He had the upper hand. I was in his world now, playing by his rules. He shimmered with victory – somnambulant yet shimmery. Weird.

'So, two tickets, one adult, one *child*, for the two forty programme of *Charlie St. Cloud*, which has already started.'

'Yes please.'

'Standard or premium seats?'

This was an interesting question I had already encountered online but which, to be honest, I still hadn't really resolved. It seemed to me that, at the prices they were charging, all seats ought to be 'premium'. After all, wasn't this the whole point of the anti-piracy thing they kept ramming down our throats: the idea that the cinema was the best (not to say the only) place to see a film, and watching at home on illegal download would be doing a disservice to both ourselves and the movie; in the long run we would all suffer. And yet here was an admission that some seats in the cinema were better (and therefore pricier) than others, leading one to conclude by default that the still-costly pleasures of 'standard' seating might not actually be up to the same high standards accorded by one's own couch. I can't be the only one to have thought this – if all the seats aren't premium, then why the hell am I paying so much for them? Moreover, in a world in which ushers are apparently considered an unnecessary extravagance, what's to stop me from simply paying for a 'standard' seat and then sitting in a 'premium' seat once I get inside the spectacularly unpoliced auditorium? The answer, of course, is nothing, as I had previously discovered after having paid through the nose for premium seats only to find some unchaperoned upstarts blithely sitting in my seats, solidly refusing – in the absence of a higher authority – to move. And why should they? They'd already paid enough to get into the wretched cinema, and frankly they wanted to be able to see the film from a reasonable vantage point. Otherwise, they could have just stayed at home and downloaded it illegally. Which, to be honest, was starting to look like a surprisingly attractive option.

Back at the ticket-office-cum-fast-food-stand, the attendant was still awaiting my reply.

'Standard,' I said firmly. 'Left-hand side by the aisle. F8 and 9, in fact.'

'Those seats are taken.'

'Yes, I know. They're taken by *me*. Those are the seats which I bought online but for which I have been unable to collect the tickets from the machine in the foyer because it does not recognise my card. So instead I am buying them from you.'

'You can't buy them from me because they're already taken.'

'Yes, taken by *me*.'

'No, just taken. I can give you G16 and 17.'

'Is either one of them an aisle seat?'

'No.'

'Are they on the left?'

'No, they're both in the middle.'

'I see. So when I said I wanted two seats on the left, one on the aisle, that didn't really make any difference, did it?'

He said nothing. The seconds ticked away. Minutes passed – I couldn't stop them.

'OK, you win again,' I blurted. 'Just give me G16 and 17 and we'll move once we get inside the cinema.'

The attendant looked outraged. 'You can't *move*, sir, its allocated seating. You have to sit in your allocated seat.'

'Which I will of course do. Unless, that is, the clone versions of me and my daughter (in whom you seem to have placed your faith) fail to show up, in which case I'll keep seats F8 and 9 warm for them.'

'The ushers won't let you do that, sir,' said the attendant, sounding increasingly like HAL the computer from *2001* telling astronaut Dave Bowman that he couldn't open the hatch for him and he was going to have to die in space after all. Clearly he'd gone to DefCon 1, and I had to up my game accordingly.

I leaned toward the kiosk window, my breath condensing on the apparently bulletproof glass, lowered my voice conspiratorially, and whispered, 'But there are no ushers . . . *are there?*'

He looked back at me in silence, with what I fancied was an expression of unspoken horror shot through with shock and awe, and garnished with a sprinkling of reluctant admiration. I had spoken the unspeakable, named the unnameable, mentioned the unmentionable; like Charlton Heston telling the starving masses that 'Soylent Green is people!' only quieter. Much quieter. 'But it's alright,' I continued in hushed tones. 'I won't tell anyone if you won't. Now just give me the damned tickets.'

A moment of electricity passed between us before normal service was resumed.

'You want drinks or popcorn?'

'No.'

'*Yes!*'

My daughter, silent up until now, was suddenly eager to get involved. We'd had this discussion before, at home and in the car, but clearly an agreement had not yet been reached. See, the thing is, I hate popcorn. Not the taste or the substance of the foodstuff itself, which is every bit as yummy and nutritious as exploded mushroom clouds of super-heated dried grain smothered in salt and/or sugar plus a cocktail of super-poisonous chemicals (Google 'popcorn' and 'chemicals' and check it out – you'll be shocked) and packed in cardboard can possibly be. As a child I used to surreptitiously chew those Styrofoam worms in which fragile electrical appliances are packed for shipping, and taste-wise there wasn't a whole lot of difference between them and the buttered delights now sold in vast quantities in cinema foyers around the world. Certainly the overall effect was the same: much munching, zero nourishment and an overpowering need to quench your thirst with whichever carbonated brand of tooth-napalm came most easily to hand. To my mind, popcorn has always been a bit like heroin: the first hit makes you want to throw up (apparently), but also leaves you with a craving to quell the nausea by ingesting industrial amounts of the very thing which made you sick in the first place. Cigarettes are the same – or so smokers tell me – ghastly, but in a moreish kind of way. The only real difference between the consumption of popcorn, heroin and cigarettes is that the purchase of a pack of 20 is a much faster and more efficient way of getting your money straight into the hands of highly organised murderous bastards than fencing it through drug dealers or fast-food franchises. Tot up the number of people who've been maimed, killed and generally ravaged by cigarettes over the past 50 years and compare it with the statistics for drug and obesity-related fatalities; the only sensible conclusion is that, where fags are concerned, the tax benefits must massively outweigh the human tragedy. If only the government could figure out a way of putting VAT on smack.

Luckily the government *have* figured out a way of putting

VAT on popcorn. Indeed, it was the 'commonly quoted' purchase tax case of Popcorn House Ltd in 1968 (come on, you must have heard of it) which gave birth to the very definition of taxable confectionery as being 'any form of food normally eaten with the fingers and made by a cooking process, other than baking, which contains a substantial amount of sweetening matter'. The VAT-keepers' guide goes on to explain that 'taste and texture' and 'time and place of eating' may also be taken into account when assessing whether an allegedly edible substance is a tax-free foodstuff or a tax-rich treat, with cinema popcorn clearly falling into the latter category. If I was the VAT man, I would person- ally add a further financial penalty for the 'noise pollution' caused by eating popcorn in a cinema auditorium, with revenues gathered from this lucrative income stream used to fund a string of retirement homes for the prematurely obsolete projectionists and ushers who lost their jobs when their employers decided that their primary business was not the projection and exhibition of movies but the sale of VAT-able fast food.

A few months ago, after complaining on my BBC blog about the ear-splitting levels of extraneous noise that currently befoul the UK multiplex experience, somebody wrote in to suggest that cinemas should offer seat sockets, into which one could plug headphones. They pointed out that many venues are already fitted with induction loops and other such aids for the hard of hearing, and surely it wouldn't be too hard to rig up a decent hi-fi outlet that would allow people to watch movies in peace. They could even bring their own headphones. This sounded like a smart idea, but head-phones don't give you the full surround-sound experience that has become such a big part of modern spectacular cinema. Moreover, the fact that I don't want to hear people eating in the cinema (or talking on their mobile phones) doesn't necessarily mean that I don't want to hear them laughing or shrieking or crying, or doing whatever else it is that movies are meant to make people do. Isn't that a crucial part of the cinema-going experience: enjoying being in an auditorium full of people sharing the same emotions en masse? If you want isolation, then stay at home and get the movie when it comes out on DVD.

Surely a far better solution would be for cinemas to employ enough ushers to allow them to do their job properly – part of which is telling people to 'Ussh!' when they start talking or rustling or munching too loudly during a performance. A few years ago, Richard Griffiths famously halted a perform-ance of Alan Bennett's play *The History Boys* at the National Theatre, London, to remonstrate with a noisy audience member whose mobile phone was proving a distraction to both the cast and audience. Yet only a year later I sat in a screening of the (disappointing) movie version of *The History Boys* at which an attendee had not one but *two* phones in his hands, using the glaring light from one to illuminate the screen of the other so that he could carry on texting. You remember that scene in Woody Allen's *The Purple Rose of Cairo* where a character reaches down from the screen and pulls an audience member into the film? If only Griffiths's imposing screen presence had been similarly able to break through the fourth wall and stick said patron's phones where the sun don't shine. But in the absence of such an intervention the film simply played on, spoilt by the selfish actions of one audience member who had no sense of cinema as a living, breathing medium which requires as much respect from its patrons as theatre. And why should he? Because as far as the cinema staff were concerned, no one seemed to care how he behaved. Once upon a time he would have been ejected from the auditorium. Now he was able to treat it as his own living room.

Things do not have to be this way. I was particularly impressed by a recent trip to a massive multiplex just outside New Orleans where, for reasons which fail me now, I had to go to see the disappointing Farrelly brothers comedy *Hall Pass* at an 11 o'clock screening on a Wednesday night. The screening was surprisingly well attended, with the ludicrous laxity of the American 'R' rating meaning that several parents had brought along children who were: a) far too young to be up that late and b) far too young to be watching a movie which contained (according to our very own British Board of Film Classification) 'strong language, sex references and crude humour'. The film sucked but the screening was great, thanks largely to the presence of a rather imposing usher who seemed to have been recently released from a steroid farm and who looked ready to use lethal force to suppress any improper behaviour. No one would have dared to take out their mobile phone or make noise with their popcorn with this man-mountain in the auditorium, and he promptly became my new best friend. Forget armed policemen, I want armed ushers! Coincidentally, someone else wrote in to my BBC blog to say that they worked in a UK multiplex, and the reason there were never any ushers around to police the screenings was because they were all too busy cleaning up all the spilled popcorn.

Which brings us back to . . .

'Regular, medium or large?' Apparently, the attendant had decided to cut me out of the conversation entirely and go directly to point-of-sale contact with the 11-or-16-year-old with whom he hadn't yet fallen out.

'Large,' she replied merrily.

'*Small!*' I shrieked, embarrassingly.

'We don't do small. Only regular, medium or . . .'

'Right. *Regular.*'

'I want large.'

We settled on medium.

'You want a drink with that?'

'No, we have our own water.'

'Did you buy it in the foyer?'

'No, I brought it from home.'

'You can't take your own water into the cinema. Only drinks purchased in the foyer can be taken into the cinema.'

'Then we don't want a drink.'

'Yes we do! I want Coke!'

'Regular, medium or . . .'

'*Regular.*'

'Diet or . . .'

'*Regular!*' I shouted again. This was getting out of hand; I was losing my grip. People around me were starting to look concerned and a tad irate. No wonder it was taking such a long time to sell tickets if people like me were holding up the line like this. Suddenly it was all becoming my fault. I had to get a grip and move on.

'Just *regular*,' I whispered. 'Very, *very* regular, OK?'

'Okey dokey,' replied the attendant with a shrug, and he shuffled off to fill my bulging order of crap, leaving the ticket queue utterly unmanned, like a stationary line of traffic waiting at a red-light signal that has suddenly decided to go for a stroll.

We all waited.

We all waited some more.

We all waited some more more.

People behind me were starting to get antsy about missing the start of their programme in a manner which seemed indirectly to be pointing the finger of blame at me – in exactly the same way that I was indirectly pointing the finger of blame at the person standing in front of me before I *became* the person standing in front of me and felt my own finger of blame pointing at me from behind. If you see what I mean.

After what seemed an eternity my nemesis returned, a medium popcorn in one hand, 'regular' Coke in the other, both spilling generously over the floor as he walked. He put them on the counter in front of him, tapped some numbers into the till, then looked up and let me have it.

'Twenty-one pounds fifty.'

'*How much?!*'

'Twenty-one pounds fifty.'

'For one-and-a-half tickets, a small Coke and a medium popcorn? You've got to be kidding!'

He heaved a resigned sigh. Presumably he'd been here before.

'Fourteen pounds sixty for the tickets, four pounds fifty for the popcorn, two pounds forty for the Coke.'

I was stunned, although honestly I had no reason to be. A couple of hours earlier I had discovered that ordering one-and-a-half premium seats online would have cost a staggering £17.80 plus a booking charge of 75 pence per ticket, pushing the total price up to £19.30. It was this 'WTF?' online revelation that had persuaded me to be a cheapskate and opt for 'standard' seating after all; for some strange reason, £14.60 seemed like just a little bit more than a tenner while £19.30 sounded like 70 pence change from a score. But now, the additional purchase of a couple of moderately sized portions of crap (solid and liquid) had moved us into the ballpark of the handsomely attired pony, and I was rapidly turning into Arthur Daley. Where was Dennis Waterman when you needed him?

The most likely answer was that he was round the back unloading huge cartons of unpopped corn, from which the cinema would ultimately make more profit than the films. As *The Times* pointed out in 2004, to cook up 145 grams of popcorn at home would cost you 4 pence for the vegetable oil, 19 pence for the popcorn, and 3 pence for the sugar. Chuck in 4 pence for the cost of the gas and the cardboard packaging, and the whole kit and caboodle comes to 30 pence – that's a profit mark-up of well over 1,000 per cent when sold in the cinema foyer. No wonder the tickets themselves are becoming secondary.

'Cash or credit card?' asked the attendant, with the merest hint of malice.

'What? Oh, credit card I suppose. Hang on – just assure me that there isn't an extra charge for paying by card.'

He smiled, said nothing, took the credit card payment, handed me the tickets, and suddenly we were neither friends nor foe.

'Next.'

I walked away feeling like I had been mugged, or violated, or defiled in some ill-defined yet essentially unspeakable manner. As I stumbled toward the screening area which housed umpteen small but separate cinemas, I caught sight of a clock which told me that it was now 2.59. Damn! The programme had started 19 minutes ago. Maybe we *had* missed the beginning of the film after all. We'd better leg it; the trailers could be all done and dusted by now. Zac could be working his magic.

No such luck . . .

We burst into the screening room just in time to see the usually loveable Martin Freeman being a bit embarrassing in yet another of those bloody awful anti-piracy adverts; you know, the ones in which actors who should know better wander round unconvincing movie sets wearing painfully casual 'everyday' clothes and thanking us poor schmucks for paying a small fortune in order to endure their self-congratulatory twaddle, thereby ensuring that we all 'enjoy the real experience' (as long as we're not sitting in the standard economy seats) of cinema 'as it's meant to be seen'. I hate those adverts almost as much as I hate being frisked for recording devices before going into press screenings of movies which, it is implied, I am likely to record and then upload to the internet for my own extravagant profit and pleasure.

For the record, if movie companies really wanted to stop people downloading illegal copies of their product, they would simply follow the example of the music industry and make that product available legally in the formats audiences want. Having spent years pursuing the creators of Napster through the courts, the music industry simply adopted the technology themselves, allowing them to generate revenue from music exchanged over the internet. CD sales may have taken a bashing, but money now pours in thanks to everything from online sales of albums to downloads of single tracks and royalties from sites like Spotify. Moreover, the production and distribution costs associated with online sales are a fraction of those incurred by pressing, packaging and shipping CDs. Look at the example of Radiohead; they made their album *In Rainbows* available online, where customers could pay whatever they liked to download it, and they still made a hefty profit in the process. If people want to go buy a pre-packaged album in a real-life shop (and, despite the march of technology, millions still do) then they can; if, on the other hand, they want to cherry-pick their favourite tracks from the internet and create their own personal portable jukebox, they can do that too. And although the record companies moaned about how the internet was going to strangle the industry (in the same way that they once complained that 'home taping is killing music' – ha ha ha) it soon became apparent that the people who downloaded music ended up buying more product than people who didn't. Far from killing music, the legacy of piracy was to reinvigorate and redefine the manner in which music was distributed and consumed – through legitimate channels.

In the case of movies, the business paradigm is eerily comparable: allow people to choose how they want to watch movies and then provide them with a service which makes them happy to pay. In an ideal world, movies would be issued day-and-date in theatrical, DVD/Blu-ray, and download or streamable formats. Customers who want the deluxe theatrical experience can pay to see the film projected on to a proper-sized screen in a public auditorium, while those who want to squint at it in bite-sized bits on their mobile phones can do just that. Everyone pays, everyone's happy and, *voilà*, the pirates are promptly squeezed out of the marketplace. This is not rocket science; it is GCSE-level economics. Moreover, it means that those who actually want to watch a movie in the cinema are spared the annoyance of being surrounded by people who would rather be fiddling around with their mobile phones, and who would now have no need to trouble the theatrical auditorium.

Several independent distribution companies in the UK have been experimenting with multi-format day-and-date releases for a couple of years now. On Boxing Day 2009, the low-budget British indie-horror flick *Mum & Dad* premiered simultaneously in cinemas, on DVD, and on download and TV pay-per-view. In the autumn of 2010, viewers of Mathieu Amalric's *On Tour* (which got a very warm reception in Cannes) and Brian Welsh's award-winning Brit-pic *In Our Name* were given the choice between watching the movie in their nearest available cinema or live-streaming it on their computer. And in spring 2011, Ken Loach's controversial Cannes-premiered Iraq War drama *Route Irish* opened in the UK as a simultaneous multi-platform release. By all accounts, the revenues accrued by these films not only matched but exceeded the profits predicted for more conventional forms of distribution. And (presumably) the pirates didn't get a look in, because their services were not required.

As always, the majors are bringing up the rear, with Warner and Fox prompting scandalous 'End of Cinema as We Know It' headlines in the UK in May 2011 with news of their proposed 'on demand' service which would make movies available for home-viewing two months after their theatrical release. This has prompted a furious response from the multiplex chains, who claim it will damage their takings – as indeed it might. But denting the attendance figures of those faceless warehouses that currently serve up the blandest of movies in the worst possible circumstances at extortionate prices can only benefit the kind of movie houses run by people who actually care about their punters and who strive for excellence in feature presentation. Why pay £8.50 to be treated like cattle in a fast-food multiplex that shows the film in the wrong ratio in a noisy auditorium when you can watch it at home on your TV for a fiver? Alternatively, why watch a film on a postage-stamp-sized screen on your mobile phone when you can see it in all its projected, widescreen glory in a well-run cinema whose patrons respect those around them and whose management thinks that the film deserves to be projected as the director intended? And if you think that such a place doesn't exist then you've clearly never been to the Phoenix in East Finchley.

Anyway, back to the multiplex and the harsh realities of Screen Seven, which, despite zombie boy's computer-based protestations to the contrary, was far from full and was handsomely supplied with available last seats on the left (aisle). OK, so the auditorium was tiny, and the seating anywhere but the back two rows was way too close to the screen for anyone over the age of 12 who had grown used to reading the paper at arm's length. Seats F8 and 9, which, you will remember, I had somehow failed to book online, were indeed available – as was a large section of the 'premium' seating, in which the very few other patrons had spread themselves out with glee. Had any of them paid extra for this enhanced vantage point? I certainly hoped not, as I guided my daughter to a premium left-hand aisle seat with nary an usher in sight to stop me. For a brief moment I felt a surging rush of victory; after all that nastiness in the foyer I had actually beaten the bastards. I had paid for a crap, cramped, and crucially 'trapped' mid-row standard seat, and now found myself ostentatiously stretching my legs out into the aisle and sinking into the plush opulence of a premium aisle seat that would allow me to watch the movie without straining or craning, or cramping my style. OK, so I had probably paid *twice*, what with all that online confusion and whatnot, and at some point in the not-too-distant future I would get a Barclaycard bill telling me that I had actually watched the movie from the vantage point of four different seats – a quadrophonic experience indeed. But sod it, for the moment I was where I wanted to be: in the cinema, in a good seat, and in good time to see the entire movie from beginning to end. Like Woody Allen in *Annie Hall*. Only with better hair.

But still not a patch on Zac Efron's hair . . .

Have I told you how much I like Zac Efron? How much his screen presence reminds me of a better time, when movie stars learned their craft in vaudeville, earned their spurs tap dancing on stage, and then signed their lives away to movie studios who would put them on a treadmill and micromanage their careers into the grave, bizarrely creating some great works of art in the process? For me, Zac was cut from the same cloth as Fred Astaire, Gene Kelly and Donald O'Connor – hard-working hoofers who put their heart and soul into entertaining their audience, and who tripped across the screen with an elegance and grace that was at once delightful and heartbreaking. Johnny Depp is the same: an anachronistic silent-movie star who seems to have been washed up on the shores of the talkies, a devotee of Buster Keaton who is not afraid to act with his body rather than just his eyes. Oh, don't get me wrong, he's absolutely rubbish in the *Pirates of the Caribbean* movies (the worst Anthony Newley impression since David Bowie, even if he insists it's meant to be Keith Richards) and ironically excruciating in *Benny & Joon*, in which he effectively plays Buster Keaton with toe-curling results. But take a look at his performance in Jim Jarmusch's monochrome Western *Dead Man* and then tell me that Depp is not one of the greatest silent actors of his generation. I once interviewed Neil Young, who did the soundtrack to *Dead Man*, and he remembered telling Jarmusch that he had made a wonderful silent movie and it would be a shame to spoil it. He went on to record what was effectively a live musical accompaniment, playing his clanging, echoey guitar direct-to-picture as if he were an ad hoc accompanist performing right there in the theatrical auditorium. To this day it baffles me that *Dead Man* is not more highly regarded or widely seen by fans of Jarmusch, Young and Depp, who must surely amount to tens of millions. If only a tenth of those who shelled out for the *Pirates* abominations had paid to buy a ticket for *Dead Man*, then intelligent independent cinema would be in far better financial shape all round. Hey ho.

As for Zac, while he's unlikely to tread the offbeat indie path any time soon (although *Me and Orson Welles* was a step in the right direction), I love the fact that he's trying to broaden his dramatic palette without alienating the tweenie fanbase who first made him a star, and without whose affections he wouldn't be where he is today. Many modern stars spend hours whingeing about how hard it is to be shackled to a hyperactively hormonal young audience, but intriguingly they only tend to do so after enthusiastically courting and winning their affections in the first place; you don't hear them bleating when no one knows them from a hole in the ground, or running around telling everybody how fabulous it is to be an utter failure – an anonymous waffle waiter rather than an overpaid teen idol. The honest truth is that today's female teenage audiences have, in general, been pretty poorly served by a movie industry that seems to think acne-ridden boys are the only demographic worth targeting. If you're a 13-year-old girl (and I understand very well that if you're reading this book then you're probably not) you have more right to complain about the parlous state of modern cinema than anyone else in the auditorium. Just as the producers of the drive-in horror movies of the fifties and sixties figured that the boys were going to be buying the tickets to the movies which made the girls seek refuge in the safety of their sweaty arms, so today's studio heads still seem to believe that the viewing market is dominated by young men and hence all movies should be aimed at them, with an occasional 'something for the ladies' thrown in to give the appearance of balance. I once heard a cinema manager attempting to tell a potential ticket-buying customer that whilst *Transformers* was essentially a boys' flick (big robots hitting each other – you know the drill) it would also appeal to girls because it had 'some romance', i.e. the sight of Megan Fox's arse bending over the bonnet of a car and some jokes about Shia LaBeouf wanking. Apparently, this is what now passes for gender equality in tweenie cinema.

Back to Zac and *Charlie St. Cloud*. The film started and

almost immediately I was annoyed. Why? Not because the film wasn't any good (which I already knew it was) but because none of us in the auditorium – whether in standard or premium seating – were seeing the whole picture, thanks to the kind of sloppy projection that has become symptomatic of the modern multiplex experience. As I have mentioned elsewhere, I am completely anal on the subject of correct screen ratios, and not only do I need to see a film from the very beginning to the very end, I also need to see the whole image *as it was meant to be projected*. And in this particular case, I doubt very much whether director Burr Steers had intended the uppermost part of his frame to be cut off. The problem was simple – the film wasn't aligned correctly, and therefore the image was spilling over the top of the screen and on to the shabby masking which supposedly marked the upper border of the picture. The solution was equally simple – either rack the picture down a few inches, or move the masking. Or change the lens, or the aperture, or something. Whatever – the projectionist would know what to do, and presumably they were about to do it.

For various reasons, the first few moments of a movie are often accompanied by a degree of image correction as the projectionist looks out from the soundproofed box and realises that something's not quite right up there on the screen. Occasionally the problem will be major: the film will be back to front or upside down, having been loaded into the projector the wrong way round, and everything has to be shut down for a few moments in order to reload. At other times the image will be the wrong shape or size, usually because the projector has the wrong lens attached, but again this can be rectified fairly swiftly once the problem has been noted. As for incorrect racking or alignment, this can be tweaked by a deft projectionist who, in an ideal world, will also have control of the black curtains and moveable borders that frame the screen. Ideally, such issues should be sorted out in advance, but as anyone who's ever worked in a fast-turnaround cinema knows, this isn't always possible. So it's generally taken as read that the first few moments of a film may involve a degree of fiddling about which no one is going to complain.

Or are they?

Frankly, at £8.50 a ticket (£10 for premium, where the picture problems would be just the same) I figure they ought to have tested the damned thing in advance. But, hey, everyone makes mistakes, and it would only take a moment to fix.

As soon as the projectionist looked at the screen they'd know it looked wrong.

Which would be any moment now.

Any moment now . . .

They'd look out of their box and realise that the top of Zac's head was missing . . .

Or at least the top of his hair, which was just as bad . . .

Worse, in fact . . .

Any moment now . . .

Just has to look . . .

Look out of their box . . .

At the screen . . .

At Zac's head . . .

And his hair . . .

Or lack of it . . .

Any moment now . . .

Any moment . . .

Any moment . . .

Any . . .

Oh, for fuck's sake.

I got up out of my seat (easy when it's on an aisle – *see?*) and strode purposefully out of the theatre in search of an usher.

There weren't any.

As we know.

So I strode all the way back down the corridor, right back to the huge queue for the 'comestibles and tickets' stand that still snaked all the way out into the foyer, and accosted someone wearing what appeared to be the uniform of the establishment in question.

'Can you tell the projectionist to check the picture in Screen Seven?' I said with what I believed to be an air of firm authority. 'The picture's spilling over the top of the screen.'

The uniformed monkey gazed at me with an air of blank bewilderment. He appeared to be just hitting puberty. Right there. Right then. Right in the middle of the lobby, by the look of him.

'Whaaaaaa?' he drooled.

I took a deep breath – this was going to be annoyingly complicated. Let's try and make it simple.

'The projectionist,' I said slowly and clearly 'in Screen Seven . . . needs to adjust the picture. Or to move the masking. By about a foot. Can you tell him? Or her? Please?'

The pubertal monkey stared at me, slack-jawed, his mouth grasping at word-like shapes but his vocal chords too bored to go to the effort of actually making a noise.

'Please?' I asked again.

The monkey turned and pulled something chunky and weather-beaten from out of the waistband of his trousers. To my amazement, it appeared to be a walkie-talkie. Could he possibly operate such a hi-tech device? Apparently so. He pushed a button and held the machine to his head, where it let out a high-pitched screeching sound, causing him to jump a little and recoil in terror (so maybe he couldn't, after all). I imagined that would be the end of it but, no, he was going to have another go. He looked at the machine again, shook it, pressed the same button, waited for the awful howling noise, got nothing, and then gingerly lifted the receiver back toward his face.

'Roger?' he whispered, hesitantly, with just a hint of fear.

Nothing.

'Roger?' he said again, this time a little louder, a little more assertive. But answer came there none. He decided to give it one last go.

'*Roger!*' he shouted into the machine at a volume which meant Roger would probably have heard were he anywhere in the cinema complex, whether the walkie-talkie was working or not. Presumably most of the audience in Screen

Seven – where I was currently missing *Charlie St. Cloud* in the same way that Zac's head was missing the screen – heard it too. So much for turning off your mobile phones for the consideration of others.

But apparently Roger had heard nothing, or if he had he was staunchly refusing to answer the call of duty. Clearly Roger had about as much enthusiasm for this cinema as I did. Then, with a flash of inspiration, monkey boy remembered something and took his finger *off* the button he had been depressing since this strange procedure began. Suddenly the machine in his hand leapt into squawking, shrieking life again, catching a raised voice mid-sentence that one could only assume belonged to the aforesaid Roger.

'. . . *your finger off the button, you muppet!*'

Monkey boy blanched and put his finger straight back on the button to silence any further outburst. Taking control of the situation, he raised his chin, brought the walkie-talkie very close to his lips (while surreptitiously turning *down* the volume control) and said in a voice which sounded uncannily like those automated train information systems that claim to be robotically sorry when your service is delayed, 'Please come immediately to the ticketing area where customer assistance is required thank you over and out.' And with that he clicked the intercom off as swiftly as possible and jammed it back down into his waistband. It was a deft move, made all the more impressive by the fact that I had been rather surprised to discover he could speak, and the combination of language skills and manual dexterity had caught me quite off guard. I wasn't

51

sure whether to applaud, like you do in the circus when a chimpanzee peels a banana with its feet while riding a tricycle and wearing a bowler hat, or to laugh, like we used to do when those unhappy primates in the PG Tips commercials pretended to push musical instruments up a flight of stairs. ('Dad, do you know the piano's on my foot?' 'You hum it, son, I'll play it.') As it transpired, neither response would have been appropriate as this callow youth clearly had no intention of making eye contact or engaging in small talk. He was not, in industrial terms, 'customer facing', although this being the case it was hard to know exactly what he was facing. It seemed to me that, when approached by a ticket-buying customer, his only response had been to send out for reinforcements, presumably to neutralise the threat to his personal space. For all I knew, the phrase 'customer assistance required' meant that he (rather than I) needed the assistance, presumably to protect him from the customer, and what was required was for me to be neutralised forthwith. Whatever, having made audio contact with 'Roger' he had apparently done his bit for queen and country, and he wasn't going to do anything else except stand there and hope I wouldn't notice him.

Out of politeness, I didn't.

So we both stood there, saying nothing, waiting for Roger, like characters in a Beckett play. Only unlike a Beckett play, Roger did actually arrive. Quite quickly, in fact. Or at least, more quickly than I had expected, considering how long everything else had taken in this bloody hellhole. For all I knew, by the time I had explained the problem to Roger, the projectionist would have woken from their slumber, looked out of their box, noticed the absence of Zac's usually fabulous hair, and adjusted the picture all by themselves, thus making my laborious intervention utterly unnecessary and making me look like a bit of a fool. Maybe I was missing out on some perfectly projected Zac right now, hanging around moaning in the lobby when I should have been relaxing in the luxurious comfort of premium seating. I was starting to wish I'd stayed put.

But here was Roger, smiling, ambulant, comparatively grown up, and apparently unaware that I had overheard his recent untempered radiophonic outburst.

'Hi, I'm Roger,' he said somewhat extraneously, but with the air of a man who was well on his way to becoming assistant manager in the very near future. Clearly Roger was the guy to be dealing with, and all my trials, Lord, would soon be over. Perhaps they were over already?

Who knew? But Roger was keen to help.

'What seems to be the trouble?' he asked, like the go-getting, problem-solving sort of chap he so clearly was.

'Well,' I began, relieved to be dealing with someone with the power to make things happen. 'It's nothing terrible. It's just that the projectionist in Screen Seven needs to adjust the picture a little because it's spilling over the top of the screen.'

'I see,' said Roger, giving every impression that he did, although with noticeably less bonhomie than he appeared to be exuding about ten seconds ago – before I started telling him about the 'problem' in Screen Seven. There was a bit of an awkward silence. I wasn't quite sure why. But I decided to fill it anyway.

'So if you could just tell the projectionist in Screen Seven to . . .'

'He's not *in* Screen Seven,' said Roger, a little tersely I thought, and with an edge of irritation which suggested he did not quite appreciate the fact that I knew perfectly well the projectionist was not literally *in* Screen Seven. He was up in the projection booth.

'He's in the projection booth,' explained Roger.

I pursed my lips a little and tried to gauge the tone of this comment. Was he having me on? Or did he actually think that I needed to be told that the projectionist was in the projection booth, rather than in Screen Seven? I decided to give him the benefit of the doubt.

'I know he's in the projection booth,' I replied, taking care to keep my tone measured and encouragingly interactive, with no trace of hostility. 'He's in the projection booth for Screen Seven and . . .'

'No,' Roger cut in assertively. 'He's in *the* projection booth. There's only one. It's very modern. All the screens are controlled from there.'

This was undoubtedly true. As we noted earlier, it has long been common practice for a single overworked projectionist to operate any number of screens in a modern multiplex, leaving them unable to attend to the deficiencies of an individual performance. The solution to this problem, according to those who run such establishments, is not to employ more projectionists but rather to install equipment that has no need of the projectionist's art. Equipment like those aforementioned digital projectors which need only to be switched on, allowing the whole movie to be perfectly projected from beginning to end without clunky reel changes or old-fashioned analogue snarl-ups, just like it does when you put a DVD on at home and simply sit back and enjoy the picture.

Have you ever done that? Slapped a DVD on and then just sat back and enjoyed the picture?

I haven't.

Why not?

Because the opportunity for error with digital information is just too great.

First up, you have to make sure that the picture is playing in the right screen ratio. Oh, I know this infuriates people, and I'm constantly being told just how annoying it is that I *cannot be in the same room* as anyone watching TV in *the wrong ratio* without reaching for the remote and correcting the grievous error forthwith. But why the hell shouldn't I, when those errors are so easy to fix? It's not like the picture doesn't look wrong, for crying out loud. And every modern television handset has a ratio-adjustment button that will happily snap between screen sizes until you arrive at the right one . . . which you will know you have reached because it's the one that *looks right*. It really doesn't matter what you're watching, whether it's a handsomely remastered copy of John Ford's *The Searchers* or the early evening broadcast of *Look North West*. It makes no difference; if the people on the screen look dumpy and squat, or squished and thin, then change the flipping ratio until they look right (unless you're watching *Sex and the City*, in which case that's how they're meant to look).

And it's not over once you've got the ratio sorted. As anyone who has ever watched a DVD will know, getting the disc to start playing is just the beginning of the fun. Since digital technology is a binary yes/no (or on/off) affair, it is entirely possible for a machine attempting to convert a string of noughts and ones into moving pictures to give up the ghost unannounced at any time, causing the picture to freeze and the player to helpfully inform you that it has encountered a 'disc error' or, less helpfully, to attempt to assure you that there simply is 'no disc' on which errors might occur. So you trudge over to the machine, take out the allegedly non-existent disc, wipe it on your T-shirt (having perhaps breathed on it first), and then put it back into the player to see if it likes it any better this time. Sometimes it does, and it will start playing from where you left off (hooray!). Other times, it will insist on going back to the start menu and make you endure those infuriatingly patronising anti-piracy messages through which it is impossible to fast forward. Most often, it will simply repeat its evidence-defying claim that there is 'no disc', leaving you to: a) start the whole process all over again; or b) shout, swear, kick the DVD player, try again, fail again, and finally end up watching *Look North West* instead. In the wrong ratio.

Do you have a picture of this 'home is where the hate is' horror in your mind? OK, now transfer that to a cinema auditorium, where the problem is magnified by the fact that everyone there has just paid ten quid for the thrill of being there, and now the bloody film's either in the wrong ratio (due to being projected through the wrong lens) or misaligned or stuck or whatever, and you can't get anywhere near the projector to kick it. I once interviewed a projectionist from a major West End cinema who told me that he refused to run a digital print of a movie unless he had a secondary 35mm back-up projector running simultaneously, but 30 seconds behind. That way, if the digital brick blipped (which they are wont to do) he could simply open up the second projector and show the rest of the film from reliable old celluloid. The great advantage of film is that it is splendidly mechanical, and if anything goes wrong it can usually be fixed with razor blades and sticking plaster in a matter of moments. The same is true of gramophone records; if the record gets stuck, you can always just move the needle on to the next groove and away you go. Not so with CDs, which when they fail run the risk of simply not playing at all. I know this to be true having worked at Radio 1 during the great advent of CDs and D-carts (digital cartridges) and experiencing first-hand the horror of TDF (Total Digital Failure), which you simply never had to face with old-fashioned analogue. Hell, if worse came to the worst, you could actually haul a segment of tape through a reel-to-reel machine *manually* and it would continue to play. OK, so the sound would wobble and warp all over the place, but at least it didn't just *stop* and leave you with nothing but silence.

Or darkness.

Or a frozen picture, which is what you get when a digitally projected film fails.

And when that happens, not only is there nothing the projectionist can do about it (unless they've got a 35mm print laced and ready to go), but most of the time there's no projectionist there not to be able to do anything about it in the first place. They're too busy being unable to do anything about a whole other bunch of screens.

Which brings us back to Screen Seven and Zac Efron's hair. Or (as I mentioned previously) the lack of it. Having ascertained from Roger that the picture was (as I suspected) not being closely monitored by a keen-eyed projectionist after all, the next step seemed simple enough – get Roger to get the projectionist to move their arse up the projection corridor and correctly adjust the image in Screen Seven forthwith, a process which would take approximately 30 seconds tops. How hard could it be?

Very hard, apparently.

Firstly, Roger refused to believe that there was anything wrong with the image in Screen Seven.

'No one's complained,' he stated firmly.

'Um, *I'm* complaining,' I replied, still unsure whether he was taking the piss.

'Well, no one *else* is complaining,' clarified Roger, theatrically casting his eye around the lobby as if searching for an angry mob with flaming torches demanding to see more of the top of Zac Efron's head. There were indeed none – I was alone in my complaint. But I failed to see how the fact that everyone else was prepared to put up with shoddy projection meant that I had to do the same myself. I was beginning to feel worryingly militant about this issue.

'Look,' I said, still struggling to maintain a veneer of politeness. 'The image is spilling over the top of the screen. It's as clear as day. Come and see for yourself.'

Roger thought about this for a moment, and then looked intently at his watch, clearly attempting to give the impression of a man who was far too busy doing his job to worry about keeping the customers happy. Then he apparently remembered that keeping the customers happy *was* his job, slapped on a plastic smile, looked me in the eye and said,

'OK, I'll check it out.'

'Great. Thanks. Thanks for that. Thanks very much.' I was pathetically relieved to have achieved such an assurance of cooperation, particularly since things had looked like they were about to turn uncomfortable. With a spring in my stride, I almost skipped my way back to Screen Seven, happy despite having now missed nearly 15 minutes of the movie. No matter, I'd seen it before, and I knew what happened. It was a shame I'd missed the car crash, because that sequence was actually done really well. But it was worth it to know that Roger was going to come and take a look at the picture, notice the fact that the top of the frame was doing battle distractingly with the top of the screen, realise I had been right all along, and then go get the projectionist to fix the problem with the merest tweak of a knob or changing of a lens. OK, so right now the image was all wrong and kept messing with the top of Zac's hair. But any moment now it would all be sorted out.

Any moment now.

Any moment.

Really soon.

Just another few moments, to give Roger the time to get up to the projection booth, track down the projectionist, drag them away from whichever other screen was currently occupying them, point out the problem, and get them to fix it . . .

Any moment now.

Coming soon.

To this theatre.

A correctly projected image.

Any moment now.

Any moment.

Any . . .

OH, FOR FUCK'S SAKE!

I sprang out of my chair, down the aisle and out into the corridor, almost breaking into a run as I headed toward the lobby. As I rounded the corner I saw Roger, idly chatting away with a gaggle of his similarly underemployed cohorts, none of whom seemed particularly interested in cinema in general, and the running of this cinema in particular. As I thundered toward him, Roger turned with the merest hint of a smirk on his face, apparently unflustered by my evident sense of outrage.

'What the hell's going on?' I demanded. 'I thought you

were going to come and check the picture in Screen Seven.'

'Yeah,' replied Roger, unfazed and more than a little uninterested. 'I did. It's fine.'

He smiled at me, as if to suggest that I should stop worrying my silly little head about such things and get back to my seat. I was doing no such thing.

'It's *not* fine,' I said firmly. 'It's cutting off the top of Zac Efron's hair. He's missing a whole foot from his head.'

'He's *what?*'

'The top foot of the picture is missing.'

'The top *few inches* of the picture is missing,' Roger corrected, patronisingly. 'It's fine.'

This statement floored me. Roger was conceding that a part of the picture – the exact amount of which was admittedly a matter for debate – was indeed 'missing', as I had been saying for the past 20 minutes. But apparently in his mind this was 'fine'. Never mind that I had paid to see the whole picture, rather than some diminished proportion of the same. I wondered whether Roger would have found it equally 'fine' if an equivalent proportion of the cost of my ticket was similarly missing; if, for example, I had handed over £13.00 rather than £14.60 for one-and-a-half seats, on the grounds that all but the top few inches of the purchase price were present and correct, and so that was 'fine'.

'But you can't see *all* of the picture!' I protested. 'How can that be fine?'

'I've checked,' said Roger, as if this somehow explained his position. Which it didn't.

'What do you mean, you've checked? You've just agreed

with me that the top of the picture is missing. I think it's a foot, you think it's a few inches — what the heck, let's split the difference and call it a "nadge". Whatever. The point is we both agree that *some* part of the picture is notable by its absence so just tell the projectionist to rack it down a bit and . . .'

'He can't "rack it down a bit" while the film is playing,' declared Roger with an air of dismissive superiority.

This sounded like utter bollocks. I decided it was time to move things up a gear, and do something I have honestly never done before: pull D-list celebrity rank.

'Listen,' I said, quietly enough to make Roger have to lean forward in order to hear what I was saying. 'I am a film critic. I have been a film critic for twenty-five years. I know the film playing in Screen Seven isn't meant to look like that because I saw it properly projected at a press screening in London four days ago, where I particularly enjoyed seeing all of Zac Efron's head, including his hair. I don't know whether you're projecting from celluloid or digital but I *do* know that his hair should feature prominently in *either* format, which it *isn't* doing in Screen Seven. I know that it is possible to correct an image on screen while the film is playing because highly qualified projectionists have been doing just that for over a hundred years. I also know that I have paid a huge amount of money to watch this film, and having done so I expect you to have the courtesy to take my complaints about the quality of the picture seriously enough to actually go and *do something about it* . . .'

Roger looked at me. I looked at Roger.

Everyone else looked at Roger and Me.

We stood there, deadlocked.

Finally, Roger went for his gun.

'The picture's fine,' he said.

And with that, he turned on his heel and strode off into the foyer.

On the journey home, I asked my daughter if she'd enjoyed the film.

'Oh yeah,' she said. 'It was great. I really like Zac Efron.'

'Did you like his hair?' I asked, in a leading kind of way.

'Umm, sure. But I meant more that I really like him as an actor. He's got a really good "dramatic range". You know, he can do happy, and sad; romantic, and tough; grown-up, but childlike. He's really good.'

'But what about his hair?' I insisted. 'Could you see it alright?'

'What do you mean? His hair was fine. Why? Didn't you like it?'

'Yes. I liked it a *lot*, but I just couldn't see it because the picture was racked too high.'

'What?'

'The picture was misaligned. It kept cutting off the top of his head. And his hair. Didn't you notice?'

'Oh yeah, but so what? You could see his face OK.'

'Yes, but you couldn't see his *hair*.'

My daughter looked at me as if I was mad.

'But, Dad, he wasn't acting with his hair, he was acting with his face.'

She thought for a moment, and then frowned.

'Is that where you went in the middle of the film? Were you having another argument with the cinema manager?'

'What? No. Well, not the manager. The *assistant* manager. Or maybe the about-to-be-the-assistant manager. Roger somebody or other. And it wasn't an argument . . .'

'*Daaad*,' said my daughter, rolling her eyes in exasperation. 'You're *always* getting into arguments.'

'I am not.'

'Yes, you are.'

'No, I'm not!'

'Yes, you are; look, you're doing it now!'

'I'm *not*!'

'You *are*. Why couldn't you just sit and watch the film? Like everybody else . . .?'

I had no answer to this. Or rather, I had an answer that was so long it would take forever to explain.

I decided to change the subject.

'OK, so you liked it?' I said, cheerfully. 'You had a good time at the cinema? It was fun, right?'

My daughter nodded.

'What did you like best about it?'

Georgia paused, looked at me with her best deadpan expression, and then said:

'Popcorn.'

Chapter Two

WHY BLOCKBUSTERS SHOULD BE BETTER

'Well, it's one for the money . . .'
Carl Perkins

Here are three absolute truths:

1. The world is round.
2. We are all going to die.
3. No one enjoyed *Pirates of the Caribbean: At World's End*.

Oh, I know loads of people paid to see *POTC3* (as I believe it is known in the industry). And some of them may claim to have enjoyed it. But they didn't. Not really. They just think they did. As a film critic, an important part of my job is explaining to people why they haven't actually enjoyed a movie even if they think they have. In the case of *POTC3,* the explanation is very simple.

It's called 'diminished expectations'.

Let me give you an example.

When I was a student in Manchester I lived in a place called Hulme, a sprawling concrete estate of industrially produced deck-access housing that had been declared unfit for families in the mid-seventies and had subsequently descended into oddly bohemian squalor. By the time I arrived in Hulme in the early eighties it was full of students who loved it, because the rent was incredibly cheap and nobody paid it anyway – the council couldn't evict you for non-payment because that would just make you homeless and Hulme was the place to which they sent homeless people after they'd been thrown out of everywhere else.

The architecture of Hulme was a strange mix of sixties sci-fi futurism and bleak Eastern European uniformity, the kind of place J.G. Ballard had nightmares about. It was grimly cinematic, so much so that the photographer Kevin Cummins had used it as the background for his iconic photographs of Joy Division, the most existentially miserable band of the seventies. At nights, as the sun went down and the lights came up around the McEwan's beer factory which wafted noxious fumes across the entire misbegotten district, it seemed more like a scene from *Blade Runner* than the landscape of a thriving northern town. At regular intervals gangs of straggle-haired youths, who appeared to have escaped from the set of *Mad Max 2,* would drift across the overpass that traversed the Mancunian Way, shopping trolleys of worthless loot pushed religiously before them and umpteen dogs on various bits of string prowling behind them picking off survivors. Occasionally, an incongruous ice-cream van would creep its lonely way from one hideously uninviting tower block to another, its broken chimes turned up to maximum volume, creating a hellish racket that was somewhere between a nursery rhyme and a death rattle. As far as anyone could tell, it was selling drugs. We called it 'The Ice Cream Van of the Apocalypse'.

Mugging was a fairly common occurrence in Hulme, as was burglary and the occasional assault by packs of wild dogs. When I first moved into Otterburn Close, my third-floor flat had a pathetically inadequate H-frame door that was one part rotten wood to ten parts flimsy 'security glass'. The first time I got burgled, the door was broken so badly that the council were unable to fix it, so they replaced it with a newfangled 'security door'. Unlike their predecessors these were largely made of wood, with three tiny window slats allowing the people inside to look *out* without allowing everyone outside to come *in*. These new doors were such a whizzo idea that everyone wanted one and the council just couldn't keep up with demand.

The next time I got burgled, they stole the door.

Such was life in Hulme.

One day, a man from the council popped in to visit a friend of mine called Phil, who had accidentally agreed to take part in a survey of some sort. All he had to do was answer a few very simple questions about the state of his flat and his experience of living in Hulme.

'How *is* the flat?' asked the man with the clipboard. 'All fine?'

'Oh yes,' replied Phil, 'all absolutely fine. Very good in fact.'

'So, no complaints?'

'No, no complaints.'

'None whatsoever?'

'No, really, everything's fine.'

'I see,' said the man from the council, apparently uncon-vinced. 'So all the services in the flat are in full working order?'

'Well,' replied Phil, 'the boiler doesn't work.'

'Ah, I see. And how long has it been out of order?'

'Well,' said Phil, 'that's hard to say because it wasn't working when we got here.'

'And how long ago was that?'

'About three years ago.'

'*Three years?*'

'Yes. About that.'

'So your boiler hasn't worked for at least three years?'

'No. But, you know, we make do . . .'

'I see. And is there anything else that doesn't work?'

'Well, of course the intercom's never been connected, so technically that "doesn't work", although it's not as if it's broken – it's just not there. And the downstairs toilet's bust. But it's only the downstairs one, so, hey. And the kitchen sink leaks, so we use a bowl. Which is fine. And come to think of it the asbestos has started to crumble and leave little white flakes all over the inside of the boiler cupboard which is probably rather dangerous. But it's not a problem because, to be honest, we rarely open the boiler-cupboard door anyway.'

'Because the boiler doesn't work?'

'No, because of the cockroaches.'

'I see,' said the man from the council, laying his clipboard on his lap. 'I'm afraid we've come across this rather a lot. It's called "diminished expectations".'

All of which is a roundabout way of saying that the people who think they enjoyed *POTC3* are simply suffering from the cinematic equivalent of long-term deprivation from the basics of a civilised existence. They are the multiplex dwellers who have become used to living in the cultural freezing cold, whose brains have been addled by poisonous celluloid asbestos, and whose expectations of mainstream entertainment have been gradually eroded by leaky plumbing and infestations of verminous pests.

They are the Audiences of the Apocalypse.

How did they get here?

The short answer is: Michael Bay.

The long answer is: Michael Bay; Kevin Costner's gills; *Cleopatra* on home video; and the inability of modern blockbusters to lose money in the long run, no matter how terrible they may be.

If you don't believe me, ask yourself this question: 'Was *Pearl Harbor* a hit?'

The answer, obviously, ought to be a resounding 'No'. For, as even the lowliest of amoebic life forms can tell you, that film was shockingly poor in ways it is almost painful to imagine. For one thing, it is '*un film de* Michael Bay', the reigning deity of all that is loathsome, putrid and soul destroying about modern-day blockbuster entertainment. 'There are tons of people who hate me,' admits Bay, who turned an innocuous TV-and-toys franchise into puerile pop pornography with his headache-inducing *Transformers* movies. 'They said that I wrecked cinema. But hey, my movies have made a lot of money around the world.' If you want kids' movies in which cameras crawl up young women's skirts while CGI robots hit each other over the head, interspersed with jokes about masturbation and borderline-racist sub-minstrelsy stereotyping, then Bay is your go-to guy. He is also, shockingly, one of the most commercially successful directors working in Hollywood today, a hit-maker who proudly describes his visual style as 'fucking the frame' and whose movies appear to have been put together by people who have just snorted two tonnes of weapons-grade plutonium. Don't get me wrong – he's not stupid; he publicly admitted that *Transformers: Revenge of the Fallen* was below even his own poor par (his exact words were 'When I look back at it, that was crap'), after leading man and charisma vacuum Shia LaBeouf declared that he 'wasn't impressed with what we did'. But somehow Bay's awareness of his own films' awfulness simply makes matters worse. At least Ed Wood, director of *Plan 9 from Outer Space*, thought the trash he was making was good. Bay seems to know better, and if he does that knowledge merely compounds his guilt. Down in the deepest bowels of the abyss there is a tenth circle of Hell in which Bay's movies play for all eternity, waiting for their creator to arrive, his soul tortured by the real-isation that he *knew what he was doing . . .*

But I digress. Back to *Pearl Harbor*. In early 2001, *Pearl Harbor* was the most eagerly awaited blockbuster of the summer season. The script was by Randall Wallace, whose previous piece of historical balderdash was the Oscar-winning *Braveheart*, a movie that allegedly advanced the cause of Scottish nationalism with its shots of lochs, thistles, and men in kilts and blue woad eating haggis to the sound of bagpipes (although most of it was actually shot in Ireland after someone cut a canny deal with the government to use the An Fórsa Cosanta Áitiúil as extras – Viva William Wallace!). As a writer who appears to have a flimsy grasp of history, and who would have us believe that it is possible for men to deliver defiant speeches whilst having their intestines removed on a rack, Wallace was the perfect choice to pen a movie about the worst military disaster in US history in which 'America wins!' The fact that *Pearl Harbor* (the movie) would attempt this revisionist *coup de grâce* in the same year that America suffered its worst attack on home soil *since* Pearl Harbor (the real disaster, rather than the movie) could not have been predicted by the film-makers. But the fact that they were making one of the worst pieces of crap to grace movie theatres in living memory should have been horribly apparent to anyone who had read that bloody awful screenplay. Bad writing is one thing – bad *reading* is unforgivable. Wallace may be a rotten screenwriter (he writes lines that even Ben Affleck looks embarrassed to deliver), but it was Michael Bay and *Pirates of the Caribbean* producer Jerry Bruckheimer who gave him the go-ahead, and who must therefore shoulder the blame.

Anyway, the film got made and released, with the full support of the US Navy who gave the film-makers access to their military hardware and staged a premiere party by a graveyard (the eponymous harbour) to the shock and awe of relatives of the dead. Hey ho. The reviews were terrible, although I was personally guilty of the most atrociously contrary humbug by attempting to claim that the movie really wasn't as utterly awful as everyone was saying. What the hell was I thinking? Looking back on it now, I shudder to remember just how lenient I had been – how I had claimed that the film offered a brainless spectacle in the now time-honoured tradition of summer blockbusters, about which I had recently written a stupidly enthusiastic article for some glossy publication from whom I was frankly flattered to receive a commission. It was a shameful misjudgement, which I will carry with me to my grave, and I fully expect to be joining Mr Bay in that multiplex in Hell, wracked by the guilty knowledge that I just stood by and allowed this horror to happen.

Never trust a critic.

Especially this critic.

Others, however, were more forthright and correctly identified *Pearl Harbor* for the cack that it so clearly was. Audiences were in agreement – the vast majority of the emailed comments that Simon Mayo and I received at our BBC 5 Live radio show from people who had shelled out good money to watch *Pearl Harbor* (I saw it at a free press preview screening – always a plus) were roundly condemnatory, and many were genuinely flabbergasted by just how boring the movie had been.

So, the film was a flop, right?

Wrong.

Wrong, wrong, wrong, wrong, *wrong*.

Listen . . .

During production, there was much trade-press tooth-sucking about the fact that *Pearl Harbor*'s 'authorised starting budget' was $135 million, a record-breaking sum back then. Bay and Bruckheimer had originally wanted $208 million, and the director was widely reported to have 'walked' on several occasions as arguments about how much money the movie should cost continued. As the story of the budget grew, Bay and Bruckheimer very publicly agreed to take $4 million salary cuts (in return for a percentage of the profits – clever) to 'keep the budget down', thereby giving the impression that every cent spent would be up there on screen. The final cost of the film was somewhere between $140 and $160 million, figures gleefully quoted by negative reviewers who spied a massive flop ahoy and predicted chastening financial losses. Yet in *Variety*'s annual roundup of the biggest grossing movies of 2001, *Pearl Harbor* came in at number six, having taken just shy of $200 million dollars in the US alone. By the time the film had finished its world-wide theatrical run, this abomination had raked in a staggering $450 million worldwide, helping to push Buena Vista International's takings over the $1 billion mark for the seventh consecutive year. No matter that almost everyone who saw the film found it a crushing disappointment – as far as the dollars were concerned, *Pearl Harbor* was an unconditional hit.

It gets worse. Having more than made its money back in cinemas, *Pearl Harbor* went on to become an equally outrageous success on DVD, the release of the money-spinning disc tastefully timed to coincide with the 60th anniversary of the original attack. Available in 'several packages, including a gift set' (and at 183 minutes, *Pearl Harbor* is the gift that just keeps on giving), the DVD included a commentary track by Michael Bay who was apparently aware that his bold attempts to make a 1940s-style romance had been misinterpreted by some viewers as simply rubbish. Presumably it wasn't the film that was at fault – it was the film's *critics* who just weren't up to it.

So why did so many people pay for it?

One answer is 'diminished expectations': the film was a summer blockbuster, which everyone (myself included) expected to be utterly terrible before they saw it, and so no one was surprised when it turned out to be every bit as dire as predicted. But why pay to see something that you know in advance is going to be a disappointment? The truth is that, like it or loathe it, *Pearl Harbor* was 'an event' – a film which made headlines long before the cameras turned thanks to its bloated budget, and which managed to stay in the headlines throughout its production courtesy of a unique mix of historical tactlessness, fatuous movie-star flashing (Kate Beckinsale reportedly displayed her naked bottom during a no-pants flypast – whoopee!) and, most importantly, enormous expense. Remember that story about Bay and Bruckheimer cutting their salaries? For whose benefit do you think that story was planted? And what about the story (dutifully repeated on the film's Internet Movie Database entry) that 'the after-premiere party for *Pearl Harbor* is said to have cost more than the production costs for *Billy Elliot*'. Or that 'Michael Bay quit the project four times over various budgetary disputes'. Or, best of all, that 'the total amount of money spent on production and promotion roughly equalled the amount of damage caused in the actual attack'.

Even though some of these stories may appear at first glance to be mocking the movie and its grotesque expense, they are all in fact a publicist's wet dream, and you can be pretty much guaranteed that the only reason we know about any of them is because some publicist somewhere told someone who would in turn tell us. This is how movie publicity works – with very rare exceptions, everything you know about a movie (at least during its initial release period) is a sales pitch. Even the reviews, about which film-makers regularly bleat and whinge and moan, are part of this sales process, raising the profile of the product. Why else would the studios go to the bother and expense of putting on private pre-release screenings for critics who may very well savage their product? If they really thought the reviews were going to hurt the movie, or have zero beneficial effect upon its box office, they wouldn't press screen them at all. That's what happens with the *Saw* movies, a rampagingly successful horror franchise that has thrived without press shows for several years now. As far as the distributors are concerned, they don't need critics to raise audience awareness (the films have a firm dumbo teenage fanbase who get their 'info-tainment' from posters, internet trailers and carefully planted tabloid-press stories), and since the *Saw* sequels are increasingly rotten to the core there's no chance of any proper critic actually filing a quotably 'good' review. I have yet to see any evidence that bad reviews can in fact damage a film's box office (more of which in Chapter Four) but the distributors of *Saw* clearly aren't taking any chances, so they just don't screen them – end of story.

With *Pearl Harbor* (which was proudly screened to critics around the world) you can be sure that the piss-poor reviews it provoked were all part of the plan. Oh, I'm not claiming that the distributors wanted the critics to hate the movie – they would have preferred glowing notices praising its universal love story and drooling over its expensive special effects. But they will have known in advance that the reviews were going to be generally negative (because the film itself was so bad) and they went ahead with those press screenings anyway. Crucially, there were no 'long lead' previews, which are used to generate positive word-of-mouth buzz and to build audience awareness of titles that people might actually *like*. Instead, the film was screened as close to its release date as possible, ensuring that by the time the reviews (good or bad) appeared, the film was available for viewing by paying punters eager to see what all the fuss was about. And, as planned, many (if not most) of those reviews referred at some point to the whopping budget, about which the publicists had been priming us all since pre-production. However scathing a particular review may have been, the reader (or listener, or viewer) would come away having been reminded that *Pearl Harbor* cost a vast amount of money, and understanding that, for the price of a ticket, he or she could see where all that money had gone. Rather than the stars, the money was the story. And in today's marketplace, that's a story which almost always has a happy ending.

This wasn't always the case. Back in the good old days, really terrible movies could actually sink studios. Because film-making is such a costly enterprise, the risk factor involved in making a movie has always been high, with lavishly mounted productions facing the very real prospect of failing to recoup. For this reason, studios and producers would attempt to build levels of certainty into big budget productions, most notably by the presence of star names (who came with a loyal following, upon whose box-office bucks you could rely) and spectacle (if the explosions were big enough, or the scenery jaw-dropping enough, people might forget that the movie itself sucked). But even with these tried-and-tested caveats, grand-scale star-studded turkeys could still sink at the ticket booths, and a string of them proceeded to do just this in the sixties. Reeling from the onset of television and increasingly out of touch with the demands of movie-goers who were no longer going to the pictures in family groups, the majors backed a series of overpriced extravaganzas such as *Doctor Dolittle*, *Hello Dolly* and – most infamously – *Cleopatra*, and got their fingers burnt in the process.

Stories of the profligacy of *Cleopatra*'s production are legend, and include $10 million worth of unusable footage having been shot in England by original director Rouben Mamoulian before the entire production upped stumps to Italy when a choking Elizabeth Taylor, who had almost died of pneumonia, was deemed unfit to work in British weather. (The only people to benefit from this situation were the makers of *Carry on Cleo*, who wound up shooting on the abandoned British sets and ultimately fared far better – both artistically and financially – than the makers of *Cleopatra*.) With a contract guaranteeing her $125,000 a week for the first 16 weeks, Taylor effectively earned $2 million (around $14 million in today's money) from *Cleopatra* before a single usable frame had been shot. Her eventual earnings from the film are generally reckoned to be in the neighbourhood of $7 million (around $50 million today), which – as Robert De Niro says in *Midnight Run* – is 'a very good neighbourhood'. At the height of its production, the movie was estimated to be costing Fox $70,000 a day, with palaces, barges and entire fleets being conjured up for service – prompting a popular quip about Fox owning the world's third-largest navy.

Originally envisaged as two three-hour epics (*Caesar and Cleopatra* and *Antony and Cleopatra*), the footage was ultimately condensed to one three-and-a-quarter-hour epic when the producers realised that nobody would want to see the first film because it was sorely lacking in the Richard Burton department. Burton and Taylor's on–off romance had by that point become the stuff of gossip sheets (they were the Brangelina of their day) and people were apparently more interested in their off-screen affairs than in their on-screen characters. By the time *Cleopatra* opened, it had cost Fox between $44 and $48 million, the equivalent of around $300 million by today's standards. Industry insiders confidently predicted that there weren't enough cinema tickets in the world to cover that kind of cost, even if *Cleopatra* turned out to be the most brilliant movie ever made. Which it didn't.

When Taylor first saw *Cleopatra* at the London premiere, she threw up.

Imagine the UK publicist's phone call from Hollywood the next morning.

'Hey, how did the screening go?'

'Oh, great. It was really great. Absolutely terrific.'

'Well that's wonderful. And how about Liz?'

'Oh, great. She thought it was terrific. Really fabulous.'

'Really? Cos everyone's saying she's been complaining about how we cut all the "motivation" out of the movie – whatever the hell *that* means. Considering how much we paid her, I'd have thought she had motivation up the wazzoo! Aha ha ha ha ha!'

'Yeah, aha ha ha!'

'But seriously, she loved it, right?'

'Yeah, she loved it.'

'How *much* did she love it?'

'Oh, loads. You could tell she was really . . . moved.'

'She was "moved"?'

'Yeah, she was moved. You know, to her stomach . . .'

'She was moved to her stomach?'

'Uh, yeah. That's right. Something like that.'

'You mean her stomach *moved* . . .?'

'Just a bit. Kinda . . .'

'Her stomach *moved* there in the *theatre*?'

'Oh no, no, nothing like that. She got to the bathroom. It's fine. She loved it. Everyone loved it. It's going to be huge. You know, *historically* huge. I think everyone's gonna be really . . .'

'Moved?'

'Yeah. Really moved . . .'

By the time first-run audiences had done with *Cleopatra*, Fox had plenty of reason to feel moved to their stomachs. After its massive initial outlay the movie recouped just $26 million in American theatrical rentals, leaving a whopping $18 million hole in the studio's coffers. In 1981, editor David Pirie's respected film publication *The Anatomy of the Movies* cited *Cleopatra* as the fifth-biggest money-losing film of all time — behind *Waterloo*, *Darling Lili*, *The Fall of the Roman Empire* and *Raise the Titanic*, although the books weren't closed on the last of these, which, Pirie's splendid book gamely admitted, was still playing to audiences of two men and a dog at the time of publication.

So was *Cleopatra* an unqualified flop?

Well, not quite.

In that same 1981 publication which listed *Cleopatra* among the all-time top ten failures, the movie also makes an impressive showing amongst the all-time box-office earners. Whatever its failings, and despite some scathing reviews from the likes of Judith Crist, audiences (who knew all about the film's ever-expanding expenses) were drawn to this gargantuan spectacle in time-honoured fashion. On opening day, *Cleopatra* had sold out in some theatres for the next four months, proving once again that big stars plus big budgets plus big spectacle equals big box office. It went on to become the biggest grossing film of the year.

So the problem with *Cleopatra* was not that it flopped per se, but that (as analysts had predicted) it had cost too much and the marketplace simply wasn't big enough to pay for it – at least not yet. When the film sold to TV, however, ABC coughed up a handsome $5 million sum to Fox that went some way to correcting the film's financial imbalances. Years later (and long after Fox had officially 'closed the books' in order to stave off any future percentage profit demands) *Cleopatra* generated yet more income thanks to the emergent home video market, and later the advent of DVD. Depending on which industry analysts you believe, *Cleopatra* actually broke even in either 1973 or 1986, thanks to worldwide sales and small-screen ancillary income, and has been turning a serviceably steady profit ever since. So, given time, one of Hollywood's biggest-ever flops ended up in the black after all.

And everyone lived happily ever after.

Eventually.

Fast-forward to 1981 and the case of *Heaven's Gate*, which is regularly cited alongside *Cleopatra* as a studio-sinking stinker. Directed by Michael Cimino, who must surely hold the title for the most egregiously overrated director of all time, *Heaven's Gate* effectively put paid to the idea that auteurs should be indulged by studios seeking prestige hits. In many ways we have Michael Cimino to thank for the fact that producers became stars in the eighties, a return to the days of old Hollywood, when Selznick was a bigger name than any of the five directors who worked on *Gone with the Wind* and only the money men had final cut.

Cimino started out as a screenwriter whose credits included Douglas Trumbull's wonderful seventies sci-fi tear-jerker *Silent Running* (one of my favourite movies of all time) which also lists Steven Bochco amongst its aspiring scribes. Bochco would go on to revolutionise American television with series such as *Hill Street Blues*, *LA Law* and *NYPD Blue*. Today, he is probably the most famous (and certainly the most successful) name associated with *Silent Running*, eclipsing even leading man Bruce Dern. But back then he was still such an unknown that his name was actually misspelled (as 'Bocho') on the UK poster for the movie, an original print of which now takes pride of place in my living room. As for Cimino, having co-written the Dirty Harry actioner *Magnum Force* and helmed the decent Clint Eastwood thriller *Thunderbolt and Lightfoot*, he embarked upon a breast-beating pet project about American soldiers having a terrible time in Vietnam which somehow bamboozled everyone into thinking he was brilliant – albeit briefly.

Quite why *The Deer Hunter* was so well received by audiences, critics and Oscar voters remains a mystery to me. Yes, the film has a few impressive set pieces, most notably the opening wedding sequence, which smacks of macho authenticity and has a nice woodsy feel and some lovely shots of trees. But after that it's ill-disciplined balderdash and baloney all the way, with symbolic games of Russian roulette being orchestrated at gunpoint by screamingly racist 'gook' caricatures in the manner of the most crass exploitation cinema. The sadistic Nazis of *SS Experiment Camp* look positively underplayed in comparison with Cimino's demonic Vietcong (whose country, we should remember, had actually been invaded by napalming Americans). It doesn't help that *The Deer Hunter* uses music known to some British audiences as the 'Gallery Theme', from the kids' TV show *Take Hart*, which would subsequently become a hit single for John Williams, The Shadows, and (most bizarrely) Cleo Laine ('He was o-o-o-o-oh, so-o-o-o-o, bee-yooooo-defullllllllll'). Legend has it that grown men were crying in the aisles when *The Deer Hunter* first played in the US. I saw it in 1979 at the Classic Cinema in Hendon and fell asleep. Years later, I walked out of a screening at Manchester University on 'political grounds'. Eventually, I saw the whole movie from start to finish when it came out on newfangled 'sell-through' video. I enjoyed it more the first time.

Others loved it, however, and Cimino was promptly declared a genius – a description with which he appeared to agree wholeheartedly. When United Artists came calling in search of a profile-raising, awards-baiting 'event' movie, Cimino pitched them a historically dubious Western – originally entitled *The Johnson County War*. Thrilled at the chance to work with a 'genius', UA gave Cimino carte blanche to go off and be brilliant, without requiring him to bring his movie in on time, on budget, or at any sensible length (his first cut ran to over five hours). Nor were UA executives allowed to view a single frame of footage before the maestro was ready to show it to them. Duly emboldened, Cimino went off and made a movie that was as expensive as it was dull, a film about which the nicest thing that could be said is that it looks lovely. Of *course* it looks lovely — entire fields were irrigated to *make* it look lovely, and cinematographer Vilmos Zsigmond was allowed to shoot only during the 'loveliest' light of 'magic hour' at the very end of each day in order to ensure that it all looked as lovely as possible. Big deal. Venice looks lovely but it still smells like a toilet. Will looking lovely stop it from sinking into the sewers? I think not.

The same was true of *Heaven's Gate* — it stank, and it sank United Artists.

Oh, and the historical stuff about the Johnson County War turned out to be hooey. I mention this only in passing.

There are, of course, several key differences between the flopping of *Heaven's Gate* and the (initial) failure of *Cleopatra*. The most obvious difference is that (as we have noted) people actually wanted to see *Cleopatra*, and did so in their thousands. The problem there was that the movie was just too costly to break even, no matter how many people went to see it. In the case of *Heaven's Gate* audiences simply stayed away in droves, with poor reviews, lousy previews (it was savagely re-cut after a disastrous premiere) and an overwhelming lack of public interest causing it to tank at the box office. If the film had been a popular hit, United Artists could conceivably have broken even on their whopping investment, which was more than could be said of Fox's sword-and-sandal escapade. But *Heaven's Gate* had zero popular appeal and, although some modern critics now claim that the film was an overlooked masterpiece, audiences have never shown any interest in it whatsoever.

Why not?

Well, first up, it's rubbish – boring, overblown and ill-disciplined, just like *The Deer Hunter* (although that was a huge hit). Yet as *Pearl Harbor* more recently proved, really poor, historically inaccurate movies can still make their money back if they feature popular stars, are packed with eye-catching spectacle and cost a fortune. Crucially, *Heaven's Gate* ticked only one of these three boxes: it was stupidly expensive. But its stars were Kris Kristofferson (who I like, but who is essentially a country and western singer), Christopher Walken (quite famous now for his weirdie dancing, but a solid second-stringer back then) and Isabelle Huppert (brilliant, but French). And looking lovely is no substitute for scenes of a spaceman with a lightsaber blowing up a massive Death Star. At least, not with that kind of budget. The truth is that *Heaven's Gate* could (and *should*) have been made for a fraction of its cost; its initial budget was $7.5 million, at which price it might have become merely an honourable failure. But at a (then) staggering $36 million, it was a dishonourable disaster, and no amount of revisionist critical reappraisal can change the fact that Cimino should never have been allowed to spend that much money to make *that* movie. What United Artists paid for was 'an event' – what they got was closer to a money pit. Indeed, respected American critic Roger Ebert rightly called it 'the most scandalous cinematic waste I have ever seen'.

In the wake of *Heaven's Gate*, UA's parent company

TransAmerica sold the ailing studio to MGM, and by 1982 *Variety* observed that 'for all intents and purposes, United Artists has disappeared as a major, self-contained production and distribution company'. Thus, the grand studio – which had been founded in 1918 by Charlie Chaplin, Mary Pickford, Douglas Fairbanks and D.W. Griffith, and whose Oscar-winning hits in the seventies had included *One Flew Over the Cuckoo's Nest*, *Rocky* and *Annie Hall* – was effectively sunk by one massively overpriced clunker.

So catastrophic was the public's response to *Heaven's Gate* that the film's title entered the lexicon of screen failure, in the same way that 'Watergate' (or simply '-gate') has become shorthand for any form of scandalous corruption. A full 15 years after Cimino's super-expensive debacle, Kevin Costner would find himself embroiled in a costly catastrophe of his own – which the press jovially dubbed 'Kevin's Gate' – *Waterworld*. Like *Cleopatra* before it, *Waterworld* had the dubious honour of being 'the most expensive movie ever made', its ever-increasing price tag sparking furious pre-release press interest (although, when adjusted for inflation, *Cleopatra*'s whopping shopping list still proved comparatively unbeatable).

Here is the pitch for *Waterworld*: Kevin Costner is a fish. Really. With gills and everything.

And a tail.

OK, so I made up the bit about the tail. But in its original drafts the script for *Waterworld* did clearly describe its aquatic hero, cast adrift in a sunken future-world, as having evolved cod-like characteristics. Six writers and 36 rewrites

later the residual gills remained, although growing nervous-
ness about the potential audience response to '*Fishtar*'
(so-named after the infamous Beatty/Hoffman failure *Ishtar*,
which lost $45 million) meant that Costner's fintastic muta-
tions were underplayed to the point of unnoticeability. What
you were left with was a straggling action-adventure epic
in which a bunch of futuristic pirates, led by a cackling
Dennis Hopper, attempted to hang on to the last of the
world's oil supplies while Costner and co searched for the
mythical 'Dryland', the coordinates of which had been
tattooed on to the back of some poor water baby whose
ancestors knew how to find Mount Everest. Or something.
It is, to be sure, a very silly film indeed, alternately boring
and jaw-dropping, with occasional interludes of watery
weirdness punctuated by explosive action sequences apparently designed as adverts for jet-skis.

It is reported that trash-maestro Roger Corman was
offered *Waterworld* at a very early stage and turned it down
because he figured it couldn't be made for less than $3
million. In the end, Universal made it for somewhere in the
region of $175 million, with Costner himself reportedly chip-
ping in $22 million of his own money to bolster his pet
project. He didn't direct the movie, as he had done with the
Oscar winning *Dances with Wolves* (also dubbed 'Kevin's Gate'
before it became a huge hit), but he seems to have had more
control over the project than nominal helmsman Kevin
Reynolds. Certainly Costner shouldered most of the blame
for *Waterworld*'s apparent failure when it finally opened to
derisory reviews and underwhelming US box-office receipts,

while its floundering studio underwent a headline-making sale to Seagram. 'It helps to remember that a mere actor can bring down a company,' carped *Variety*, adding that, 'Anyone who thinks that Kevin Costner didn't have a role in Matsushita unloading MCA/Universal to Seagram's Edgar Bronfman Jr. is dreaming.'

So was Costner the new Cimino?

Not quite. For whilst *Heaven's Gate* had indeed crippled United Artists with its ludicrous costs and dismal takings, *Waterworld*'s books are somewhat harder to balance. Yes, the film took only $88 million at the American box office, of which as much as 45 per cent could have been retained by the cinemas themselves. And yes, with its sinking sets, hurricane-warning delays, rewrites, reshoots and massively troubled production history the film ended up costing far more than it ever should have done – certainly more than the on-screen results merited. But as the budget became the story, so worldwide public interest in the movie grew; this was demonstrated nowhere more clearly than in Japan, where *Waterworld* was actually marketed with giant billboards declaring it to be 'the most expensive Hollywood movie ever made'. It worked – despite the lousy reviews, Japanese punters flocked to see what all the fuss was about, turning *Waterworld* into a hit in this crucial Asian territory. Around the world the experience was the same; in the UK alone, *Waterworld* racked up a very respectable $7 million at the box office, making it one of the year's most solid earners. I was working at Radio 1 when *Waterworld* opened here and I remember very clearly putting together an uncharacteristically businessy piece for *Newsbeat*, whose editor specifically instructed me to 'concentrate on the money. No one cares about the film, just how much it cost.' In a way he was right – the combination of the Seagram sale and the film's astronomical budget had indeed made *Waterworld* far more newsworthy than a film about a talking fish might otherwise have been. (Did anyone but me give a damn about *Howard the Duck*?)

But the truth is that, after hearing all those news stories, people *did* start to care about the film, enough to pay to see where all that money had gone. Because, in the end, money is the one unsinkable commodity in Hollywood. And little by little, *Waterworld*'s fortunes started to turn around. As part of the sale to Seagram, Matsushita 'ate the film's $175 million production costs' (*Variety*); this left Seagram to reap the benefits of its worldwide revenues, which wound up totalling around $250 million. After a perhaps predictably poor Stateside run, the movie actually became something of a cash cow for its new owners, doing better in foreign territories than anyone could have predicted.

And then there were the ancillary sales – the television rights and (more importantly) the booming video sales. Remember, according to some industry analysts *Cleopatra* had finally gone into profit in the mid-eighties, with soaring 'sell-through' video sales paying off the debts the film had so miserably failed to recoup in cinemas. The book-balancing power of the small screen had been understood by Hollywood ever since NBC had paid $5 million for the TV premiere of *Gone with the Wind*, with CBS stumping up another $35 million for 20 subsequent airings over the next 20 years. At around the same time that Michael Cimino was merrily putting paid to UA with his auteurist overspend on *Heaven's Gate* (for which his contract, incidentally, specified no penalty for the director's financial and artistic indulgences), the more wily producers of *American Gigolo* were pre-selling their $5 million production to ABC for $6 million (they would have got $7 million but John Travolta bailed, leaving Richard Gere's spectacular buns to save the day).

With the rise of VCR in the early eighties (the format had been little more than a novelty sideline in the seventies), video sales became every bit as lucrative as TV deals. By the time *Waterworld* splashed into cinemas, the idea that healthy video sales could, at the very least, offset unrecouped theatrical losses was gaining more and more traction. This appeared particularly true for big-budget cinema failures which, it transpired, were far less likely to flop on VHS, where audiences seemed to have different demands and viewing expectations. Although spectacle and star names alone had never been enough to guarantee box-office success for cinema movies, such ingredients proved effectively infallible in the home-viewing market, where anything that looked like a 'proper movie' (as opposed to a straight-to-video cheapie knock-off) could find a surprisingly eager audience. All a film needed to become a home-viewing hit was 'marquee recognition' – the sense that the film you were taking home to watch on your telly had previously had its name emblazoned on the front of your local cinema, where you had clocked it and failed to watch it, but resolved to catch it on video at a later date. In the case of *Waterworld*, the press attention that its big screen release had garnered meant that the video release had marquee recognition to spare, and as a result the video enjoyed the kind of solid chart-topping success that had proved so elusive in American cinemas. Never mind the theatrical losses, on video *Waterworld* was a hit.

As the video market expanded, it soon became clear that more people were watching movies at home than in theatres – a fact we now take for granted but which seemed frankly staggering 20 years ago. In this new marketplace, the role of the cinema box office would ultimately become secondary to the profits accrued by video and later DVD sales, for certain titles – the ancillary markets having effectively become the primary markets in terms of money. While *Heaven's Gate* producer Stephen Bach had insisted that no one paid much attention to ancillaries until the mid-seventies, by the mid-nineties the distributors of many lower-profile releases were viewing cinemas as a loss-leader to boost all-important video sales. In the eighties, when I worked for the British industry paper *Video Trade Weekly*, I wrote a feature on the increasingly common practice of 'theatrical plat-forming' – a marketing strategy which involved taking a movie that was clearly designed and destined for the video market, and shoving it into a cinema for a week in order to increase its home viewing value. Crucially, it made no difference if the film flopped or attracted terrible reviews; all that mattered was that it had seen the inside of a cinema and could therefore be shelved alongside the 'premium' rather than 'straight-to-video' titles in Blockbuster, thereby increasing its saleability.

The apotheosis of this trend came with the UK video release of Brian Yuzna's underrated rubbery shocker *Society* in 1990, a terrifically twisted fantasy in which a young boy discovers that the rich are not like you and me, but are in fact shape-shifting aliens. A cult favourite amongst the horror cognoscenti, Yuzna's directorial debut boasted eye-popping rubbery mutations courtesy of an eccentric Japanese FX whizz who went by the somewhat self-explanatory name of 'Screaming Mad George'. During their regular shape-shifting orgies, the wealthy weirdos would indulge in an act of slimy pseudo-sexual congress called 'shunting', in which their bodies would melt and merge into a sea of sticky, fleshy gloopiness, a pulsating mass of shuddering, undulating orgiastic meat with outcrops of recognisable human features – an arm here, a head there, and way over yonder something vaguely resembling an anus. During the film's head-scrambling climax, our human hero punches his hand up an alien's rectum and right up into its head, pushing out its eyeballs before grabbing hold of its face from within and then swiftly withdrawing his arm, turning his adversary inside out through his arsehole! It's quite a moment, all achieved without the use of CGI, thanks to the very tactile miracle of good old-fashioned foam latex.

Ah, those were the days.

But I digress. The point of this brief excursion into the fabulous realms of what Yuzna called 'plastic reality' is that the owners of the UK distribution rights to *Society* perceived this horror oddity to be essentially a video title whose value could nonetheless be increased by the briefest of theatrical releases. The fact that the film was actually something of a genre gem which garnered a few genuinely glowing reviews mattered not a jot. When it came to announcing this forthcoming title in *Video Trade Weekly*, the distributors took out a full-page advert, upon which was emblazoned not adulatory quotes from important critics or eye-catching stills of monster fun from the movie but instead a giant snapshot of the Prince Charles Theatre in London's Leicester Square, the marquee of which duly confirmed that on one particular rainy afternoon this esteemed cinema was indeed showing *Society*. As with so much video marketing, it was a move that was at once stupid yet brilliant: stupid because it suggested that no one had any idea just how great this little movie really was; brilliant because they understood that no one *cared* about the quality as long as the damn thing had been projected inside a movie theatre at least once. Which *Society* demonstrably had.

As for the blockbuster releases, a successful theatrical run remained crucial, but increasingly the risk of a box-office failure could be underwritten by the insurance policy of the VHS and DVD markets in the same way that TV licensing had long been underwriting cinema. Nowadays, falling DVD sales and the rise of pirate discs are jointly blamed for the movie industry's imminent collapse, which is apparently just around the corner. It isn't, and anyone who worries that the majors, who do the most vociferous whining about these subjects, are actually cash-strapped needs their head examined.

Suffice to say that Hollywood currently sees home-viewing sales as a market worth protecting and only the very naïve (or nostalgic) believe that the financial future of the film industry lies solely, or even *primarily*, with cinemas.

As for *Waterworld*, far from becoming what *Variety* called 'the disaster which the film industry needed to start a serious course correction', it actually ended up demonstrating just how unsinkable the big-budget 'event movie' template really was if backers were willing (and able) to play the long game. *Cleopatra* took over a decade to pay for itself; *Waterworld* probably managed the same feat in less than five years. And although no one likes to admit it, we probably have the strangely twisted template of *Waterworld* to thank for the existence of *Titanic*, which went on to become the biggest-selling and (stop me if you've heard this one) 'most expensive' movie of all time.

Like *Waterworld*, *Titanic* was a waterlogged production with a dodgy script which ran massively over-budget, and which was widely predicted during its ever-expanding production period to be a lavish vanity-project disaster in the making. As we all know, it went on to make $1.8 billion worldwide and is currently being digitally dicked around for re-release in 2012 in eye-boggling commemorative 3-D (more of which later). Yippee. The fact that *Titanic* is not a great film is somewhat beside the point – its world-beating success speaks for itself. What is important is that it was allowed to be made only a couple of years after Costner's alleged water-related 'flop', with Fox and Paramount jointly shouldering the burden of its out-of-control costs. In what turned out to be a terrifically smart move, Paramount took the domestic rights for a capped sum of $60 million, with Fox handling worldwide in return for picking up the rest of the production tab. (They figured the excess cost couldn't be much more than $40 million. Doh!) As total costs spiralled from $100 million to $200 million, Paramount found themselves in the enviable position of having paid a fixed rate for a film whose widely reported budget just kept growing and growing – with headline-grabbing results. Fox, meanwhile, were left wondering if *Titanic*'s international box office could get close to matching the $167 million made by *Waterworld* outside the US, which would at least go some way toward recouping the whopping $140 million they had accidentally ended up sinking into the film just to get the damned thing finished. The only thing that kept their hopes afloat was the fact that *Waterworld* was a terrible film (*Titanic* couldn't possibly be any worse) and it still managed to turn a buck. If *Titanic* was any good at all, they might just get away with it . . .

Nearly $2 billion later, some of us were still wondering why *Titanic* didn't become *Fishtar* after all. With hindsight it's easy to be blasé about Cameron's canny audience manipulation, but there's just so much wrong with *Titanic* (at least from the perspective of an old fart like myself) that its success still gets under my skin. It's bothered me for years. Some months after the film's record-breaking release, I found myself in the company of Paramount boss Sherry Lansing, and felt impelled to tell her just how grievously the film had failed in my all-important eyes. To her infinite credit, she listened patiently and politely while I explained how Cameron had dropped the ball with a film that was about to win 11 Oscars, including Best Director and Best Picture.

Here's what I said . . .

First up, the big problem with *Titanic* is that it isn't *A Night to Remember*. Whereas the latter is essentially a film about Englishness in crisis (and is therefore interesting), the former is a film about Hollywood in hysterics (and is therefore annoying). In *A Night to Remember*, the band played on. In *Titanic*, Celine Dion sang.

Any questions?

Next, the stars. According to James Cameron's honking screenplay, Rose is a naïve, innocent rose (geddit?) who, whilst being dragged across oceans by her caddish fiancé (whose money will secure her family's future), falls for the altogether more worldly-wise Jack, who has spent the last few years whoring his way around Europe with one-legged prostitutes. Sadly, while Kate Winslet has the appearance of a woman of substance, Leonardo DiCaprio doesn't look old enough to be out on his own. You don't want Rose to shag him, you want her to adopt him.

DiCaprio was, of course, cast as Jack on the strength of his starring role in Baz Luhrmann's *Romeo + Juliet*. In *Titanic*, he would effectively reprise this doomed-pretty-boy schtick, playing another floppy-fringed upstart with the hots for a socially unobtainable prom-queen type who would go weak at the sight of his unsheathed rapier. The only real difference would be that, whereas Juliet kills herself after Romeo kicks the bucket, Rose's heart would go on and on and on and on . . .

Then there's the script itself – Shakespeare it ain't. If the iceberg hadn't sunk the bloody boat, then the dialogue would surely have done so. Among *Titanic*'s more memorably awful lines, one stands out in my mind; it is the moment when, as the butt-end of the sinking boat starts to creak up out of the water and various CGI souls fall dramatically off the deck, Rose grabs Jack and says helpfully, 'This is where we first met!' It's a line that makes me want to stand up and scream, 'Yes I *know* that's where you fucking met, I've been watching the movie for the last *two hours* (as has everyone else) and we all *watched* you meet there, and frankly if I'd known you were going to come up with crap like *that* at a moment like *this*, then you would both have been better off throwing yourselves to an icy death in the first place . . .'

All of which brings me to the crux of the *Titanic* problem, which is this:

From the minute the ship hits the iceberg, I don't *care* what happens to Jack and Rose; all I can think about is the army of jolly Oirish-dancing types who are now drowning below decks, along with all the other badly sketched, incidental caricatures whose lives seem so much less important to the film-makers. I don't care if Jack drowns, or if Rose goes on to have loads of grandchildren, only to return years later to drop expensive jewellery into the sea.

I just don't care (and I'll care even less in 3-D).

Sherry Lansing, God bless her, sat through all the above with a look of serene amusement on her face. And then, when I'd finished, she put down her glass of chilled mineral water, folded her extraordinarily elegant hands under her chin, smiled charmingly, and said, 'The problem with you is that you're not a teenage girl.'

And she was right. In every possible way.

The fact is that I am not (and have never been) a teenage girl. Consequently, I did not buy into the Rose and Jack love story in the way that armies of teenage girls were doing all around the world. And not doing just once; the real genius of *Titanic* was that its core audience went to see it time and time again. When you start analysing the mind-boggling box-office figures for the movie, you very quickly realise that repeat viewing played a significant factor in the film's success. As the makers of the *Twilight* series have since discovered, the teen-girl demographic may be hard to crack, but if you succeed the rewards of their eternal devotion are substantial. To all intents and purposes, Bella and Edward are the latter-day Jack and Rose. The difference is that the *Twilight* movies don't cost £200 million to make. (Maybe that's why I like them so much more than *Titanic*.)

As for myself, I would have ditched Jack and married Billy Zane, who has better hair (all of it wigs!) and who seemed to be the only actor in *Titanic* who really understood the film's cheesy B-movie roots. Plus, anyone who has David Warner for a butler is OK in my book.

But the real question is whether *Titanic* could have broken even *without* the teen-girl support network. Would it have done all right if Kate and Leo hadn't captured the pubescent imagination? Of course it would. Why? Because it was a really expensive 'event movie' featuring huge special effects of the kind that just don't lose money anymore. For a year before the film hit theatres, the papers had been full of its gargantuan budgetary requirements. The casting of Winslet had sparked a press furore which some have compared to the 'search for Scarlett' hoo-ha that accompanied *Gone with the Wind*. And the promise of watching a really big boat sink in glorious widescreen detail had all the spectacular allure of watching a really big boat go belly-up in Irwin Allen's *The Poseidon Adventure* (cost $5 million; US gross $93 million), or watching a really big building burn in Irwin Allen's *The Towering Inferno* (cost $14 million; US gross $116 million), the latter of which had also laid the template for *Titanic*'s 'shared liability' co-production, with Fox and Warner splitting the bill.

The fact is that even if *Titanic* had zero romantic appeal, it still would have made its money back. Eventually. For proof, look no further than *Pearl Harbor*, which gives us a unique insight into what *could* have happened to *Titanic* if it had turned out to be really rubbish. For in the end, what is Michael Bay's monstrosity if not a cack-handed remake of James Cameron's hit? Just look at the key ingredients:

Historical tragedy? Check.

Sinking boats? Check.

English rose actress? Check.

American hunks? Check.

Awful pop theme song? Check.

Massive expense? Check.

Engaging love story? Er . . .

Just think of the business *Pearl Harbor* could have done if Michael Bay had shown any genuine talent for putting recognisable human emotions on screen, if he was anything more than a peddler of grand-scale mechanical porn. Bay admitted that some people didn't 'get' the love story in *Pearl Harbor*, but it still took $450 million worldwide. Imagine how much more it could have taken if those people had actually *liked* it.

The difference between *Pearl Harbor* and *Titanic* is that, for all its faults, *Titanic* really worked for the devoted section of the audience who loved the movie and went to see it loads of times. These were the people who turned it from a sure-fire investment into a runaway success. These are the people to whom the producers owe a debt of gratitude, the people who made *Titanic* the most successful movie of all time (until *Avatar*). But make no mistake – without them, the movie would still have recouped its costs in the end. In the worst case scenario, if *Titanic* had been viewed as utter, utter crap by everyone who saw it, it still would have been *Pearl Harbor: The Prequel* or *Waterworld: Part Deux*.

And, as we have seen, in financial terms that's not the very 'worst' after all.

Event movies no longer flop.

Nowadays, they just 'underperform'.

In fact, for an expensive movie to really break the bank in the current marketplace it has to be a genuine 'non-event', and the biggest non-events around have a horrible tendency to be comedies. There's an age-old maxim that laughter is priceless but comedy should be cheap, and nowhere is this truer than in the cinema. Time and again, film-makers have fallen flat on their faces by imagining that there's something inherently amusing about extravagant expense. There isn't. Blowing up aircraft carriers and sinking huge boats may be fun, but it's not funny. Crucial difference. If audiences pay to see a film-maker spending hundreds of millions of dollars doing something really stupid (like Costner with *Waterworld*), then they don't want to laugh *with* the movie – they want to laugh *at* it.

It is significant that over the course of a career which has included horror films, sci-fi romps, historical epics, literary adaptations, war movies, action adventures and even a ghostly romance, the only time Steven Spielberg has come genuinely unstuck was when he decided to make a really expensive comedy. In some ways, his bloated Second World War farrago *1941* can be seen as a companion piece to Michael Bay's *Pearl Harbor* – a film which takes a historical tragedy (America's bloody war with Japan) and turns it into a dreary farce. Both movies are bloated, baggy, boring, fantastically ill-judged, bum-numbingly long, and ludicrously wasteful in terms of dollars spent for enjoyment had. The only real difference between these two stinkers is that Spielberg wanted his audience to laugh while Bay wanted them to cry. Both directors failed badly in their respective endeavours, but whereas Bay still scored a financial hit by virtue of his movie's non-comic 'event' status, Spielberg took a bath because nothing sinks faster than an unfunny comedy, regardless of how much cash you throw at it. (Incidentally, when I raised the spectre of *1941* in an interview with Spielberg himself, he conceded that extravagance had indeed got the better of him but insisted that the film had *not* lost money in the long run – it had merely 'underperformed' in the short term.)

A quick glance at the list of money-losing, non-event failures of the past 25 years reveals unfunny comedy as the killer ingredient every time. In 1987 the aforementioned *Ishtar*, a 'romantic comedy' in which Warren Beatty and Dustin Hoffman play lousy lounge singers stumbling into a web of Middle Eastern intrigue, proved that spending $51 million in the pursuit of cheap jokes really was no laughing matter. Just over a decade later, Beatty would star in another money-haemorrhaging failure – the 'middle-aged sex comedy' *Town & Country* – which proved rather less welcome than a dose of the clap. Finally released three years after production began, the film's ever-spiralling budget hit a reported $90 million, but it managed to gross less than $7 million in the US, committing the threefold sins of: a) costing far too much; b) not being spectacular; and c) trying to be funny – a lethal combination.

It is arguable that comic misjudgement was the undoing of the nineties 'action comedy' flop *Hudson Hawk*, which racked up bills of $70 million, some of which was reportedly spent on teams of special-effects men who laboured to 'fix' Bruce Willis's receding hair. If the film had been played straight, as no more than an extravagant adventure with a big star and a few dazzling visual set pieces, director Michael Lehmann (reportedly nicknamed Michael 'Lame Man' on set) might just have walked away from the wreckage in one piece. I remember being at a press screening for *Hudson Hawk* at the Odeon Leicester Square, where the stunning silence that greeted the movie's endless stream of self-referential in-jokes was broken only by the sound of fellow critic Kim Newman and me howling like hyenas. The more no one else laughed, the funnier *Hudson Hawk* became (at least for Kim and me), and at the end of the screening we pretty much had to crawl out on our hands and knees, having been doubled-up with paralysing merriment for so long. But the film's failure to hit anyone else's funny bone meant that it took a pitiful $17 million in the US (although it did, inevitably, become something of a 'hit' on video). A few years after that screening I was on a radio show with Willis's co-star Richard E. Grant, who described *Hudson Hawk* as 'a steaming hot pile of elephant droppings'. When I told him how much I had enjoyed it he was genuinely shocked, and not a little outraged. The film had kicked the crap out of TriStar's already crumbling finances, and Grant was still gamely struggling to put the stench of its failure behind him. Yet as recently as June 2011, the thoroughly respectable *Sight & Sound* magazine published a passionate defence of *Hudson Hawk* that listed it as one of the overlooked multiplex gems of the past 30 years, not least because 'as the Mayflower twins, Sandra Bernhard and Richard E. Grant are among the best comic villains ever'. If there is a lesson to be learned here, it is that comedy (unlike sheer spectacle) is a toxically unpredictable commodity, which simply *cannot* be relied upon to tickle an audience's fancy and which, if mishandled, will blow up in a film-maker's face.

For further proof of the dangers of misjudging expensive

laughs, look no further than Renny Harlin's 1995 pirate comedy *Cutthroat Island*. The film (which regularly appears in lists of all time flops, as indeed does Roman Polanski's comparable *Pirates*) cost and lost about the same amount as *Hudson Hawk*, although it is no worse a movie than *Pirates of the Caribbean*, which duly made a fortune rehashing the same tired riffs a decade later. But crucially *POTC* wasn't sold as a 'comedy' – rather, it was marketed as a spectacular thrill ride in the mould of *Indiana Jones*, a fantastical adventure packed with eye-popping spectacle which just happened to contain a few take-it-or-leave-it jokes. In fact, according to all reports, the studio were genuinely terrified when they first saw the rushes of Johnny Depp doing his 'humorous' Keith Richards impression and begged director Gore Verbinski to get him to tone it down, for fear that his outrageous gurning might actually kill the movie. The last thing the money men wanted was an expensive movie (based on a popular fairground ride) that depended upon making the audience laugh for its success rather than simply bludgeoning them with stars and whizzo special effects. Their fears turned out to be unfounded when it transpired that audiences were actually charmed by Depp's shambling antics – a response which still baffles me to this day – and *POTC* became a socking great hit. But the fact remains that, had Depp's humorous schtick fallen as flat with a mainstream audience as it did with me, the film could have joined *Cutthroat Island* in the ranks of overpriced failures which have demonstrated that (in the words of Woody Allen) insufficient laughter is grounds for divorce.

The *ne plus ultra* of this rule was the 2002 Eddie Murphy 'comedy fantasy' *The Adventures of Pluto Nash*, for which divorce proceedings swiftly gave way to a restraining order that prevented the movie from getting within a 50-mile radius of its intended audience. Costing $100 million, almost none of which it recouped on its horrendous theatrical release, *Pluto Nash* left Castle Rock executives crying into their cappuccinos when Murphy deemed the movie too embarrassingly unfunny to promote. Just think about that for a moment – a film which is so staggeringly lacking in laughs that even Eddie Murphy didn't want to be associated with it. How unfunny could that be? This is the same Eddie Murphy who once 'joked' that director John Landis was more likely to work again with Vic Morrow (who was decapitated on the set of *Twilight Zone: The Movie*) than with him, but who still signed on for Landis's *Beverly Hills Cop 3* when the fat pay cheque was dangled before his eyes. The same Eddie Murphy who torched his chances of winning an Oscar for his stand-out role in *Dreamgirls* by donning the fat suit for *Norbit*, which was released in time to remind Academy members just how ghastly he could be. The same Eddie Murphy whose greatest role to date has been providing the voice of Donkey in the *Shrek* movies, proving conclusively that one thing he is guaranteed to get right is talking out of his ass. When a comedian of that calibre tells you that *Pluto Nash* doesn't meet his quality-control standards, you know you need to steer well clear, which movie-goers did in their millions. In 'absolute financial terms' (i.e. regardless of any adjustments for inflation or ancillary sales) *Pluto Nash* was long-regarded by some industry watchers to have accrued the biggest theatrical money loss *ever*: somewhere in the region of $96 million – a figure which easily overshadows the losses of Kevin Costner's super-serious 1997 dud *The Postman* (aka 'Post-Apocalyptic Pat'), which flopped for being expensive but solidly unspectacular, but which would surely have done even worse if Kevin had told jokes.

While *Speed Racer* (no stars), *The Alamo* (little spectacle) and *Sahara* (*Hudson Hawk*-y humour) all posted losses in the noughties, the only recent movie to bear catastrophic comparison with *Pluto Nash* is the Robert Zemeckis produced *Mars Needs Moms*, which had an estimated budget of something in the region of $150 million but which took a paltry $21 million in the US and $35 million in total worldwide – a figure which should make even Eddie Murphy laugh. There are umpteen reasons why Zemeckis's folly failed to recoup (a movie costing that much needs to be a spectacular star-studded 'event' rather than a limp motion-capture comedy featuring the voices of Seth Green and Joan Cusack) but, as we shall see in the next chapter, the real explanation for its monstrous reception may well have more to do with a collective audience protest against the overpriced tyranny of 3-D than with any innate dramatic failings.

In the meantime, we are still left with the general rule that bona fide event movies featuring proper stars, massive visual extravagance and newsworthy budgets are still a depressingly safe bet as long as you're not banking on making anyone laugh. All of which raises a very simple question: if an event movie can make its money back no matter how unpalatably awful it may be (as long as it abides by a fairly simple set of rules) why not make something really good just for the hell of it? If the presence of a whopping budget, a retina-scorching spectacle and a beezer cast list is all you need to break even, why bother to make something as terrible as *Pearl Harbor*? Why not go hell for leather and make something decent? If financial success is all but guaranteed in the long run, doesn't that actually offer the most extraordinary artistic freedom?

Or look at it this way . . .

Every time I complain that a blockbuster movie is directorially dumb, or insultingly scripted, or crappily acted, or artistically barren, I get a torrent of emails from alleged mainstream-movie lovers complaining that I (as a snotty critic) am applying highbrow criteria that cannot and should not be applied to good old undemanding blockbuster entertainment. I am not alone in this; every critic worth their salt has been lectured about their distance from the demands of 'popular cinema', or has been told that their views are somehow elitist and out of touch (and if you haven't been told this then you are not a critic, you are a 'showbiz correspondent'). This has become the shrieking refrain of 21st-century film (anti)culture – the idea that critics are just too clever for their own good, have seen too many movies to know what the average punter wants, and are therefore sorely unqualified to pass judgement on the popcorn fodder that 'real' cinema-goers demand from the movies.

This is baloney – and worse, it is pernicious baloney peddled by people who are only interested in money and don't give a damn about cinema. The problem with movies today is not that 'real' cinema-goers love garbage whilst critics only like poncy foreign language arthouse fare. The problem is that we've all learned to tolerate a level of overpaid, institutionalised corporate dreadfulness that no one actually *likes* but everyone meekly accepts because we've all been told that blockbuster movies have to be stupid to survive. Being intelligent will cause them to become unpopular. Duh! The more money you spend, the dumb and dumberer you have to be. You know the drill: no one went broke underestimating the public intelligence. That's just how it is, OK?

Well, actually, no. You want proof?

OK. Exhibit A: *Inception*.

Inception is an artistically ambitious and intellectually challenging thriller from writer/director Christopher Nolan, who made his name with the temporally dislocated low-budget 'arthouse' puzzler *Memento*. Nolan unfashionably imagines that his audience are sentient beings, and treats them as such regardless of budget. *Memento* cost $5 million, had no stars or special effects, aimed high nonetheless, expected its audience to keep up, and reaped over $25 million in the US alone. *Inception* cost $160 million, had huge stars and blinding special effects, aimed high nonetheless, expected its audience to keep up, and took around $800 million worldwide. See a connection here?

Nolan earned the right to make a movie as intelligent and expensive as *Inception* by grossing Warner Bros close to $1.5 billion with *Batman Begins* and *The Dark Knight*, both of which can best be described as arthouse movies posing as massive franchise blockbusters. I remember being genuinely stunned by the level of invention at work in *Batman Begins*, and burbling to Radio 5 Live listeners that it was 'far, far smarter than any of us had the right to expect from a movie which cost that much'. But why shouldn't it be smart? Why shouldn't we expect movies that 'cost that much' to be worth it? Because we have been told for too long that popular movies must, by their very nature, be terrible, and we've all learned to accept this horrendous untruth.

As for *Inception*, the idea that a 'mainstream' audience could embrace a movie that includes the lines 'Sorry, whose dream are we in?' and 'He's militarised his subsconsious!' would seem anathema to the studio heads (and their mealy-mouthed media minions), who have been telling us for decades that dumb is beautiful. Yet Nolan has become one of the most financially reliable directors working in Hollywood without ever checking his intellect in at the door. Did no one ever explain the rules to him? Did he miss a meeting?

Don't get me wrong; *Inception* isn't perfect, nor is it 'stunningly original', as some would have you believe. The plot, which revolves around explosive industrial espionage played out within the interlocking layers of an unsuspecting psyche, is essentially *Dreamscape* with A-levels and draws upon a number of populist sources, ranging from Wes Craven's horror sequel *A Nightmare on Elm Street: Dream Warriors* to Alejandro Amenábar's Spanish oddity *Open Your Eyes* (later remade in Hollywood as the inferior Tom Cruise vehicle *Vanilla Sky*). It is also, in essence, an existential Bond movie: *On Her Majesty's Psychiatric Service*. But like great pop music, groundbreaking cinema rarely arrives *ex nihilo*, and the fact that Nolan seems to have watched (and loved) a lot of genre trash in his time merely increases his significant stature in my eyes. Too many blockbuster movies nowadays seem to be made by people who hate cinema, who have seen too few movies, and who have nothing but contempt for the audiences who pay their grotesquely over-inflated salaries.

So, did *Inception* become a money-spinning hit *because* it boasts a really smart script?

I'd like to think so, but honestly, no.

Would it have taken less money if it had been less intelligent?

Maybe. Probably not. Who knows?

Would it have taken *more* money if it been less intelligent?

Maybe. Probably not. Who knows?

Would it have made anything like that amount of money if it didn't include:

a) an A-list star

b) eye-popping special effects

c) a newsworthy budget?

Definitely not.

So what does the success – both financial and artistic – of *Inception* prove? Simply this: that (as I may have mentioned before) if you spend enough money, bag an A-list star and pile on the spectacle, the chances are your movie will not lose money (unless it's a comedy), regardless of how smart or dumb it may be. Trying to be funny may be a massive risk (fail and your movie goes *down*) but trying to be clever never hurt anyone. Clearly, the exact *amount* of money a movie will ultimately make will be affected to some degree by whether or not anyone actually *likes* it; *Titanic* couldn't have become a record-breaking profit-maker if some people hadn't wanted to see it twice, and whatever my own personal problems with the film I concede that loads of people really do love it to pieces. But the fact remains that, if you obey the three rules of blockbuster entertainment, an intelligent script will not (as is widely claimed) make your movie tank or alienate your core audience. Even if they don't understand the film, they'll show up and pay to see it anyway – in just the same way they'll flock to see films that are rubbish, and which they don't actually enjoy. Like *Pearl Harbor*.

This may sound like a terribly depressing scenario – that multiplex audiences will stump up for 'event movies' regardless of their quality. But look at it this way: if the audiences will show up whether a movie is good or bad, then does the opportunity not exist to make something genuinely adventurous with little or no risk? If the studio's money is safe regardless of what they do, artistically speaking, why not do something of which they can be proud? If you're working in a marketplace in which the right kind of gargantuan expense all but guarantees equivalent returns, where's the downside in pushing the artistic envelope? Why dumb down when the dollar is going up?

Why be Michael Bay when you could be Christopher Nolan?

In fact, despite the asinine whining of those cultural collaborators who have invested their fortunes in the presumption of the stupidity of others, the blockbuster market arguably offers a level of artistic freedom that no other sector of film financing enjoys. The idea that creative risk must be limited to low or mid-priced movie-making (where you can in fact lose *loads* of money) while thick-headed reductionism rules the big-budget roost is in fact the very opposite of the truth. As David Puttnam has been saying for years, the biggest risk in Hollywood at the moment is making a mid-priced, artistically adventurous movie which has a great script but no stars or special effects, i.e. the kind of film that studios now view as potential financial Kryptonite. It is this area in which producers can most legitimately be forgiven for following a policy of cultural risk avoidance, because it is here that monetary shirts may still be lost. Remember – *The Shawshank Redemption*, a prison drama with no marquee-name stars or special effects, actually *lost* money in cinemas (it cost $35 million, of which it recouped only $18 million in its initial release period) before it went on to become one of the most popular movies of all time on home video. If it had cost $200 million, starred Tom Cruise and featured a couple of explosive break-out sequences, it would have broken even in the first few weeks – guaranteed.

For further proof of money's ability to make more money, look at the list of the most expensive movies of the past 20 years and see how infrequently they have failed to turn a profit, regardless of quality. Sam Raimi's baggily sub-standard *Spider-Man 3*, which even the fans agree was a calamitous mess (unlike the first two instalments) cost $258 million and grossed $885 million worldwide. *X-Men: The Last Stand*, which tested the patience of devotees of both the comic books and the movies, ran up a bill of $210 million but still raked in

$455 million worldwide. James Cameron's *Avatar* (aka *Smurfahontas*, or *Dances with Smurfs*) cost $237 million and (if we include the unnecessarily extended 'Special Edition' re-release) has achieved global box-office takings just shy of $2.8 billion.

Even David Fincher's utterly up-itself *The Curious Case of Benjamin Button*, an upmarket indulgence in which Brad Pitt plays a man who lives his life backwards, managed to balance its $150 million costs with worldwide box-office takings in the region of $329 million, thanks in part to well-placed news stories about its ultra-expensive special effects. If you take the oft-repeated industry maxim that a film must gross twice its negative cost (the price of actually making the film before incurring print, publicity and distribution costs) in order to earn its keep, then all of these movies were bona fide hits. Working on the same ratio, Bryan Singer's dangerously star-free 2006 superhero flick *Superman Returns*, featuring Brandon 'Who He?' Routh, 'underperformed' at the box office, with takings of $390 million just failing to balance its official cost of $209 million (as opposed to the $270 million some reported) although ancillary revenues would certainly have pushed it into profit. Compare that with Spike Jonze's *Where the Wild Things Are*, which I really liked (although crucially my kids didn't) but which only a fool would have financed to the tune of $100 million, since it contained no stars (Catherine Keener is an indie queen, James Gandolfini a safe bet only on TV) and boasted deliberately unspectacular (but nonetheless costly) special effects. Like *Heaven's Gate*, *Where the Wild Things Are* was a movie whose budget was totally out of whack with the financial realities of what was on-screen, and it has been widely described as a chastening flop. Unlike *Heaven's Gate*, however, Jonze's folly still took around $100 million in theatres worldwide and has since recouped more on DVD and TV, meaning that the level of its 'failure' is far from studio-sinkingly spectacular. Once upon a time, a film like *Where the Wild Things Are* would have ended Spike Jonze's career and sent industry bosses tumbling from high windows. Today, it is merely a curio from which everyone will walk away unscathed.

This is the not-so-harsh reality of the movie business for top-end productions in the 21st century. For all the bleating and moaning and carping and whingeing that we constantly hear about studios struggling to make ends meet in the multimedia age, those with the means to splash money around will always come out on top. So the next time you pay good money to watch a really lousy summer blockbuster, remember this: the people who made that movie are wallowing in an endless ocean of cash, which isn't going to dry up any time soon. They are floating on the financial equivalent of the Dead Sea, an expanse of water so full of rotting bodies turned to salt that it is literally impossible for them to sink. They could make better movies if they wanted, and the opulent ripples of buoyant hard currency would still continue to lap at their fattening suntanned bodies. If they fail to entertain, engage and amaze you, then it is because they can't be bothered to do better. And if you accept that, then you are every bit as stupid as they think you are.

This is no time to be *nice* to big budget movies. This is the time for them to start paying their way, both financially *and* artistically . . .

Last summer, while attending the Society of Cinema and Media Studies conference in downtown Los Angeles, I found myself with a day to spare and decided to take the kids to Universal Studios to 'do' the celebrated movie tour. Since movies seem to be in the process of mutating into glorified theme park rides, Universal were on to a winner with their celebrated trundle through a series of mocked-up movie sets in which famous screen moments are recreated in front of your very eyes, in a cheerfully clanking, grinding sort of way. Here, for example, was a clapboard mock-up of the town of Amity, built around a large lake from which a jolly rubber shark would emerge at four-minute intervals to terrorise your tour bus (this shark, incidentally, was both more convincing and more reliable than 'Bruce', the mechanical monster with which Spielberg was saddled during *Jaws*, and which kept on breaking down). Further on was a subway station that collapsed and imploded around you in homage to the seventies disaster epic *Earthquake*, a film which famously employed 'Sensurround' sound to give its audiences the collective collie-wobbles. Elsewhere, a crashed airplane belched smoke and flames amidst an apocalyptic landscape of smashed houses and broken streets, painstakingly constructed to resemble the scenes of devastation through which Tom Cruise stumbled in the recent remake of *War of the Worlds*. Actually, I'd stumbled through them myself a couple of years earlier when filming a documentary about Spielberg for BBC2. Having met the director in his idyllic Amblin offices (which are snuggled away in a quiet corner of the Universal lot), I mentioned that we were going to take a wander around the studio and maybe shoot some links on the appropriate exhibits, to which Spielberg enthusiastically replied, 'Oh yeah, that *War of the Worlds* one is really . . . cinematic.' Which indeed it was.

As indeed it ought to be, frankly, considering the price of admission for those not lucky enough to be 'wandering around' after shooting the breeze with Steven Spielberg. In my altogether less glamorous role as a schlubby father of two (rather than a hoity British television presenter), I forked out $280 for the privilege of dragging my kids around Universal Studios for the day, insisting that we proceed at breakneck speed from one overcrowded attraction to the next without ever stopping for water or toilet breaks or whatever, on the basis that the more rides we went on, the less the comparative cost of each automated adventure. I am always like this at theme parks, behaving more like a general engaged in a military intervention than a father enjoying a nice day out with his kids. If I had my way, we'd show up two hours before opening and then, as soon as the gates open, blitz our way through all the rides before the crowds had a chance to catch up, ticking everything off by 10.30 a.m. and thereby allowing me to *relax* for the rest of the day. This never happens, however, and so my enjoyment is always tempered by a sense of gnawing anxiety that we're not getting our money's worth and a desperate need to do more in order to ensure that everything costs less. Comparatively speaking.

Inevitably, as we stood queuing in the broiling heat (the primary pastime of US theme parks) I started to add up the vast sums of money involved in the creation and exploitation of Universal's rides, and wondered whether their potential profit margins were ever factored into the original costs of movie production. Crucially, all the rides were related to hit movies, which made perfect sense; who's going to pay to go on a ride that's a spin-off of a film they never wanted to see in the first place? I noted with interest that the *Hulk* attraction, which was being built the last time I'd been there, had mysteriously disappeared, presumably because the movie itself had 'underperformed' so spectacularly (cost $137 million; took $242 million, which is as close as you can get to a flop nowadays). No such fate had befallen the *Backdraft* inferno in which I had also done some filming for a Channel 4 documentary about the indefatigability of disaster movies, way back in 2002. Having filmed several lengthy links that were specifically timed to coincide with the carefully choreographed explosions, I knew my way around this attraction, and knew exactly where to stand for the family to get the best view of the fiery action. As promised, we were all duly cooked by the ensuing excitement. It was just like being in a real burning building. Yay!

As late afternoon rolled around, and we'd ticked off all the 'important' attractions (including *Terminator 2: 3-D* and *Shrek 4-D*), we decided that we'd ease up a little and take in something altogether less popular. So, with duly lowered expectations we strolled over to the *Waterworld* arena, a vast tank of water where extravagant high-wire structures were decked out to resemble the set of a movie which (according to popular mythology) had been a total flop, which no one had gone to see, and which had indeed precipitated the sale of the studio in whose backlot we were now standing.

It should have been a ghost town. Yet 15 years after it first failed to make a bigger splash, *Waterworld* was doing faster business than ever. The arena was packed – you had to fight for a seat. And as the stand-in stuntmen jet-skied into view, spraying water as they skimmed hither and thither, falling and flying and generally flailing around as things went 'KABOOM!' around them, the crowd went mad: cheering the guy who didn't look anything like Kevin Costner, booing the guy who looked a little bit like Dennis Hopper, and generally pretending to understand a storyline which hadn't made any sense in the first place – not that it mattered. The whole show lasted about 20 minutes, at the end of which the entire cast got encores and standing ovations. It was like watching a rock band. Only wet.

As we all straggled out of the arena, I did a bit of O-level mental arithmetic and calculated (dividing the cost of admission by the number of shows/rides we'd seen/been on) that the *Waterworld* knees-up had cost me somewhere in the region of $28, about the same amount it would have cost to take the family to the cinema. All of which meant that a decade and a half after its damp-squib opening weekend, *Waterworld* (in some form or another) was still generating a steady stream of cash, still making the money it was meant to have lost, and still attracting paying punters who presumably wanted to see what all the fuss was about.

'Did you enjoy that?' I asked the middle-aged man who was sitting in the crowd next to us, his offspring similarly in tow, all of them enthusiastically vocal during the performance.

'Oh yeah,' he replied, 'it was great. We got soaked.'

'Did you ever see the movie?' I asked.

He frowned.

'What? The *Waterworld* movie? No. I don't think so. Oh, hang on . . . maybe on TV. I'm not sure. Or maybe video. Yeah, I think it was on video.'

'But you didn't see it in the cinema?'

'No. On video.'

'What about your kids?'

'No, man, they're too young.'

'To watch the film?'

'They weren't even born when it came out.'

'But they knew about it?'

He looked at me as if I was an idiot.

'Yeah, of course they *knew* about it. *Everyone* knows about it. It's *Waterworld*. It's huge, man. Huge . . . like *Jaws*, you know . . .'

'Did you ever see *Jaws*?'

'No.'

'But did you go on the ride?'

'Yeah, it was awesome.'

He paused for a moment, then added, 'You see *Jaws?*'

'Oh sure,' I replied. 'Loads of times.'

He thought about this for a while, and then almost as an afterthought asked, 'Was it as good as *Waterworld* . . .?'

'Are you kidding?' I replied aghast. '*Jaws* is a *million* times better than *Waterworld*!'

The guy looked taken aback.

'A million times better than *Waterworld* . . .' he said, shaking his head, apparently overwhelmed by such a prospect.

'Wow' he said finally, 'that must be *really* good . . .'

Chapter Three

THE INEVITABLE DECLINE OF 3-D

'O pointy birds, O pointy pointy . . .'
John Lillison

Picture this . . .

A one-eyed man is standing on a railway track in the middle of a desert, the straight line of the track stretching off toward the horizon, disappearing eventually into the distance. Far, far away down the line, a small black dot starts to grow in size, slowly at first but with increasing rapidity. As the dot grows, it gradually begins to take the form of a steam engine: a big, black beast with an aggressive tooth-like cow-catcher on the front, a silver circular emblem above this and a giant, funnelled chimney stack on top. You know, like the ones you see in cowboy films which inevitably get held up by men wearing scarves over their faces, one of whom turns out to be Brad Pitt with a beard. Only this one doesn't get held up. Instead it just continues to get bigger and bigger. And as it gets bigger, the one-eyed man is able to hear the noise the engine is making – a great honking, steaming, squawking cacophony of biliousness – accompanied by the clattering and clanging of its weighty steel wheels on the iron of the railway track. The engine continues to get bigger and louder and clearer, and as it does so the amount of track the one-eyed man can see stretching away from him inexorably diminishes, blocked out by the growing spectre of the steam train. Eventually the train is so large, and the amount of track still visible so small, that the one-eyed man can see almost nothing but the big, black engine with the looming cow-catcher that seems almost bigger than him. The sound of the engine is deafening, the sight of the steaming funnel transfixing and the rate of their comparative growth in size positively alarming. And at the very last moment, just before the engine ploughs into the man and turns him into a human skid-mark, our monocular anti-hero thinks:

'Damn, if only I could see in 3-D.'

Or how about this . . .

You're sitting in the Empire, Leicester Square, arguably the best cinema auditorium in the country, watching a reissue of David Lean's epic masterpiece *Lawrence of Arabia*. About 40 minutes into the screening (which, incidentally, is unencumbered by other badly behaved patrons kicking your seat from behind, or obstructing your view from in front, or annoying your ears from the side) we get to the epochal shot that introduces Omar Sharif's character, Sherif Ali, who appears out of the distance, riding majestically upon a camel. It's a long shot, beautifully framed and held for what seems like an eternity (in fact, around two minutes – with edits), far longer than classical wisdom tells us is appropriate. At first, it's almost impossible to make out the tiny shape in the distant landscape, but as Sharif and his camel come closer, falling gradually into focus, the sense of regal mystery is overpowering, awe-inspiring, transcendent . . .

Except that in the alternative universe of this hypothetical example, David Lean has decided to shoot this scene in 3-D. So, rather than marvelling at the clarity of the camerawork, the composition of the shot and the emotional power of the scene, you are instead squinting at a smudgy image through uncomfortable and ill-fitting glasses, which have darkened the brightness of the screen by around 30 per cent, have caused the colour saturation to decline into something approaching a pastel smudge, and are in the process of giving you a headache in order to create artificially the illusion of depth through a bizarrely concocted polarised parallax process that your brain does not recognise from 'real' life. As Sharif approaches, two competing images of him wrestle with your right and left eye, messing with your head, which could quite happily have worked out from a monocular image that what you are looking at is not a man and a camel magi-cally growing in size but a man and a camel gradually getting *nearer and nearer*.

How would your brain know this? Well, loads of ways, including focus, depth of field, occlusion (nearer objects getting in the way of further objects), comparative colour saturation (distant objects being naturally desaturated in comparison with nearer objects), comparative brightness (ditto) and – perhaps most obviously – comparative size.

Oh, and sound. All the ways, in fact, in which movies have been telling us whether something is near or far away for over a century. And all without having to wear those bloody silly glasses.

The human brain is so agile and so developed in its under-standing of monocular visual information that it can (and, more to the point, *will*) impose a sense of spatial awareness, including distance and nearness, on to even the most basic image in which only one of those signifiers mentioned above is at work. Don't believe me? OK, try this test. Look at the two pictures below.

As you can see, they are in black and white. (If they're in red and blue then you're still wearing those rubbish cardboard glasses that came with your recent DVD purchase of *Piranha 3-D* – take them off now!) These pictures contain no spatial clues in terms of stereoscopy, focus, depth of field, occlusion, comparative brightness and/or colour saturation. Or sound. Obviously.

So, what do you see? Unless you're being really bloody

minded (and that may be the case) I'll wager that what you see is a man standing by a fence that is of constant size, but that recedes in size as it moves from the foreground at the left of the picture to the distance in the middle of the picture. In the first picture, the man is standing some way away, and therefore appears to be quite small. In the second picture, the man has moved closer, and therefore appears larger.

That's what you see, isn't it?

OK, so how about if I tell you that in fact what you are looking at is a picture of an irregular quadrilateral shape (with bisecting lines) which is presented face on, and is simply larger on the left than on the right. As for the man, that is in fact *two* men – one big, one small – situated in the same place in relation to the weirdly shaped thing that is most definitely not a fence.

Got that?

Good.

Now look at the picture again. What do you see?

Be honest.

What you see is a fence stretching away into the distance and a man walking toward you, isn't it? Oh, you can *make* yourself see the irregular quadrilateral thingy and the stationary giant and the dwarf if you *try*, in the same way that you can look at one of those line drawings of a cube and then see it turned inside out if you concentrate hard enough. But even as you do so, your brain is still telling you that what you're looking at is not flat or 'two-dimensional' at all. Your vision may be effectively monocular, and the picture may be cruddy hand-drawn black-and-white 2-D, but your brain, which is a thing of wonder (unless perhaps you are Michael Bay), sees in 3-D. Naturally.

So, that being the case, why is Hollywood currently spending so much time and so much money trying to convince us that unless we play ball with their latest movie fad, we're just not seeing the big picture? Why is James Cameron telling us that 'everything looks better in 3-D' and waving Smurfs in our faces to prove it? Why am I getting a headache watching *Clash of the Titans*, a movie that was shot in 2-D but has been 'converted' to 3-D to make it 'better' when it actually now looks far worse? Why did Warner Brothers blithely announce in the summer of 2010 that the same conversion process was going to be applied to *Harry Potter and the Deathly Hallows: Part 1* despite the fact that everyone clearly *hated* it on *Clash of the Titans*? And why is Martin Scorsese, the one-time doyen of edgy American New Wave cinema, now looking me straight in the eye and telling me that 'while you and I are sitting here talking, we're talking *in 3-D*' as if that somehow justifies making a new movie that we'll all have to watch through those bloody silly glasses?

What's *wrong* with this picture?

Let us be absolutely clear about this: 3-D cinema is a con. For a start, it's *not* 3-D; rather, it is a technical illusion that uses an artificial 'parallax effect' (the process through which your left and right eye see slightly different images) to confuse your brain into thinking that flat images on a flat screen are either nearer or further away than a designated 'point of convergence'. At least, that's what it's meant to do; in terms of audience experience, the system is at best flawed, producing 'wall-eye', 'ghosting', 'unfusable images' and a range of other equally exciting sounding optical blips, along with those old favourites headaches and eye-strain – any one of which should be enough to put off potential viewers. But the current 3-D revival is not about enhancing the audience's cinematic viewing experience. On the contrary, their entertainment is entirely secondary to the primary purpose of 21st-century 3-D, which is to head off movie piracy and force audiences to watch badly made films in overpriced, undermanned multiplexes. It is a marketing ploy designed entirely to protect the bloated bank balances of buck-hungry Hollywood producers. It is not a creative leap on a par with the advent of colour or sound; if it were, it would not have faltered on so many previous occasions.

Far from being new and exciting, 3-D cinema is the oldest trick in the book – as old, in fact, as cinema itself. And there's good reason why it has been consistently rejected by audiences for more than a hundred years.

Listen . . .

In his snappily entitled book *Stereoscopic Cinema and the Origins of 3-D Film 1838–1952*, Ray Zone notes that the patent for Edison's Kinetoscope (patent no. 493,426), issued on 14th March 1893 and titled 'Apparatus for Exhibiting Photographs of Moving Objects', 'had several stereo claims [and] depicted an optical system with two lenses for stereoscopic viewing of moving objects'. Apparently Edison never got round to using the system, but clearly the concept of 3-D moving pictures actually predates the projection of film.

At around the same time, a 3-D motion picture system was being patented by British photographer-cum-inventor William Friese-Greene, an eccentric character referred to by the British Film Institute's 'ScreenOnline' as 'the most maddening figure in early British film history [who] obsessively patented insufficiently thought out devices'. These early 3-D outings were clunky and cumbersome and clearly had no future – although having seen Tim Burton's 'converted' stereoscopic *Alice in Wonderland* I'm starting to wonder whether those 19th-century experiments could possibly have looked any worse.

Then, in the mid-1890s, the Lumière brothers began startling audiences with the projection of their experimental short film *L'arrivée d'un train en gare de La Ciotat*, aka *Arrival of a Train at La Ciotat*, aka *The Arrival of the Mail Train*, a thoroughly immersive 2-D experience that effectively gave birth to the modern popular cinema that has been with us ever since. Various controversies attend the first public screening of this documentary short, ranging from the date of the performance (either late 1895 or early 1896 depending on whom you believe) to the effect the film had upon its audience. Slightly less than a minute in length, the film shows (as the title suggests) a train pulling into a station, the image of the engine growing in size as it moves toward the camera, starting in the right of the frame and moving across to the left, filling one side of the screen, with the passengers on the platform occupying the right side of the frame (and initially occluding the view of the distant train). If you can't quite picture that (it's amazing how hard it is to describe something really simple) then just YouTube it. It'll take you less time to watch than boiling the kettle. Don't worry, I'll wait . . .

. . .

. . .

Done? OK, so now we're all on the same page. Great. Anyway, according to folklore, when audiences first saw this film (either in a Parisian cafe in December 1895, or – more probably – in January 1896) they were so overwhelmed by the sight of the approaching locomotive bearing down upon them that some ran screaming to the back of the room while others attempted to vacate the premises forthwith. No matter that the audience weren't wearing 3-D glasses or having forced perspectives rammed in their faces through complex dual-image projection and separation systems. Nosirree, audiences saw an allegedly flat-screen image of a train coming toward them and understood it well enough to run in the opposite direction.

Or did they?

Magazines at the time certainly reported 'fear, terror, even panic' in response to early screenings of *L'arrivée d'un train*, reactions that the Lumière brothers (who were nothing if not showmen) would have exploited to the hilt. And why not? As Whale, Hitchcock, Spielberg et al. would discover over the next hundred years, nothing sells movie tickets like a really good scare. Yet eminent scholars have since written at great length about the lack of hard factual evidence to support accounts of the crowd-shaking effects of *L'arrivée d'un train* and in recent years a rather more contentious theory has been forwarded as to the source of those stories. You want to hear it? OK, pay attention . . .

As is often noted, the Lumières (like so many other photographic pioneers) had been playing around with stereoscopy for some time, and in 1935 (or possibly 1934 – accounts vary) Louis exhibited a 3-D remake of *L'arrivée d'un train* to the French Academy of Science. (Such a film may have been viewable on a stereoscope as early as 1903, but only by one person at a time.) Is it possible that it was in fact this later 3-D screening of the early silent classic from which audiences fled in terror? Has history somehow conflated the reactions to these two very different versions of *L'arrivée d'un train* and imposed the hysteria provoked by the latter upon the former? Was the real power of the image contained not in its motion, but in its stereoscopy?

In a word, no.

Think about it. By the end of the 19th century, audiences had become familiar with the phantasmagorical fairground projections of ghost trains and funhouses, with zoetropes and whirring animation devices, with shadow-shows and cleverly orchestrated tricks of the light that could make apparitions appear as if by magic. They had also seen 3-D photographs, which date back to the 1840s. But the projection of a realistic moving image was still new enough to produce startled and even fearful reactions amongst those faced for the first time with the minute-long film of an oncoming train.

Yet the history of cinema moves fast, and by 1915 audiences were happily settling down to D.W. Griffith's spectacular epic *The Birth of a Nation* (a cinematic milestone marred by its unfortunate fondness for the Ku Klux Klan) and wondering whether noisy snacks would be available in the interval. Come the twenties they were being treated to Cecil B. DeMille taking a walloping bash at *The Ten Commandments* and listening to Al Jolson telling them they ain't heard nothing yet, thereby signalling the death knell of silent cinema. By the time the thirties rolled around the emergence of full-colour three-strip Technicolor seemed set to make black-and-white movies a thing of the past (although mainstream monochrome cinema would bravely soldier on for another 30 years). All of which meant that the audience who saw Louis Lumière's newfangled 3-D train film in Paris in 1935 would have been about as cine-literate as most movie-goers are today, well versed in the all-singing all-dancing razzamatazz of mainstream block-busters, and highly unlikely to have been sent screaming from the theatre by the sight of an approaching train – 3-D or not 3-D. Moreover, if you actually bother to watch Louis's 3-D remake (which I have), you'll discover that the approaching train very quickly breaks the left frame, just as it did in the original, but thanks to miracle of 3-D this means that the train never appears to come *out* of the screen at all, merely to approach it. Doh!

Nope, the truth of the matter is that if anyone ran away from *L'arrivée d'un train* (which they may not have done but, hey, print the legend) then they would have done it in 1896 rather than 1935, and the train from which they were fleeing would have been black-and-white, silent and two-dimensional. It is *this* version of *L'arrivée d'un train* that has passed into popular folklore because this is the version that everyone saw and talked about for years to come. As for the 3-D version, who the hell has even heard of it? Be honest – unless you're a scholar of early cinema or an enthusiastic devotee of the tortured history of stereoscopic movies, then this late entry in the filmography of Louis Lumière (who had effectively stopped making movies in 1901) is little more than a footnote, a curiosity, an intriguing but ultimately ephemeral bit of movie trivia – much like 3-D itself. In a strangely poetic way, *L'arrivée d'un train*, one of the first films ever made, contains within its genetic pattern both the blueprint of all future cinema and the proof of the obsolescence of 3-D. It exists in two versions, and only one of them is any good.

What does all this prove? Simply that in their role as pioneers of modern movie-making the Lumière brothers very quickly discovered both the magic and the limitations of cinema. They patented their Cinématographe in 1895, toured the world with their amazing device in 1896, patented an Octagonal Disc Stereo Device in 1900, and then effectively gave up film-making to pursue other projects, having concluded that 'the cinema is an invention without any future'. Others were more stubborn – for better or worse – and experiments with allegedly new cinematic formats, including 3-D, continued throughout the 20th century. According to Ray Zone, the first public presentation of 'anaglyph' motion pictures in America took place in 1915 at the Astor Theatre, New York, where viewers got to experience the dreary brown smudge produced by wearing those red-blue glasses (a process that dates back to the mid-19th century) that have now become shorthand for 'old school' 3-D. Multiple anaglyph shorts followed, with the 1922 feature *The Power of Love* (which many cite as the first ticket-paying 3-D feature) reportedly (and perhaps apocryphally) allowing the audience to watch alternate endings through either the red or blue lenses. How's *that* for a gimmick? In 1936, the anaglyph oddity *Audioscopiks* was nominated for an Academy Award in the splendidly self-explanatory Best Short Subject: Novelty category. (If only *Avatar* had been eligible for a 'novelty' award . . .) In the same year, Edwin H. Land started demonstrating his version of the polarised 3-D system with which we are now all depressingly familiar, and which we are all being assured is once again the future of cinema.

Meanwhile, in Nazi Germany, Goebbels had become a 3-D fan, his propaganda ministry commissioning 'Raum film' (or 'space film') productions such as *So Real You Can Touch It* and *Six Girls Roll Into Weekend* which kicked off a long-standing Third Reich obsession with 3-D (they were also into occult magic, numerology and time travel). Later, and with some poetic justice, the Allies used 3-D photography to identify and destroy Nazi missile silos in 'Operation Crossbow', reckoned by some to be the world's first 3-D powered military operation.

Outside of warfare, however, 3-D remained little more than a novelty, with film studios and movie-goers continuing to show little interest in or enthusiasm for the format, despite its great technical leaps forward. And then, in the early fifties, everything changed, and the reason for the change was not artistic but financial, driven not by consumer demand but by studio pressure. Sounds familiar? As always, the main impetus for the so-called 3-D revolution in cinemas was the need to compete with the home-viewing market, which was threatening to put a major dent in box-office figures. In the early fifties, the greatest threat to cinema (at least as far as the studios and theatres were concerned) was the rapid rise of television, with oversized sets becoming more established items of household furniture than three-piece suites and handy heated hostess serving racks. Why pay good money schlepping the family to the local fleapit when you could all watch stuff at home for free?

The movie industry's answer was to big up the whole 'theatrical experience', with widescreen framing and projection, scorching colour, epic spectacle and inevitably pointy-pointy 3-D all doing their damnedest to lure punters out of their sitting rooms and back into the cinemas. In 1952, *Bwana Devil* offered audiences 'A Lion in your lap! A lover in your arms!', neither of which (like that hoary old joke about lobster thermidor) you were going to get at home. In 1953, Jane Russell starred in the stereoscopic romp *The French Line*, the tagline for which promised that 'She'll knock BOTH your eyes out' (oo-er, missus). Meanwhile Jack Arnold's *Creature from the Black Lagoon* delivered a man in a rubber suit with weird gills emerging from the watery depths and looming toward the camera with his arms outstretched – an image that still holds an enduring fascination for nostalgic horror and sci-fi fans today. Until fairly recently, this delightfully creaky creature-feature had a place in history as the only 3-D movie to spawn a successful stereoscopic sequel, *Revenge of the Creature* (boasting an early appearance by Clint Eastwood), although by the time they got round to shooting the third instalment, *The Creature Walks Among Us*, the 3-D craze had run its course and it was back to good old 'flat-screen' business as usual.

Alongside such high-kicking anomalies as *Kiss Me Kate*, the two 3-D titles that everyone seems to remember and revere from this period are *House of Wax*, the first 3-D film to boast stereo sound, and Alfred Hitchcock's allegedly epochal *Dial M for Murder*. In 2005, my partner Linda Ruth Williams and I programmed a 'History of Horror' season at London's National Film Theatre in which we included a 3-D screening of *House of Wax*, the film which had briefly established horror legend Vincent Price as the reigning 'King of 3-D' (he went on to star in *The Mad Magician*, *Son of Sinbad* and *Dangerous Mission*, all shot and widely projected in 3-D). The print we showed was old and somewhat colour-faded, and we'd had some difficulty securing the rights to screen it since Warner Bros. was in the process of remaking *House of Wax* and had therefore withdrawn the old version from circulation – a traditional marketing ploy designed to prevent a remake being unfavourably compared to the original. As it turned out, the new version of *House of Wax* (which was made in 2-D) was notable only for a scene in which Paris Hilton is violently dismembered on-screen, a gruesome highlight that drew uncomfortable murmurs of approval from audiences. Anyway, in my introduction to the 1952 *House of Wax* I pointed out that the audience, who were all peering at me through their retro 3-D glasses, were about to watch a movie the director had never seen, because (as any fule kno) André de Toth famously had only one eye, and was therefore monocular. Significantly, this didn't stop him from helming what was to become one of the most respected stereoscopic movies of the period, a 'Natural Vision 3D' production, publicity for which promised that 'Beauty and Terror meet in your seat' with the movie coming 'Right at you!' to ensure that 'The hand is at your throat . . . The kiss is on your lips . . .' Not for de Toth, however, who could only see the film in 2-D but who always said that it looked just fine to him that way. Vincent Price later remembered that de Toth would 'go to the rushes and say "Why is everybody so excited about this?" It didn't mean anything to him.'

Is there not a lesson to be learned here?

As for *Dial M for Murder,* there's no doubting the film's enduring artistic stature, and it's easy to see why today's 3-D pioneers constantly refer to it as a format-justifying landmark. In my own experience as a 3-D-sceptical film journalist, I have had everyone from John Lasseter to Martin Scorsese attempt to convince me that stereoscopy is an artistically valid cinematic process by citing the precedent of *Dial M for Murder.* With Hitchcock at the helm, Ray Milland and Grace Kelly as the leads, an already proven stage-screenplay by Frederick Knott and a soundtrack by Dimitri Tiomkin, *Dial M for Murder* was always going to be a cut above the exploitation schlock on which 3-D thrived, and its champions still point to it as proof of the 'immersive' qualities of the format. No one, they argue, complained about being alienated by the usual pointy-pointy clichés of 3-D when it came to *Dial M*; on the contrary, audiences were drawn *into* the story, which continues to thrill and engross viewers to this day. It's a good argument, sadly undermined by the fact that the main reason no one complained was that almost no one ever saw *Dial M* in 3-D. Released simultaneously in 2-D and 3-D versions, the film promptly became a flat-screen hit, with 3-D prints being left to moulder on the shelf until they were nostalgically revived in the eighties. And, as far as anyone can tell, the audiences who lapped up the 2-D version didn't go complaining to theatre managers that the movie was in any way 'non-immersive'. Because it wasn't. As for Hitchcock, he significantly never went near 3-D again, having clearly decided that the whole thing was a waste of time and money. (Six years later Hitchcock would make *Psycho* – recently voted the Greatest Horror Film of All Time – in black and white. So much for the inevitable march of technology.)

The reasons 3-D failed to set the world alight during its so-called 'golden age' in the early fifties were pretty similar to the reasons it still sucks today. Although the initial novelty value was high, audiences and critics soon started complaining about the eye-strain, headaches and smudgy darkened pictures that inevitably resulted from the donning of 3-D glasses. (The Russians had experimented with a lenticular screen 3-D process which worked without glasses in the forties, but the strict viewing angle significantly limited audience size.) More significantly, the fleeting rise of 3-D happened alongside the emergence of CinemaScope's anamorphic widescreen system which was itself referred to in publicity puffs as offering an immersive 3-D experience due to the sheer size and scale of the projected image. Promotional materials for Fox's CinemaScope flagship *The Robe* showed the actors' faces apparently breaking the boundaries of the screen in the manner of 3-D posters, while the tagline called it 'the miracle you can see *without* glasses!' Unlike Cinerama, which had made the front pages in 1952 with its curved screen and interlocked triple projectors, CinemaScope's anamorphic systems compressed a widescreen image (later standardised at 2.35:1, nearly twice the width of the traditional 'Academy' 1.33:1) onto a single 35mm film strip, thereby rendering it both impressive and (more importantly) widely available. Although Cinerama would continue to offer a deluxe viewing experience akin to today's IMAX theatres, it was Fox's more populist system which effectively killed 3-D, proving that 'immersion' in a picture had nothing to do with stereoscopy and everything to do with 'Scope.

In the wake of 'Scope and the subsequent competing anamorphic systems that made widescreen pretty much standard fare, 3-D crawled back into the cupboard, and audiences got on with enjoying cinema in all its immersive monocular glory. Oh, stereoscopy never went away: in the sixties, the 3-D novelty was used to flog a number of cheapie anaglyph exploitation creature-features, while the development of the 'over/under' process that printed two widescreen images, one above the other within a single square frame, allowed for polarised projection from a single strip of film (although the image remained dark and less than pin-clear). In 1966, *Bwana Devil* helmsman Arch Oboler enjoyed some 'Space Vision' success with the sci-fi romp *The Bubble* ('The picture floats off the screen and over your head!'), while in 1969 *The Stewardesses* promised to 'leap from the screen onto your lap' thanks to the miracle of StereoVision, which squished two anamorphic images side by side on to the same frame. Costing a mere $100,000, *The Stewardesses* went on to serve up a hefty $27 million at the box office, making it (in terms of cost-to-profit ratio) the most successful 3-D movie ever. Think about that; with its conservatively estimated price tag of $250 million, *Avatar* returned its initial investment costs at a paltry profit ratio of 1:12, while *The Stewardesses* raked in an arousing 1:270. Forget Smurfs in Space, when it comes to 3-D nothing sells like Hooters on a Plane. And if the success of stereo-scopic knockers doesn't tell you everything you need to know about the 'artistic validity' of 3-D then, frankly, I don't know what will.

This delightful downward trend continued into the seventies, the decade's stereoscopic highlight being Paul Morrissey's *Flesh for Frankenstein*, to which Andy Warhol lent his moniker (but nothing else, as with its 2-D sibling *Blood for Dracula*) in the manner of a man signing a blank canvas for a) the hell of it and b) profit. *Flesh for Frankenstein* is actually my favourite 3-D film because it perfectly showcases the format's novelty trash aesthetic, boasting Udo Kier dangling offal in the audience's faces whilst imploring them to 'fuck life in the gall bladder!' In the eighties the Italian stereoscopic Western *Comin' at Ya!* and the Charles Band cheapie schlocker *Parasite 3-D* (Demi Moore's first starring role, folks) were followed by a slew of horror sequels, all of which appear to have been released in 3-D largely because producers realised they already had the numeral '3' in the titles. First out of the gate was the somewhat clumsily named *Friday the 13th Part III in 3-D*, which was swiftly retitled to the rather more punchy *Friday the 13th Part 3-D*, thus kicking off a titular triptych trend. Linda and I showed *Ft13thPt3-D* (which people forget marks the first time Jason actually dons the now iconic hockey mask) alongside *House of Wax* and *Flesh for Frankenstein* at our NFT horror season as part of a 3-D triple-bill. I mention this again in order to offer proof that, despite everything, I'm not just a total killjoy when it comes to the daft pleasures of stereoscopy. On the contrary, I think there's something stupidly fun about watching horror film-makers throw eyeballs out of the screen at you and flip dripping gizzards (and, of course, gall bladders) in your face – but that's all it is: stupid fun. Trashy, schlocky, stupid fun.

At least, that's what it is at best. At worst, it's *Jaws 3-D*, which followed hot on the heels of *Ft13thPt3-D* but entirely lacked the sleazy charm of its dumbo, trendsetting predecessors. Whereas *Parasite* cost less than $800,000 and *Ft13thPt3-D* really pushed out the exploitation boat at $4 million, *Jaws 3-D* was a big-budget family-friendly venture which cost over $20 million and featured neither extreme gore, whacko weirdness nor cheesy T&A – the only real reasons to watch a 3-D film. Set, boringly, in a SeaWorld theme park, *Jaws*

3-D was an utter stinker that is meant to have begun life as a spoof script entitled *Jaws 3: People 0*. According to legend, the story was about a studio struggling to flog a second dead-horse sequel to *Jaws*, and opened with author Peter Benchley being eaten alive in his swimming pool. There were also roles for a naked Bo Derek and some space aliens in shark suits, apparently. Joe Dante, who had helmed the *Jaws* rip-off *Piranha* (recently remade in 3-D with more gratuitous nudity and blood), was tipped to direct but then Universal got cold feet when they realised that spoofing their biggest hit would be akin to 'fouling in your own nest'. So the joke was over – more's the pity. Instead, cameraman Chris J. Condon (who shot *The Stewardesses* and handled the stereoscopy on *Parasite*) was enlisted to lens a dull-as-ditchwater straightfaced *Jaws* knock-off which respected writer Richard Matheson (who had worked with Spielberg on *Duel*) would subsequently disown, commenting that 'the so-called 3-D just made the film look murky. It had no effect whatsoever. It was a waste of time.'

Stop me if you've heard this one.

In fact, the most interesting thing about *Jaws 3-D* is the way in which it perfectly illustrates the other great technical flaw of forced stereoscopy – namely, the bizarre phenomenon of miniaturisation. As fans of *Father Ted* will know, there are 'cows that are small, and cows that are far away', and our brains are usually able to distinguish between the two thanks to a range of visual and aural information that is no way hampered by monocularity. Occasionally we can be fooled; there are loads of monster movies which have attempted to convince audiences that giant beasties are terrorising normal-sized people by (for example) holding a lobster very close to the camera and getting the actors to stand very far away and scream into mid-air. It may work for a moment, but pretty quickly our brains do the maths and realise it's just a crap perspective trick – which is why so many monster movies only show their monsters for a very short time indeed. With 3-D cinema, the problem is compounded by the fact that eye-catching stereoscopy only really kicks in if an object is really quite close to us, way in front of the point of convergence upon which the right and left images match up. Although forced parallax can make backgrounds seem comparatively far away, it's only fore-ground action (on or in front of the point of convergence) that audiences actually tend to notice, justifying the use of those bloody silly glasses for which, incidentally, they've just paid a bloody silly price. Thus 3-D film-makers traditionally like to wave things right in front of our eyes at regular intervals – hence the (in)famous paddle-ball sequence from *House of Wax* which has nothing whatsoever to do with the plot, but which is invariably the one 3-D trick everyone remembers after seeing the movie.

In the case of *Jaws 3-D*, director Joe Alves clearly under-stood that (given the crap title) people were going to come to see the shark *in 3-D*, and thus he and Chris Condon set about making the fish leap out of the screen at the audience in time-honoured tradition. The problem was that this partic-ular shark was meant to be about 35 foot long, a whopper even by Great White standards, and conveying this sense of size whilst making the most of the 3-D illusion was never going to be easy; the more three-dimensional the shark got, the closer it appeared to be, and therefore the smaller it looked. Only in the long shots, where the stereoscopy had little effect other than depth, did the shark look suitably sizeable; in all the close-ups, it just looked like an angry guppy attempting to bite your nose off whilst hanging in mid-air about three feet in front of your face. The effect was hardly jaw-dropping. Watching the movie in 1983 at the Cine City cinema in Withington, Manchester, I remember actually attempting to swat the irritating minnow-like monster out of my immediate field of vision; the 3-D was clearly 'working', but not in the way the film-makers wanted.

Jaws 3: 'D' Nil.

Having proved a thoroughly damp squib at the box office (the film took less than $90 million worldwide, compared to the $470 million taken by the 2-D *Jaws*, or even the $209 million by the utterly rubbish *Jaws 2*) and been kicked around town by critics (it was nominated for five Razzies, including Worst Film), *Jaws 3-D* sank without trace, taking stereoscopic cinema down with it – the third time the process had tried and failed to become the new future of cinema.

Considering its previous failures, one may ask why any major studio (such as Universal, who owned the *Jaws* franchise) would have tried to revive 3-D in the first place. The last time, the answer had been television; this time, it was home video. Toward the end of seventies, VCRs – which had been around as an unwieldy and hugely expensive accessory for some time – gradually started to look like a viable and affordable home-viewing option. Although initially thrilled that they could sell feature films to video stores at around £80 a pop, the studios soon realised that the prospect of staying at home and watching a movie was rapidly becoming more appealing than paying through the nose for the privilege of seeing a film in a multiplex screen the size of a shoebox. If you could rent a video for £1.25 or £2.50 a night and invite your friends and family to watch it with you, then why on earth would you pay to go the cinema where the screen was the same size as your TV? I remember coughing up £4.00 to see *The Evil Dead* in a barely functioning cinema at the Screen 1–5 in Manchester in the early eighties, and then passing a video store on the way home which would have rented it to me (and my assembled mates) for a quid! Luckily, I didn't have a video machine at the time, but if I *had* I would have gone straight back to the cinema and demanded my money back. (Some patrons did just that, and in the wake of the popularity of *The Evil Dead* on video, cinema distributors started demanding a fiercely guarded 'theatrical window', the length of which remains a hotly contested issue to this day.)

As had happened in the fifties, the solution to the problem of exponentially declining cinema ticket sales was to attempt to make the theatrical experience something worth paying for. If you're old enough to remember just how lousy most British multiplexes were in the early eighties, then you'll remember how rapidly they smartened up their act as the age of video dawned. Whereas in the seventies single-screen cinemas had simply been partitioned off to run more films on smaller screens, the later eighties saw a return to the kind of spectacular widescreen entertainment that had saved the day 30 years earlier. This was the decade in which Lucas and Spielberg served up such circus-like fare as the *Indiana Jones* movies, which revelled in unabashed on-screen spectacle and went to town with stereo and surround sound. Lucas may be a terrible director, but he was a brilliant producer who really understood the art of noise, and the rise of his trademarked THX-certified sound systems put paid to the godawful tinny whining most people had come to expect from disheartening trips to the movies. While cinema in the fifties had widened its horizons by widening its screens, in the eighties it promised to immerse the audience further in a blissful sea of sound. For, as radio graduate Orson Welles famously observed, the best pictures are the ones you see with your ears.

Once again the small screen had apparently threatened the future of cinema. Once again cinema had responded by upping its game and offering audiences a more immersive and spectacular theatrical experience. And once again 3-D turned out to be nothing more than a dead-end – the wrong answer to the eternal question of what people really want from the movies.

'But wait!' I hear the massed ranks cry. 'Aren't you just being a miserable Luddite? A facetious technophobe? An old fart who longs for the good old days and hates any form of change? If you're so against 3-D, then why not rail against the advent of colour? Or sound? Weren't these once little more than exotic "gimmicks" which the naysayers claimed would never catch on? What about the cynics who complained that the arrival of "talkies" would herald the death of "proper" cinema, or that the shadowy majesty of monochrome cinematography could never be matched by the fancy-schmancy addition of reds and greens and (heaven forbid!) blues? Why don't we just go back to black-and-white silent movies with live musical accompaniment? That would make you happy, wouldn't it, you miserable curmudgeonly old bastard?'

Well, to be honest, yes it would. At least up to a point. As someone who's spent quite a lot of time accompanying silent movies, I have indeed been thrilled by the resurgence of interest in these oft-forgotten works that seems to have flourished since the turn of the century. Spurred on by the retrospective fervour that attended the 100th anniversary of the 'invention of cinema' (a moving feast, which seemed to last from 1996 to 2003 depending on whose history books you were reading) many modern movie-goers were inspired to seek out reissued silent gems and to experience the wonder of a live soundtrack first-hand. It wasn't just cineastes who got in on the act. In 2004, the Pet Shop Boys unveiled their new score for Eisenstein's 1925 classic *Battleship Potemkin* at a free concert and screening in Trafalgar Square, at which packed crowds heard the Dresdner Sinfonika accompany a movie many of them had very probably never seen before. In 2007, I introduced Robert Ziegler conducting The Matrix Ensemble for a live performance of Joby Talbot's newly written score for Alfred Hitchcock's *The Lodger* at the popular Latitude Festival, where a packed field of revellers was hushed in awe by the spectacle of sight and sound. And earlier this year (to my enormous pride), I got to introduce a screening of *Blackmail* at a packed Barbican Centre, where the BBC Philharmonic Orchestra played Neil Brand's spine-tingling (and often wonderfully comedic) score, the first new orchestral score to have been commissioned for a British silent drama since the advent of sound. I was even persuaded to look again at Giorgio Moroder's attempts to make *Metropolis* relevant to a modern audience by slapping a blooping synthpop score (interspersed with offerings from the likes of Adam Ant) all over it – although I must confess that I remain unimpressed by its alleged charms.

One of the most rewarding moments of my career came when my skiffle band, The Dodge Brothers, teamed up with Neil Brand to present a live accompaniment to the long-forgotten Louise Brooks movie *Beggars of Life* at a uniquely 'carbon-neutral' screening, as part of the inaugural New Forest Film Festival in September 2010. The movie itself is a surprisingly gritty gem: a 1928 tale of a hobo who goes on the run with a young waif after she kills her stepfather, by whom she has been repeatedly molested. In order to disguise his new companion, our hero (handsomely played by Richard Arlen) advises her to dress 'like a boy', at which point Brooks dons an old hat and battered trouser suit and somehow becomes even more stunningly beautiful than she was before. (People talk about movie stars having the ability to 'draw the camera's eye', but few have ever managed this trick as well as Brooks. The camera doesn't just look at her – it falls in love with her, brings her flowers, recites poetry outside her balcony, and finally offers to cut off its own ear in service to her radiant charms.) Conjoined in their outsider status, our star-crossed couple hit the rails, their paths intermingling with those of a bunch of drunken renegades led by the top-billed Wallace Beery (perhaps best known to younger audiences through a passing reference in the Coen brothers' best film *Barton Fink*, where the titular scribe is told by his cigar-chomping boss, 'It's a Wallace Beery wrestling picture, ferrcrissakes! You know the drill – big men in tights!'). Everything becomes spectacularly twisted and it ends up with kangaroo courts, love and death struggles, and an almighty train wreck featuring a real train really falling down a really large ravine. For real. Apparently the wreckage is still out there, a twisted heap in the Carrizo Gorge, somewhere in the desert of Southern California. Brooks (who performed her own stunts, including running along the boards of the moving train) was rightly told to be afraid of director William Wellman because 'he's a maniac'. As it turned out, she was more than a match for his much-vaunted madness.

Anyway, back to the New Forest Film Festival. Because the festival had a mandate to be 'sustainable', someone came up with the bright idea of powering the projector by bicycle. A few months earlier, Linda and I had seen someone furiously pedalling away on a single bike mounted upon a car alternator, which in turn powered a small projector throwing an 'experimental' silent short film on to a tiny screen at the Larmer Tree Festival in Dorset. If you could do that with one bike, what could you do with ten? With the help of a company called Magnificent Revolutions, we managed to rig up a powerful projector to an entire bank of bikes, all of which chugged away at full power for the length of time it took *Beggars of Life* to play to 350 people, while The Dodge Brothers provided acoustic skiffle accompaniment throughout. The bikes were far from silent, but somehow the whirring, clunking sound of the wheels seemed to replicate the sound of an old projector, providing an authentically wheezing backdrop to a live musical score that involved all manner of banging, crashing, bluegrass banjo and gob-iron wailing. At the end of the screening, a gaunt-faced gentleman with piercing eyes and strangely distinctive teeth (and apparently wearing a tea-cosy on his head) came up and shook our hands and told us that he couldn't remember the last time he'd enjoyed himself so much at the cinema.

It was Richard O'Brien, creator of *The Rocky Horror Show* — a hero of mine.

For a moment my life felt strangely complete.

So yes, I *do* have a powerful hankering for the days when films were performed rather than just screened, and directors understood that film (unlike theatre) is first and foremost a visual medium in which dialogue is *not* the driving force. Another of my personal heroes, Mike Figgis, once spoke passionately to me about how the advent of sound and the introduction of recorded speech had, ironically, brought to an end the universal language that once had been a defining factor of pure cinema. Figgis recalled how immigrants arriving in America from Europe were first processed at Ellis Island, where a silent film screening (with live musical accompaniment – 'silent' film was never silent) would be used to explain to them the wonders of the New World that awaited. The film would have had neither recorded sound (obviously) nor intertitles (illiteracy and language barriers would have rendered them useless), but somehow the images conveyed enough information to orientate the newcomers and prepare them for what might otherwise have been an intolerable culture shock. For Figgis, the moment film became a verbal, rather than a visual and musical, experience it also became a slave to the boundaries of language – its scope no longer universal, but national, perhaps even regional. To be sure, the director was not decrying the use of recorded sound, with which he has experimented throughout his career, most notably on the bizarre Lynchian rumblings that accompany his best and most underrated movie *Liebestraum*. But he understood that whatever else may have been gained, something had also been lost when dialogue became the primary ingredient of cinematic exposition. Australian director Peter Weir said something similar when I interviewed him onstage at BAFTA in 2010, on behalf of the David Lean foundation. Recounting the difficulties he had experienced dealing with certain Hollywood executives, Weir remarked in an offhand way that 'their problem is that they don't read the script. Oh, they read the *dialogue*, but that's *all* they read.' Weir went on to explain that when signing on to direct *Witness* he had made a point of making the executives listen to him tell the story of the film, going on to describe in detail the opening shots, which depict an apparently ancient community living amidst the modern world. There wasn't a single word of dialogue in his description, but the essence of the film was encapsulated in the verbal pictures he drew for them. By the time he signed the contract, he was confident that they were all seeing the same film, as distinct from simply hearing the same words.

All of which is a very roundabout way of saying that I not only accept, but actively embrace, accusations that I have an accentuated fondness for the early forms of cinema for which many of my most shrill opponents have neither the time nor the patience (nor indeed the intelligence, wit and integrity). Screw 'em, I say – it's their loss. But as to my aversion to 3-D being comparable with a desire to wipe sound and colour from the film-maker's palette – that is sheer corporate ass-licking balderdash. 3-D is *nothing* like sound or colour; you know it, I know it, everybody knows it. And for proof, one need look no further than the public's willingness to embrace sound and colour, in stark comparison to their long-standing resistance to 3-D.

Look at the evidence. Experiments with sound cinema were being carried out at the turn of the century, with picture synchronisation being the greatest hurdle. By the 1920s, Warner Bros. was using the 'Vitaphone' system to provide aural accompaniment to a string of short features, and in 1927 *The Jazz Singer* put sound features on the map. By 1929, silent cinema was as good as dead in Hollywood, although in some territories such as China and Japan, silent and sound cinema coexisted throughout the thirties. But by the forties, even the films produced in the world's poorest economies were being made with sound, without which they were deemed internationally unsaleable. Nowadays, we have surround sound in our homes and wouldn't settle for anything less at the pictures (although the all but silent French film *The Artist* has just become a huge hit in Cannes). As for colour, Thomas Edison was hand-painting prints of Annabelle Moore dancing for his Kinetoscope attractions as early as 1894, while Georges Méliès reportedly employed 20 or so women in Montreuil to hand-paint frames from *A Trip to the Moon* with production-line efficiency. In 1905, Pathé Frères introduced a stencil colour process, while film tinting continued to be popular throughout the twenties and thirties, and was even used as late as 1951 for the sci-fi feature *Lost Continent*. Meanwhile, three-strip Technicolor, which had become popular in the thirties, heralded the arrival of full-colour cinema, which would co-exist with black-and-white features for decades before effectively becoming industry standard in the sixties; by the early seventies, *no one* was making monochrome features as a matter of course, only as a matter of *design*. Unless specified otherwise, all movies were in colour.

The same is true of widescreen cinema in all its various forms. Today films shot in the squarer ratio of 1.33 have become rare enough to draw complaints when correctly projected in cinemas, such as Andrea Arnold's critically acclaimed feature *Fish Tank* or Kelly Reichardt's *Meek's Cutoff*, both of which sent patrons scurrying to the projection booth claiming that the sides of the picture were missing. Even TV programmes (once the last bastion of old school 4x3

'Academy' framing) are now standardly shot and broadcast in 16x9 (or, in cinema terms, 1.77:1). In short, widescreen has become normal screen, with screen dimensions ranging from 1.85:1 to 2.39:1 being what everyone expects from the movies.

Crucially, all these innovations (sound, colour, 'Scope) were accepted almost at once by the movie-going public, despite the technical teething problems that each encountered. Early soundtracks were scratchy, distorted and often out of sync; colour was patchy, irregular and unreliably changeable; widescreen projection was costly, cumbersome and (in its earliest multiple-projector incarnations) given to break down at regular intervals. Yet, despite these manifest failings, the public never expressed enough disenchantment or lack of interest for the studios simply to give up and move on to the Next Big Thing. On the contrary, the progress of all three formats has been more or less a continuum, a steady rise in public acceptance and expectation halted only by the failure of technology to come up with the goods at an affordable price. Oh, there were long periods during the early silent era when film-makers who had experimented with sound decided that the process of matching images with dialogue was simply more trouble than it was worth. But as soon as reliably synchronised sound and film became both possible and practical, audiences took to it with alacrity. At no point did they decide that, actually, they weren't that interested in this new 'novelty' after all, or realise that another advancement altogether was the true way forward.

In this respect, 3-D is unique. Despite being as old as film itself, stereoscopic cinema has been rejected by audiences and superseded by competing 'revolutionary' formats on at least three separate occasions in the same century. Unlike colour, sound or 'Scope, its driving force has always been industry need rather than consumer demand. Whereas other systems have had to prove their worth in cash terms from the get-go, 3-D has been thrust (like the lion in *Bwana Devil*) into the laps of movie-goers by studios desperate for audiences to embrace the format whatever the cost. Like Microsoft attempting to ram their latest version of Word down our throats when most of us were happy with the old one, the inevitable move toward a stereoscopic future has been pushed from the rear rather than led from the front, foisted upon consumers who have been told what to want and then forced to pay for something they never asked for in the first place.

You want proof? OK, here's proof – *Clash of the Titans*. Not the 1981 Ray Harryhausen production which, to be honest, was never the maestro's finest work (and in which, despite the title, titans never do actually clash). No, I'm talking about the aforementioned 2010 Louis Leterrier remake starring *Avatar* graduate Sam Worthington, whose previous success has a lot to answer for. As we have already observed, James Cameron's 3-D spectacular took just shy of $2.8 billion at the worldwide box office, making the director the proud helmsman of the two biggest money-making films of all time, neither of which had been burdened by a half-decent script. In the wake of *Avatar*'s bum-numbing stereoscopic success, every half-witted Hollywood producer without an original thought in their coke-addled heads decided that 3-D was a cash cow and all future products must be forced to conform to this glutinous economic paradigm forthwith. Never mind the fact that Cameron had spent years gazing at his own navel trying to figure out how to make a game-changing movie in a medium which no one had liked for almost a century. Say what you like about *Avatar* (that it's infantile, overlong, shamelessly derivative, wildly patronising, and laughably lacking in humour from start to finish – which it *is*), at least its creator *believed* in the technological innovations apparently required to bring the damned thing to the screen. (According to an interview in *Entertainment Weekly*, he also believed that *The Hurt Locker* would have been improved by being in 3-D.) Never mind the fact that the film looks a million times better in 2-D (clearer, brighter, sharper), or that Pandora is a far more immersive world when not viewed through the alienating annoyance of polarised lenses that make everything seem dark, dingy and dismally diminutive. At least Cameron *thought* he was doing the right thing – like Tony Blair deciding to invade Iraq, only with less tragic results.

In 2010, punters wishing to see *Clash of the Titans* (more fool them) were asked to stump up a surplus charge in order to pay for the 3-D glasses that would enable them to experience the miracle of stereoscopy which made the movie such an allegedly unmissable experience. Unfortunately the film (which had gone into production long before *Avatar* broke box-office records) had, as noted previously, been designed and shot in plain old 2-D, in which format the director had originally intended it to be shown. However, in the wake of *Avatar*'s 'game-changing' success, it was declared that movies had to be in 3-D in order to be hits. So *Clash of the Titans* was handed over to a bunch of computer nerds, who set about digitally reconfiguring the images to impose a clumsy illusion of stereoscopy upon a picture which was never intended to be anything but monoscopic. To achieve this retrofitted 3-D effect, the techies took a parallax hammer to the background footage, imposing an eyeball-twisting illusion of depth that caused the unfazed foreground images to appear *flat* but *nearer*. Then they repeated this trick in reverse (negative parallax) on some of the pointier foreground images, making them appear even nearer, and even flatter. The result was not a fully rounded 3-D experience – it just looked like a bunch of flat things happening on opposing planes of flatness. In the business, this apparently common phenomenon is referred to as the 'cardboard cut-out' effect – meaning that the cast of *Clash of the Titans* were not just wooden, but cardboard. Thanks for that. A similar process was applied to equally dismal effect on Tim Burton's *Alice in Wonderland*, producing results so piss-poor that 3-D evangelist James Cameron took to the press to badmouth the kind of 'slapdash conversion' processes that were giving 3-D cinema a bad name. Even Michael Bay, the reigning champion of artistically bankrupt blockbuster cinema (and latterday advocate of 'real' 3-D), announced that he was 'not sold right now on the conversion process'. Which is rather like Max Clifford declaring that he's worried about certain forms of press coverage lowering the general tone of news reporting.

In the case of *Clash of the Titans*, the clear consensus was that the retrofitted 3-D had damaged rather than enhanced the movie, an opinion shared even by those who made the film. Although initially obliged to say only positive things, Sam Worthington later ruefully admitted that 'I think . . . we kind of let some people down' (you *think?*). Leterrier was more forthright, telling *The Hollywood Reporter*: 'I was saying to them, "Don't make it so much like a ViewMaster – so puffed up." It was not my intention to do it in 3-D. It was not my decision to convert it in 3-D . . . Conversions, they all look like this. *Alice in Wonderland* looked like this. The technology was not ready.'

If you've seen *Clash of the Titans* both in theatres and on 2-D Blu-ray disc (which I have, because that's my job) you'll realise just how 'not ready' the technology really was, and just what a mess the conversion made of an otherwise merely bland fantasy remake. The film may not be much good in pristine 2-D, but it's a hell of a lot better (brighter, clearer, more focused) than it was in a screwed-up 3-D conversion. Yet even devoted fans of Louis Leterrier and his explosive *oeuvre* (I have an ongoing weakness for his *Transporter* movies which, for me, are essentially homoerotic male wrestling pics posing as action adventures) were bullied into watching *Clash* in a format for which it was neither designed nor intended. Worse still, they were made to pay for the privilege. Just think about that: Hollywood execs take a vaguely watchable film, make it all but unwatchable, and then ask you to pick up the cheque.

Smile and wave, boys, smile and wave . . .

In many ways, the depressing case of *Clash of the Titans* is symptomatic of the fraudulence of the entire 3-D fad through which we are currently suffering. Not only does it highlight the technical shortcomings of the process, but more importantly it demonstrates that the current 3-D craze has nothing to do with what's on screen and everything to do with what's in your wallet. Terrified by piracy and goggle-eyed by the spectre of *Avatar*, Hollywood studios told audiences that 3-D was the future, and then made sure that it was by any means necessary. And it worked, at least for a while: *Clash of the Titans* took around $450 million worldwide – not quite what the suits were hoping for perhaps, and certainly not a patch on *Avatar*'s box-office bonanza, but still far better than the spectacular floppage this mishandled stereoscopic mess of a movie clearly deserved to suffer. Duly emboldened, the executives declared that *all* future blockbusters would be released in 3-D, whether their creators and/or audiences liked it or not. Suddenly 3-D was not an option; it was an order, an edict, an inevitability.

Not everyone fell in line, thank God. Christopher Nolan was an outspoken critic of the dimness and colour desaturation caused by wearing 3-D glasses, complaining in particularly erudite terms about the loss of 'foot lamberts' (a measurement of light used in relation to the projected image). 'On a technical level it's fascinating,' he explained, 'but on an experiential level I find the dimness of the image extremely alienating.' Nolan's long-time cinematographer Wally Pfister (more of whom in Chapter Five) was rather more blunt, calling 3-D 'a fad' – go Wally! Despite huge industry pressure, Nolan insisted on shooting *Inception* in 2-D rather than throwing his hat in with the stereoscopic mob, thereby scoring (as we have seen) one of the biggest hits of the year. In the autumn of 2010, Nolan confirmed that his third Batman movie, *The Dark Knight Rises*, would also be a 2-D production with key sequences shot in the IMAX format (the modern equivalent of Cinerama), which, he argued, offered the most immersive experience available. Yet even Nolan sounded a note of caution, pointing out that he couldn't fight the market pressures if audiences demanded 3-D in future. 'There's no question that if audiences want to watch films in stereoscopic imaging,' he confessed, 'then that's what the studios will be doing, and that's what *I'll* be doing . . .'

The unanswered question behind this carefully worded statement is whether or not audiences really do *want* to watch films in 'stereoscopic imaging', or whether they are merely doing what they've been told to do by studios attempting to squeeze the maximum amount of profit out of the minimum amount of artistic effort. John Boorman once said that movie-making was essentially a process of turning money into light and then back into money again, but in the age of 3-D it seems to have become a process of turning money into *less* light and then back into *more* money – whether the audience like it or not.

The nadir of the dimness issue came in May 2011, when it was revealed that a multiplex chain in the Boston area of America had been projecting 2-D movies through 3-D lenses, causing light loss of up to a staggering 85 per cent! According to a report in the *Boston Globe*, the Sony digital projectors used by AMC (and others) require the attachment of a special lens, which alternates rapidly between two polarised images in order to project movies in 3-D. Unfortunately, this lens was being left on the projectors even when 2-D films were being shown, resulting in a dramatic darkening of the image. 'A walk through the AMC Loews Boston Common on Tremont Street one evening in mid-April illustrates the problem,' wrote journalist Ty Burr. 'Gloomy, underlit images on eight of the multiplex's 19 screens (theaters 5, 8, 9, 10, 11, 13, 15, and 18, to be specific). These are the auditoriums using new digital projectors that are transforming the movie exhibition business, machines that entirely do away with celluloid . . . A visit to the Regal Fenway two weeks later turned up similar issues: "Water for Elephants" and "Madea's Big Happy Family" were playing in brightly lit 35mm prints and, across the hall, in drastically darker digital versions.'

Such 2-D darkening was drastic enough for director Peter Farrelly (helmsman of *Hall Pass*) to 'complain loudly' about the lousy presentation of promo screenings for his film. 'Farrelly went from one screening where the 3-D lens had been removed,' reported the *Globe*, 'to a second in which the lens was still on, and he couldn't believe his eyes. "I walked into the room and I could barely see, and my stomach dropped," the film-maker said. "The first screening looked spectacular and the second was so dark, it was daytime versus nighttime. If they're doing this for a big screening, I can't imagine what they do for regular customers. That's no way to see a movie."'

According to the paper, the reason 3-D lenses were being left on for the screening of 2-D films was that removing them required the attention of someone qualified to do so – i.e. a trained projectionist, of whom (as we have previously noted) there are so few left nowadays. Moreover, thanks to the insane levels of anti-piracy software now built into digital projectors, cinemas have become scared of messing with the machinery *at all* for fear that it will simply shut down and lock them out, thereby effectively closing one of their screens. Faced with the choice between allowing an unqualified staff member to fiddle around with a projector they didn't really understand or simply letting the audience suffer up to 85 per cent light loss, cinema managers apparently opted for the latter. And, as ever, the customer pays the price.

So, is 3-D here to stay this time? Ask anyone within the industry and they'll tell you that too much money has been spent to turn back now. Experiments are currently afoot to develop projection systems that will allow 3-D movies to be viewed without glasses (the holy grail) while home-viewing systems employing various forms of 'autostereoscopy' are already on the market. Yet so far the outlook remains distinctly dodgy, despite the vast amount of money that has been spent. Take-up on 3-D televisions has been at best sluggish, and game-makers Nintendo have already had to issue health warnings about their new 3DS handheld consoles, stating that the autostereo (or 'glasses free') effect may damage the eye development of the young and produce nausea and headaches amongst adults. (Some sales pitch, huh?)

Meanwhile, despite the best efforts of Hollywood, cinema-goers have been steadily losing interest in 3-D in exactly the same way that they did in the twenties, the fifties and the eighties. While James Cameron may have told *Entertainment Weekly* in 2010 that '3-D movies are still performing well above their 2-D versions', more viewers chose to watch *Despicable Me* in 2-D than 3-D that year, despite the fact that kid-friendly digital animation is considered to be the one genre for which audience enthusiasm is most fervent. (When even the kids don't care about 3-D, the end is most definitely in sight.) The trend continued in the summer of 2011 with *Pirates of the Caribbean: On Stranger Tides,* the first stereoscopic instalment in the series, for which 2-D screenings accounted for around 60 per cent of audience figures in the all-import-ant opening weekend – a whopping slap in the face for 3-D. A few weeks later, only 45 per cent of *Kung Fu Panda 2*'s opening weekend business was for 3-D screenings, with 2-D once again winning the popular vote.

Nor did the so-called 'stereoscopic revolution' stop audi-ence attendance figures plunging to their lowest level in 15 years in 2010, marking a major drop from 2009 and strongly suggesting that 3-D might not be the answer after all. In an article unambiguously headlined 'Attendance Crumbles in 2010', *Box Office Mojo* scribe Brandon Gray pointed out that, although 'the industry shoved 3D down people's throats in the wake of *Avatar*'s success', the apparently impressive sales figures these films racked up in 2010 'boiled down to more money from fewer people. The 3D premiums alone (the differences between 3D and regular ticket prices) accounted for an estimated $600 million of the total box office'. Or, to put it another way, fewer people ended up paying more money for less entertainment. Whichever way you spin it, that's not a success story in the making.

The real bombshell, of course, came early in 2011 when (as noted in Chapter Two) the 3-D motion-capture digimation *Mars Needs Moms* took an intergalactic bath of the highest order. Costing somewhere between $150 and $175 million (depending, as ever, on your sources) and taking a measly $35 million worldwide, this otherwise unremarkable fantasy made headlines by flopping in the way that really big movies just don't do any more. Attempting to explain this astonishing anomaly, *The New York Times* concluded that *Mars Needs Moms* had become the focus of 'a consumer referendum for 3D ticket pricing for children', the public voting with their feet by staying away in droves. Writing in the *Independent*, Geoffrey Macnab claimed that 'a simmering backlash' against over-priced 3-D had finally 'reached boiling point', and quoted Belgian film producer/director Ben Stassen's suggestion that 'People might reject 3-D as a whole and say the hell with that.' The article was headlined 'The $175m flop so bad it could end the 3D boom.' Meanwhile, back in Hollywood, the plugs were being pulled on producer Robert Zemeckis's long-planned 3-D remake of *Yellow Submarine*, and Disney shut the doors on his ImageMovers Digital studio.

It was a proper old-fashioned disaster – cinema's first fully fledged 21st-century train wreck – in 3-D!

Whether or not this all adds up to audiences throwing off the stereoscopic shackles is still a subject for debate.

Like the banks that we all paid to bail out after they destroyed our economy, 3-D may simply be considered too big to fail. And no matter how lousy the movies are or how much we may hate them, they're certainly not going to disappear overnight; the studios and multiplexes have too much invested in the format to let it die without a fight. As I write, Jeffrey Katzenberg is complaining that Hollywood has simply let viewers down with a slew of inferior 3-D fare, but he remains confident that films like Michael Bay's *Transformers: Dark of the Moon* and Spielberg's *The Adventures of Tintin: The Secret of the Unicorn* will reinvigorate waning audience enthusiasm. And, of course, we all have *Titanic 3-D* to look forward to in 2012. But will 3-D be dead in the water by then – again?

In 2010, after spending millions of dollars attempting to convert *Harry Potter and the Deathly Hallows: Part 1* into 3-D, Warner Bros. finally got wind of public dissatisfaction with the process and decided to release it in 2-D instead, with record breaking results. At the time of writing, advanced ticket sales for the 2-D version of *Deathly Hallows: Part 2* are outstripping their 3-D counterparts. You don't have to be a wizard to figure that the writing is on the wall . . .

Meanwhile, a string of 'respectable' directors such as Wim Wenders, Werner Herzog and, of course, Martin Scorsese have all dabbled in 3-D, and although Wenders has declared himself wedded to the format, others are less evangelical. We have yet to see how Scorsese's *Hugo Cabret* fares with critics and audiences, but the slate of projects he has lined up to follow it is notably lacking in 3-D outings. As for

Herzog, he's declared that having made *Cave of Forgotten Dreams* in 3-D, he has no intention to use the format again and remains every bit as sceptical about its unsuitability for narrative cinema as he was before. When I told him that I saw *Cave* in both 2-D and 3-D and much preferred the former, initially he replied that I was 'intellectually warped', which I took as a compliment. Later he conceded that stereoscopy was inherently non-cinematic, and promised not to do it again.

If 3-D has a creative future, it seems more likely to be in the arena of home entertainment than in expensively refitted cinemas. And it's probably not sports coverage but computer gaming, with its key facet of interactivity, which is most perfectly poised to explore the virtual-reality capabilities of 3-D.

As for 3-D movies, other than *Flesh for Frankenstein* I've only seen two stereoscopic productions that didn't leave me feeling underwhelmed. One was a spin-off of *Honey, I Shrunk the Kids*; the other was *Terminator 2: 3-D*, Cameron's dry run for *Avatar*. Crucially, both were short films, projected on to screens vast enough to (almost) overcome 3-D's bizarre propensity for miniaturisation. More importantly, neither were 'films' in the classic sense; they were in fact part of theme-park rides – short thrill trips displayed in amusement parks, accompanied by vibrating seats, steam showers, laser shows, blasts of hot and cold air, and live actors running around the auditorium. They were fun, a reminder that cinema started life as a carnival sideshow. But that's all they were.

Today, studio executives are attempting to drag us all back to the fairground, to take the *Pirates of the Caribbean* formula to its logical conclusion and simply replace art with the roll-on, roll-off mechanics of the critic-proof theme-park ride. There's nothing new about this – in fact it's the oldest trick in the book. But then 3-D has never been the future of cinema.

It is, was and always will be the past.

Chapter Four

WHAT ARE FILM CRITICS FOR?

'They neither reap, nor sow, nor harvest.
They are malignant lilies of the field.'
William Peter Blatty

What are film critics for?

No, really, what purpose do they serve?

In a review of my previous book, *It's Only a Movie*, *Empire* magazine stated that 'critics watch all the movies so that we don't have to'. I disagree. I don't think critics should do the job of watching movies for you. I don't even think they should do the job of telling you which movies to watch. Or what you should think about them. No, I think critics should do the job of watching all the movies and then telling you what *they* think about them in a way which is honest, engaging, erudite and (if you're lucky) entertaining.

Beyond that, you're on your own.

When I first started reviewing movies, it never occurred to me that anyone else would care what I thought of a film. As a schoolkid, I went to the pictures as often as possible, saw everything I was allowed to see, and then kept notebooks

in which I would scribble reactions to each week's screenings. Back then, in the age before video and DVD, 'reviewing'
was a way of preserving the movie – however good or bad
– for my own future entertainment, writing reminders to
myself which would allow me to 're-view' films I had seen
only once in the cinema. I was writing for no one's benefit
but my own, and felt no sense of responsibility toward readers
(of which there were none), film companies, movie-makers
or cinema chains in my praise or damnation of a particular
film. After all, it wasn't as if my opinions could have any
effect upon the film or its potential audience, was it? The
only person I had to be true to was me, and my job was to
describe accurately the experience of watching a film in a
manner vivid enough to make it come to life once more –
for better or worse.

One of the first films I remember reviewing in this way
was *Dougal and the Blue Cat*, the feature-length animated
spin-off from the TV show *The Magic Roundabout*, which
remains a touchstone text to this day. I was about eight
years old and the film had such a powerful effect on me
that I felt positively compelled to commit my thoughts to
paper, for fear of losing the strange tingle of its eerie spell.
I wrote down everything I could remember: snippets of
dialogue ('What a place; worse than Barnsley'); freeze-
framed images (Buxton, the blue cat, trapped in the terrifying Room of Dreams); even the tune of 'Florence's Sad
Song' (which I attempted to work out on the piano), a few
notes of which would send me off into a world of cinematic
rapture. Some months later, I was with my mum in

Woolworths in North Finchley, where we found a cut-price soundtrack album for *Dougal and the Blue Cat* that included most of Eric Thompson's brilliant narration and all of the songs. I begged mum to shell out the 99 pence it cost to buy that LP, then took it home and played it to death. Every time the record hit the turntable, the movie would start to play in my head and I would feel compelled to write about it once again. I ended up filling almost an entire notebook with my quasi-critical responses to this film, discovering new depths in each subsequent replaying. It wasn't until 1989, when *Dougal and the Blue Cat* was finally released on newfangled video, that I actually got to watch the movie again in real life, as opposed to in my head. What was surprising was just how much the genuine article departed from my carefully constructed memory. For one thing, there were chunks of dialogue that had been trimmed from the record for reasons of time and which now seemed to have no right to be in the film at all. More bizarrely, I had completely re-imagined a couple of key sequences on the basis of my first hastily scribbled notes, and therefore for almost 20 years I had been effectively watching a version of the film that didn't actually exist. The film was still brilliantly strange and bafflingly inexplicable, but not in quite the way I had imagined.

Lesson number one: the way anyone experiences and remembers a film may bear only a passing relation to the movie itself.

Other movies I saw as a child might have been less rewarding, but that didn't dampen my fervour in wanting to write about them. I remember spending hours trying to capture in words exactly what was wrong with *The Odessa File* (the short answer was that it wasn't anything like as exciting as the trailer, which featured a man being pushed under a train – an image which still haunts me) and why *Earthquake* sagged in all the sequences when the 'Sensurround' was switched off (which was most of the movie). In each case, I was trying to describe not only the movie but my reaction to it, as if those palpable immediate responses could be bottled, corked and kept like a fine wine, to be sipped from at will in the future.

Soon I needed to broaden my horizons and to review films that were technically off-limits to someone of my tender age. I was 11 years old when I saw my first 'AA' movie, a classification that forbade entry to anyone under the age of 14. The film was Mel Brooks's *Blazing Saddles*, about which I knew almost nothing (other than the fact that I wasn't allowed to see it). One Saturday afternoon, a schoolfriend called Nick Kennedy and I decided to try and blag our way into a screening at the Classic Hendon, a three-screen cinema which (we had been reliably informed) had a somewhat lax door policy with regard to the age of its patrons. We agreed to meet at Hendon Central Tube station at 1 p.m. with a view to catching the 1.30 p.m. performance in Screen One, on the understanding that if we were refused entry because we looked too young then we could go and see *The Paper Chase*, starring Timothy Bottoms, in Screen Three instead. I'd already seen *The Paper Chase* and didn't think much of it (although I did fall a little bit in love with Lindsay Wagner), but seeing a movie was always preferable to not seeing a movie and I was quite happy to sit through it again because I knew I would enjoy writing about it afterwards. But what we *really* wanted to watch was *Blazing Saddles*, and to this end we had both agreed that we would do our best to 'look older'.

For reasons which frankly now fail me, I decided that the best way to 'look older' was to wear a cravat. And so it was that I arrived at Hendon Central station wearing white and blue training shoes, thick burgundy cords, a denim jacket that I had borrowed from my sister and a bright yellow T-shirt with some appropriately scruffy motif ironed on to the front, all topped off with a paisley cravat recklessly thrown around my neck at what I considered to be a maturely cavalier angle. In my head at the time, this combination made me look like a grown-up. Looking back, I realise that it probably made me look like Jodie Foster in *Taxi Driver*.

Nick, who had arrived looking exactly the same as he always did, was horrified.

'Why are you dressed as a girl?' he asked.

'I'm not dressed as a girl,' I replied, somewhat taken aback. 'I'm dressed as a grown-up.'

'Well, why are you wearing a girl's scarf round your neck?'

'It's not a girl's scarf,' I protested. 'It's a "cravat".'

'A *what*?'

'A cravat. It's what grown-ups wear. Grown-up *men*.'

Nick looked unconvinced.

'It's purple,' he said, after examining it further. 'Girls wear purple.'

'It's *not* purple,' I retorted somewhat defensively. 'It's "paisley". Paisley is completely different to purple. Just like cravats are completely different to scarves. This is not a purple, girl's scarf. It is a paisley, man's cravat.'

Nick thought about this for a moment whilst making a pained, wincing expression. Perhaps he was trying to imagine a proper grown-up man wearing such a garment and having the testosterone-fuelled panache to pull it off. Would Sean Connery have got away with it? Quite possibly. Plastered all over the Tube station at that very moment were posters of Connery wearing nothing more than thigh-high boots and a red-leather posing pouch advertising his new X-rated sci-fi movie *Zardoz*. He even had a ponytail and he still didn't look like a girl. We really wanted to see *Zardoz*, but since we were currently struggling to look 14, the chances of being able to pass for 18 seemed infinitesimal. Perhaps we could try the posing pouches. Or perhaps not.

'They won't let you in,' said Nick firmly. 'You look like a girl and they won't let you in.'

'But if I take it off, then I just look like me, and I'm not fourteen and they'll *know*,' I whined.

'How will they know?' Nick demanded. 'If they ask you how old you are, you just say that you're fourteen. It's simple.'

But herein lay the rub. For, being an anxious and essentially law-abiding soul, I had actually gone and asked my parents for their permission to attempt to bunk into a movie that I was technically too young to see. And my dad, in what I now consider to be a brilliantly political answer, had told me that he appreciated my being honest enough to ask and therefore didn't mind me going, as long as I didn't lie about my age. If the person at the ticket office asked me how old I was, then I had to tell them the truth – that I was 11. If no one asked, then the responsibility was theirs and not mine, in both a moral and legal sense.

Genius.

The problem with this strategy was that it required me looking old enough for the person in the ticket booth not to feel the need to ask my age in the first place, since I was so evidently a cosmopolitan teenager who did this sort of thing all the time. Hence the cravat. Obviously. Without this embellishment I was just a dorky kid. And not a very tall dorky kid at that. Things were different for Nick. He was impressively tall for his age. Plus he had loads of dark curly hair, which made him look a bit like Kevin Keegan during his ill-advised perm period and which also added a further couple of inches to his height. As for me, the reason I was wearing training shoes rather than more grown-up leather shoes was because I'd stuffed some newspaper under my heels to give me a smidgen of extra height, and you could only do that with shoes soft enough not to crush the tops of your feet when you tied them up. By which I mean training shoes. The unfortunate side effect of this heel-stacking, however, was that it made me walk a bit funny, like someone tottering upon newly purchased stilettos to which they were not yet comfortably accustomed.

Like I said – Jodie Foster in *Taxi Driver*.

Anyway, against his better judgement Nick decided not to argue the point any further, and so we both headed out of

Hendon Central station and up the magnificent concrete esplanade that led into the Classic Cinema. Nick strode purposefully, like a man on a mission to see a movie. I hobbled along behind him, like an underage transvestite with ongoing ligament issues. We made it up the steps. Just. And then into the foyer, where Nick boldly headed straight for the ticket office whilst I cowered behind him, hoping that no one would notice me.

'Two for Screen One,' growled Nick, in an unusually low and guttural voice that he clearly believed made him sound terribly grown-up, but actually made him sound mad and a little bit dangerous. So now we were an underage tranny and a serial killer. Great. I fiddled nervously with my cravat, suddenly wishing that I'd taken Nick's advice and thrown the damned thing in the bin. I had a pain growing in my calf muscles from walking on the newspaper and I was starting to sweat like someone in the throes of a coronary attack. My neck was itching, my scalp was prickling and I was having difficulty breathing. I started pulling at the cravat as if it was somehow strangling me and in the process made it tighter, so it did indeed start to strangle me. My head began to turn purple, matching the purple-hued paisley of what now looked, more than ever, like a big girl's scarf. My knees began to wobble, the room began to swim, and for a moment I thought I'd have to be ambulanced off like those punters who had been regularly stretchered out of screenings of *The Exorcist* in this very cinema.

It was all over.

The game was up.

The gaff was blown.

The ruse was rumbled.

We were both clearly going down . . .

'You want chocolate raisins?'

What?

'Or chocolate peanuts? I like raisins.'

Nick was walking nonchalantly toward the sweet counter, which back then was a rather more low-key affair than the extravagant popcorn and nachos fast-food outlets that dominate the foyers of modern multiplexes (see Chapter One). Back then you got to choose between a small cardboard box of stale raisins coated in chocolate or a small cardboard box of similarly prepared nuts. If you were in a really flashy cinema, you also had the option of gorging yourself on a 'Frankie's Hot Dog', a steamingly inedible comestible. Other than that there was nothing – you went to the movies to watch, rather than eat.

'Um, raisins are good,' I gasped, still unclear as to what exactly had happened at the ticket stand. Presumably we'd been rumbled and were now going to watch *The Paper Chase*. Again.

'So what happened at the ticket office?'

Nick looked at me, in my purple girl's scarf and stack-heeled training shoes, sweating like a water buffalo, unsteady on my legs.

'No problem,' he said in an off-hand fashion. 'Raisins then, is it?'

I struggled to get a grip on the situation.

'What, you mean we got in?'

'Yeah, of course.'

'In to Screen One?'

'Yup.'

'In to Screen One which is showing *Blazing Saddles*?'

'Like I said.'

'And they didn't ask your age?'

'Nope.' Nick paused for a moment before adding, 'Nor yours. Although the man behind the counter did look rather oddly at you. Well, not "oddly" considering the fact that you're dressed as a girl.'

'But, crucially, a fourteen-year-old girl?' I asked.

'Apparently so,' said Nick, before bursting into wild hooting laughter of the kind that would clearly attract the attention of the management if we weren't careful. Overwhelmed, I grabbed Nick's arm and bundled him toward Screen One as fast as possible, his shrieking merriment continuing all the way through the door, down the aisle and into the seats, of which we apparently had our pick. There were only ten or 20 other people in the auditorium, and glancing around I noticed that most of them looked no older than Nick and me. Finally wrenching that bloody cravat from around my strangulated neck, I sat back and started to laugh myself, and as far as I can remember I didn't stop laughing until the end credits of the movie had run and Nick and I were attempting to gather ourselves in the street outside the cinema.

As far as I was concerned, *Blazing Saddles* – with its AA-rated farting cowboys and mildly saucy songs – was just about the funniest film I had ever seen. I honestly couldn't remember having had more fun in the cinema *ever*, and that was pretty much what I wrote in my notebook when I got home and settled down to 'review' the movie. I sat there for hours struggling to remember all the best lines, the crudest cracks, the naughtiest sight gags, the stupidest bum jokes – all were committed lovingly (and almost certainly inaccurately) to paper so that I could enjoy them over and over again. Even though I had never heard Marlene Dietrich's Frenchy singing 'See What the Boys in the Back Room Will Have' in *Destry Rides Again*, I was tickled pink by the parodic drone of Madeline Kahn performing 'I'm Tired' as the 'Teutonic Titwillow' Lili Von Shtupp, and took particular pride in my phonetic attempts to capture her cod-German accent ('I'm doyyyered, doyerred ov be-ink ad-moyyerred . . .'). Many of the jokes I clearly didn't understand (Mel Brooks's 'Gov' in voluminous undershorts, retiring behind a curtain with his secretary whilst announcing 'Gentlemen, affairs of state must take precedence over the affairs of state!' for example) but I found them funny anyway. The truth, which I gradually came to realise whilst writing that review, was that having actually gotten into the screening in the first place I would have found almost anything hilariously entertaining. Clearly my insane excitement about the convoluted subterfuge that had been used to gain entrance to my first ever AA-certificate film had caused my reactions to become massively over-cooked, and when writing about the movie I was writing as much about my own state of mind whilst watching it as about Mel Brooks's achievement in making it.

Decades later I remain fiercely aware of this powerful element of film criticism; that what the reviewer brings to the cinema is every bit as important as what's up there on the screen. Oh, you can dress it up with authoritative-sounding analysis and rigorous contextualisation, both of which are important components of 'proper' film criticism (more of which in a moment). But the fact remains that your response to a movie will always be (first and foremost) just that – *your* response. Over the years those responses will change, and the more movies you see the more sober your reaction to each new film tends to be. This is particularly true of horror movies, or more precisely scary movies. The first time you see someone closing a bathroom cabinet and catching sight of the killer's reflection in the mirror, chances are you'll jump out of your skin. But by the time you've seen that same gag done a hundred times or more, the effect is rather lessened. That doesn't mean that it can't still be scary; rather that it has to be executed with a little more flair, panache and wit to have the desired effect. The same is true of comedy. The first time I watched a bunch of cowboys breaking wind in *Blazing Saddles*, I laughed so much I thought I was going to soil myself. Nowadays a fart joke has to be really well-timed and splendidly executed to raise a titter, even though farting remains inherently funny.

The point is that, having now worked as a 'professional film critic' for over 25 years, I am certain that my reviews and responses are every bit as subjective as they were when I first scribbled down a few ramshackle notes in order to remind myself just how much fun I'd had watching *Blazing Saddles* whilst dressed as Jodie Foster in *Taxi Driver*. How else do you explain the fact that I honestly think the eighties Hollywood romp *Breathless*, starring Richard Gere, is better than Jean-Luc Godard's epochal *nouvelle vague* masterpiece *À bout de souffle*?

Really.

Oh, I could give you loads of explanatory guff about how Jim McBride's ridiculous remake is more of an honest rock'n'roll picture than Godard's over-praised original; how the use of LA locations is really striking and original; how Gere's preening gambler-on-the-run is a more entertaining self-regarding anti-hero then Belmondo. I could even sell you a line about how McBride's recurrent use of the Silver Surfer riff is a clear forerunner of the films of Kevin Smith and Quentin Tarantino that were to look so modern in their trash-culture obsessions over a decade later. But the truth is that I first saw *Breathless* at a cheap screening in South Manchester one Saturday evening when I was in a terrifically good mood for reasons which I cannot now remember, and only caught up with *À bout de souffle* years later as part of a belated and somewhat gruelling attempt to fill the massive gaps in my film knowledge because by then I was working as a 'proper critic'. As a consequence, I have rather fonder memories of *Breathless*, even though I know in my heart that it is the lesser piece, because the first time I saw it felt less like work and more like fun. Also, I have always had a pathetic soft spot for Richard Gere, and the image of him singing along to Jerry Lee Lewis while sporting a frankly terrible array of trousers and Cuban heels just fills me with joy every time. So, if you ask me as a 'proper film critic' whether you should watch *Breathless* or *À bout de souffle*, I will tell you that while I wouldn't wish to make your viewing choices for you and the weight of academic history is clearly with the latter, frankly I'll take the former any day.

This sort of rampant subjectivity and lack of authoritative judgement is often frowned upon by those who believe that critics should be somehow impartial, but the truth is that, to a greater or lesser degree, every critic is constantly guilty of letting their personal feelings get the better of them. This doesn't matter when you're a 12-year-old writing reviews for no one's benefit but your own. But is it different if your reviews are read by others out there in the 'real world'? Do your responsibilities change if your potential audience extends beyond the confines of your own bedroom?

Well, yes and no.

Back in October 2010, a YouGov poll was published which concluded (amazingly) that I am the 'most trusted' film critic in the UK. Yes, you read that right: most trusted. Go figure. Apparently, three times as many people trust my judgement above all others on movie-related matters as the number that trust *Empire* or *Total Film*, the country's best-selling movie magazines. It sounds like a ringing endorsement until you discover that the huge tidal wave of assured popularity upon which I surfed constituted a mere 3 per cent of people polled. Just think about that – the most trusted film critic in the country is trusted by only *3 per cent* of the population.

Admittedly, governments have claimed landslide victories on dodgier statistics than that (we are currently being ruled by a coalition for whom nobody voted), but even my old sparring partner Alastair Campbell would have to concede that such a result hardly constitutes a popular mandate. In case maths isn't your strong point, that statistic means that for every three people who think 'Mark Kermode loved/hated that film, therefore it must be great/rubbish', there are 97 others who think:

a) I disagree with Mark Kermode on *everything* so that film's probably rubbish/great.

b) I don't *care* what Mark Kermode thinks about anything; he's more annoying than Mick Hucknall (see previous book).

c) Who the hell is Mark Kermode?

Indeed, rather than proving that I am the most trusted film critic in the country, the YouGov poll merely suggests that the public don't trust film critics – *any* film critics – full stop.

This is as it should be. Anyone who believes that an individual critic's personal responses to a film are in any way definitive is a fool. No matter how much people blather on about certain reviewers having the 'popular touch', the fact is that you cannot second-guess anyone else's reaction to a movie. This being the case, the only honest thing to do is to be upfront about your personal prejudices and allow the reader, listener or viewer to pick their way through your opinions, duly warned.

Yet while your opinions may be yours and yours alone, the job of 'proper' film criticism does also require a degree of factual and historical research and accuracy that is anything but subjective, and without which those opinions are nothing but hot air. For example, imagine you're in a pub with someone you've never met before and about whom you know nothing other than the fact that they seem friendly enough. Somehow the topic of conversation turns to movies. You ask them what they've seen recently, and they reply, 'I've just been to see *Saw VII* and it's rubbish.' After politely correcting them on the issue of the title ('Ah, you mean *Saw 3D,* aka *Saw: The Final Chapter,* aka *Saw 3D: The Final Chapter*') your first follow-up question should be: 'And what did you think of the other six?' If they reply that they haven't seen any of the previous *Saw* franchise instalments, then you may conclude that:

a) they are not part of the film's target demographic;

b) they don't like horror films; or,

c) they are a person of discernment and taste who recognised *Saw 3D* as the rubbish it so clearly is.

Crucially, you have no idea which of these propositions is true and therefore you have no way of judging whether this person's pithily expressed opinion has any merit or weight. If, however, they reply that they have seen all *seven* of the *Saw* movies and thought they really tailed off after the first outing, you might conclude that:

a) they are a glutton for punishment;

b) they really like horror movies; or,

c) they are a person of discernment, taste and (crucially) track record who recognised *Saw 3D* as the piece of rubbish it so clearly is.

The point is not that someone who hasn't seen all the *Saw* movies has no right to think that *Saw 3D* is rubbish, nor indeed that such an opinion should not be entirely sound, merely that one might reasonably wonder about the basis on which that opinion was reached.

At the end of April 2010 I did an onstage event with writer and critic Kim Newman, who probably knows more about horror movies than anyone. Kim had recently updated his essential work *Nightmare Movies* – an exhaustive, author-itative and extremely entertaining overview of 'Horror on Screen Since the 1960s' – and our talk at the BFI Southbank was to celebrate the publication of the new edition and to discuss the ways in which horror cinema had changed over the past 20 years. I was surprised to find that Kim had devoted almost an entire chapter of his new book to the legacy of Eli Roth's *Hostel* movies, which I found depress-ingly dull but which he argued were an important corner-stone of the contemporary horror market. Crucially, Kim didn't say he actively liked either *Hostel* or *Hostel: Part II*, or indeed the slew of so-called 'torture porn' slashers into which subgenre the *Saw* sequels also fell. But simply not liking a movie didn't mean that it could merely be dismissed or ignored, at least not for a film critic whose reputation is built upon an encyclopaedic wealth of knowledge. And, according to Kim, 'like it or not, *Hostel* was the most signif-icant horror film of 2005'.

A few weeks later, Kim and I went to a preview screening of the cartoony vampire-slayer romp *Priest* in 3-D, which I was really looking forward to because, just as with Richard

Gere, I have a bit of a thing for Paul Bettany. The film turned out to be a major disappointment – noisy, empty and (worst of all) not a patch on Bettany's previous collaboration with director Scott Stewart, the splendidly silly *Legion*. Despite the fact that it attracted almost universally stinky reviews I had enjoyed the hell out of *Legion*, in which Bettany plays a renegade archangel who hacks off his wings and picks up an Uzi in defiance of a God who is waxing wroth and then some. Set in a roadside cafe in the middle of the desert, that film had a sparky comic-book wit and featured excitingly diverting set pieces in which the possessed minions of the apocalypse are mown down by the kind of heavy artillery fire sorely missing from the Book of Revelation. (When it comes to the Bible, it's all slings and swords and plagues of beasts and boils, but there's a notable shortage of intercontinental ballistic missiles with massive atomic warheads, which is a shame.) Judged alongside the comparably themed Keanu Reeves dud *Constantine* (similarly ridiculed by most mainstream critics, but an entirely different beast), *Legion* really held its own. And it was way more fun than the overblown guns-and-religion Schwarzenegger smash-'em-up *End of Days*, in which Arnie attempts to redeem the human race by shooting and punching devils in the face. So, within its own admittedly rarified subgenre, *Legion* was a hit in my book.

Anyway, as we sat down to watch *Priest* I mentioned to Kim in passing that I had recently been asked a specific question about *Saw V* (which was rubbish) and was ashamed to admit that I couldn't recall a single scene that I could posi-tively identify as being from that particular episode, as opposed to any of the other six instalments. 'Ah,' replied Kim sympathetically, 'I have the same problem with *Saw IV*. I can tell you something specific about all the rest of the *Saw* movies but I can't remember a single distinctive thing about *Saw IV*. It really bothers me . . .'

The fact that it bothered Kim is what makes him such a great critic, and I half expected him to scurry home and watch *Saw IV* (which is rubbish) all over again just to fill in that gap in his otherwise all-encompassing knowledge. And it's precisely because of this dedication to the cause that I'd rather hear what Kim has to say on the subject of *Saw 3D* than someone who hasn't religiously ploughed their way through the rest of the series first.

In fact, if you just hold on a minute, I'll give him a call right now and get his verdict.

Ring ring.

'Kim Newman.' (He always answers the phone like that.)

'Hi, Kim. It's Mark.'

'Oh, hi.'

'I just wanted to check something. What did you think of *Saw 3D*?'

'Disappointingly flat.'

'Great, thanks. Bye!'

Click.

The fact that both Kim (who knows loads about horror films) and some bloke down the pub could come to the same overall conclusion about the relative merits of *Saw*

3D (it's rubbish) is neither surprising nor ultimately important. Opinions are like arseholes: everyone's got one, and everyone thinks theirs is the only one that doesn't stink. What's important is the context in which the opinion was reached and the manner in which it is expressed. This is the difference between film criticism and pub talk. Pub talk can be all opinion and nothing else; film criticism, if it is done properly, should involve opinion, description, contextualisation, analysis and (if you're lucky) entertainment. These are the five essential ingredients of a 'proper' film review, and they are what separate the bedroom ramblings of somebody writing about movies for no one's amusement but their own and the published reports of someone (like Kim) for whom film criticism is a lifelong vocation.

To illustrate these essential elements, here are five short reviews of *Saw 3D*, each one adding another key ingredient:

1) Opinion:

Saw 3D is rubbish.

2) Opinion and description:

Saw 3D is a horror film that is rubbish.

3) Opinion, description and contextualisation:

Saw 3D is the seventh episode and the first stereoscopic instalment in a long-running horror series, and it is rubbish.

4) Opinion, description, contextualisation and analysis:

Saw 3D is the first stereoscopic instalment in a series that began life as a tortuously inventive low-budget chiller but which has descended over the course of six sequels into gory, boring torture porn which is rubbish. '

5) Opinion, description, contextualisation, analysis and entertainment:

It took the once-inventive but increasingly depressing *Saw* series seven movies to resort to the hackneyed headache of 3-D, but despite the promise that this is 'The Final Chapter' (just wait until the sums say otherwise) you keep wishing those protruding spikes would leap a little further out of the screen and puncture your eyeballs to ensure that you never have to watch rubbish like this ever again.

OK, so that last example wasn't particularly entertaining, but I never said that I was any good at marshalling the five essential elements of proper film criticism, merely that I could identify them. Kim did it more pithily and came up with a better joke. The best joke I ever heard about the *Saw* series was from a listener to my Radio 5 Live film review show who had gone to a 7 p.m. multiplex screening of the fifth instalment (the one about which I couldn't remember a single distinguishing feature) and had taken great delight in being able to stride up to the ticket office and demand: 'One to see *Saw* Five in Six at Seven.' This began a long-running theme that found listeners seemingly planning their entire evening's entertainment on the basis of a numerical pun such as 'One to 3-D *Thor* in Five at Six', which I found ludicrously entertaining.

But to the point: what's important about these five golden rules is that all of them relate to one's duty either to the reader or oneself, and none of them take account of any possible debt to the film in question. An early editor of *Empire* magazine is reported to have told his aspiring critics always to remember that 'these people [film-makers] are not your friends', that critics should owe their allegiance to no one but the reader. Inevitably, this has proved a hard rule to follow because the kind of access to the stars that shifts magazines can swiftly be withdrawn in the face of harshly honest criticism. But despite the flimsy illusion of glamour, the truth is that being a film critic really has nothing to do with being liked, and even less to do with being a 'friend of the stars'. People constantly ask me if I know such-and-such a star or whether I hang out with some film-maker or other, and the answer is almost invariably 'No'. The reason is simple: if done properly film criticism should maintain a safe distance from film-making because, just as good taste is the enemy of art, so intimacy and cosiness are the enemies of honest criticism. In an ideal world, film critics would have no friends amongst the film-making fraternity. In fact they would probably have no friends, full stop. Nor would they nurture any ambition to become film-makers themselves.

Nope, a good film critic should, by their very nature, be the kind of person who would get thrown off movie sets, and thrown out of movie industry parties – an unwanted outsider to whom nothing is owed and from whom nothing is expected by the people who actually make movies. So, when a Z-list British 'actor' and 'personality' recently became the latest in a long line of affronted luvvies to threaten to beat me up for mocking his rotten films, I felt a sense of pride that I was still able to provoke such a violent reaction. This is just part of the job: if you're honest about the parlous state of some movies, then you have to be ready for the people who make those movies to start bleating about how they're going to kick your head in for being mean and disrespectful about their craft. In this particular case, said affrontee actually devoted three whole pages of his newly published autobiography to repeating his widely viewed YouTube promise to 'put something right across [my] faakin canister' for laughing at his risible Dick Van Dire cockney-geezer shtick. It's a threat he continues to repeat ad nauseam; even as I write, I see Dick has once again told the press that he will headbutt me and break my 'faakin nose' because I 'don't take [him] seriously as an actor'.

Actually, I don't take him seriously, full stop.

Luvvies are like this, even the mockney ones. To be fair, this particular drug-snorting Groucho-club habitué (who has 'done Pinter and stuff like that') was probably upset at having recently torched his career by publicly advising a fan to cut his ex-girlfriend's face (a joke, apparently – ha ha ha), thereby becoming the only person ever to get fired from *Zoo* magazine for being *too* sexist – quite a feat. This faux pas had irreparably damaged his box-office appeal, with his most recent movie attracting only 24 punters on its opening weekend in UK cinemas, grossing a record-breakingly pitiful sum of £205. So, presumably he was cross and wanted to blame someone for his professional misfortunes, and in such circumstances the easiest person to blame is always a critic. This despite the fact that, according to that YouGov poll, no one pays any attention to critics in the first place.

This is a familiar pattern: an actor or film-maker shoots themselves in the foot with a really rubbish movie and then runs around blaming the critics, to whom no one listens anyway. In 2009, the usually jovial Kevin Smith directed an inept buddy-cop action-comedy called *Cop Out*, which featured Bruce Willis phoning in his laziest performance to date. The movie, which began life with the altogether saucier title *A Couple of Dicks*, was (as you might have guessed) rubbish, and I paid £7.50 to watch it in a cinema with five other people, all of whom had also paid and all of whom also remained stony-faced throughout. The reason I had paid to see the film rather than catching it at a free critics-only preview screening was because Kevin Smith (whose work I have enjoyed and championed in the past) had taken to the internet to complain about over-privileged critics seeing his films for free and then unfairly rubbishing them in public.

As with so many of his internet ramblings (and indeed several of his recent movies), Smith's complaint was scattershot, sloppy and – to be honest – somewhat lacking in the humour department. But it garnered international attention after respected American critic Roger Ebert issued an equally irate riposte, prompting a public spat that generated variously misleading internet reports (shockingly, such things exist) about Smith having declared war on critics, and critics duly circling the wagons and closing ranks.

What Smith actually said was that the critics who were enthusiastically sticking the boot into *Cop Out* were applying unfairly highbrow critical standards to what was essentially a fluffy piece of fun. After all, the movie wasn't called *Schindler's Cop Out*, now was it? (Smith's words, not mine.) So why were people complaining that it was stupid, empty-headed trash, when that was exactly what it was meant to be? He went further, comparing the howls of derision that had greeted preview screenings of the film to the schoolyard bullying of a disabled child. His exact words (and I encourage you to check the veracity of this quote for yourself because it sounds like I must be making this up) were: 'Writing a nasty review for *Cop Out* is akin to bullying a retarded kid who was getting a couple of chuckles from the normies by singing AFTERNOON DELIGHT . . . All you've done is make fun of something that wasn't doing you any harm and wanted only to give some cats some fun laughs.'

It's hard to know where to begin in unpicking this silliness. Let's start by imagining the shrieking indignation that would surely have ensued if a critic had had the poor taste to liken Smith's movie (which the director ought to have known was not up to snuff) to a 'retarded kid'. Said critic would have been promptly hounded out of a job by everyone from indignant film-makers to rightfully outraged equal-opportunity campaigners. Yet the director managed to do just this, whilst simultaneously complaining about all the other bad things that critics had said about his clearly sub-par film. Nor was it a slip of the tongue. Several months after *Cop Out* had finished 'underperforming' in theatres, Smith could still be found proudly rolling out the same ill-considered simile, telling MovieWeb (for example) that 'these dudes came at it like it was a retarded kid in class'.

The nub of Smith's argument (which is repeated endlessly in defence of the abysmal mainstream tosh that we are all apparently required to 'celebrate' in the name of fatuous inclusivity) was that the critics had no right to judge his film by their own unfairly highbrow standards, as if the movie required the support of a special-needs network in order for its true potential to be realised. Which is a bit rich considering that, at a cost of $37 million, *Cop Out* was hardly 'underprivileged' independent fare. On the contrary, it was a mid-priced studio movie with a star whose usual catering expenses could probably have covered several genuinely needy (and genuinely good) independent productions. Yet money (or the lack of it) swiftly became the central tenant of Smith's complaint as he fell back on that old faithful mantra about critics not even paying to watch the movie — so, huh, what do they know?

'Realized whole system's upside down,' he continued in his internet rant. 'So we let a bunch of people see it for free and they shit all over it? Meanwhile, people who'd REALLY like to see the flick for free are made to pay? Bullshit: from now on, any flick I'm ever involved with, I conduct critics' screenings thusly: you wanna see it early to review it? Fine: pay like you would if you saw it next week.'

So I did. I skipped the free preview screening and paid to see *Cop Out* on its first Friday morning performance at the Vue cinema in Shepherds Bush, where it duly stank the place out. Honestly, I had more fun having back surgery. As far as I could tell, no one else in the cinema was enjoying it either, but just to be sure I sidled up to a lone saddo (like me) on the way out and muttered something about that being 'the biggest load of bollocks I've seen in a while'. He nodded in agreement, made a vague grunting noise, and then turned on his mobile phone, which bizarrely played the theme tune from *Beverly Hills Cop*. Clearly, this was a guy who knew a decent mainstream buddy-cop comedy flick with a Harold Faltermeyer soundtrack when he saw one, and from what I could tell by his general demeanour he hadn't just seen one. If he'd been in my shoes (i.e. if he'd been about to walk a few hundred yards up the road to Television Centre in order to go on air and tell the world what he thought of *Cop Out*) I don't think he'd have been much kinder than I was.

Sure enough, despite its megastar lead and prominent advertising campaign, *Cop Out* opened in the UK box office at number 12 – behind *Furry Vengeance* (then in its third week) – taking a measly £64,935 in 127 screens, while Werner Herzog's altogether more oddball and adventurous *Bad Lieutenant: Port of Call New Orleans* (which cost $10 million *less*) took £178,953 in 129 screens. So perhaps the snot-nosed critics weren't so out-of-step with popular taste after all.

This kind of indignant strop is, of course, just the latest in a long line of film-maker tantrums that almost inevitably accompany the drubbing of a really poor film. And it will surely come as no surprise to learn that film-makers are far less inclined to complain about how awful critics are when their latest work is being hailed as the next *Citizen Kane*. Indeed, even when the notices are at very best moderate, film distributors still use critics to sell their product, often taking their words entirely out of context for use in print advertising to give the appearance of independent verification of value. For example, when reviewing the terribly ordinary 1992 romcom *Jersey Girl* (not to be confused with Kevin Smith's terribly terrible 2004 rom(non)com of the same name) for London's *Time Out* magazine, I noted in passing that, although the movie was a bit of a duffer, leading lady Jami Gertz was generally 'a joy'. I meant this in contrast to leading man Dylan McDermott, whose performance was, frankly, plank-like. But when ads for the movie appeared, the phrase 'A joy – *Time Out*' was emblazoned beneath the movie's title, thereby suggesting that this esteemed organ had given the film a whopping thumbs-up.

This is business as usual; taking quotes out of context is common practice. My good friend Trevor Johnston once began a review of the ropey erotic thriller *Color of Night* with the phrase 'Hypnotic. Compelling. Stunning. Bruce Willis' latest crime against celluloid is a special kind of bad', only to find ads for the movie emblazoned with the words 'Hypnotic. Compelling. Stunning – *Time Out*'. Similarly, when reviewing the Kirstie Alley comedy *Sibling Rivalry*, Nigel Floyd made it quite clear that he hated the movie. 'From the moment Alley screws charming, grey-haired stranger Sam Elliot to death you know this is going to be a stiff,' he wrote, with little room for misinterpretation. 'As for the scene where she has to remove a condom from the corpse's rigor mortised dick . . . Laugh? I almost changed my method of contraception.' Imagine his surprise when ads for the movie appeared boldly emblazoned with the apparently laudatory phrase 'Laugh? I almost changed my method of contraception – Nigel Floyd'.

After this has happened to you a few times you start to wise up, and any critic who knows the ropes (which clearly neither Trevor nor Nigel nor I did back then) learns to write in a convolutedly 'bulletproof' style that specifically sidesteps the use of quotable phrases. Unless, of course, a critic wants to be quoted on film posters, which many do because it serves to increase their otherwise irrelevant standing. And it seems to me that, generally speaking, the more 'poster quotable' a reviewer is, the less substantial or worthwhile their reviews are for the reader, viewer or listener. I refer you, for example, to the lone laudatory quote that adorned gigantic posters for the dodgy Simon Pegg comedy *Run, Fatboy, Run*: 'At last, the comedy of the year! Simply perfect. Go now.'

After scrabbling around on the internet, I discovered that the author of this quote is 'the most read, most watched, most listened to showbiz reporter in the world', which surprised me because I'd never heard of him, and had therefore assumed that he'd been made up by the film's publicity department. This does happen. In 2001, *Newsweek* journalist John Horn revealed that a writer named 'David Manning', who had long been supplying enthusiastic quotes for lousy movies, was in fact a fictional character conjured from thin air by a movie marketing executive. Manning, who supposedly worked for *The Ridgefield Press* (a real local newspaper, which had no knowledge of the scam), was quoted as having

written rave reviews of titles such as the grisly Rob
Schneider comedy *The Animal*, an appalling affair which
made me understand how a fox can chew its own leg off
in order to escape a hideous ordeal of entrapment, but
which Manning more charitably called 'Another winner!'
(I have a ridiculous theory that the reliably awful Schneider
has photographs of Adam Sandler doing unspeakable things
with farmyard animals, because I can't come up with any
other explanation as to why the super-successful Sandler
keeps giving him roles in his movies.) Manning also lavished
praise upon Paul Verhoeven's *Hollow Man*, a severely
compromised studio product that the director himself later
told me should more rightly have been called 'Hollow Film',
but one with which Manning could find no fault. Other
duds championed by Manning included *The Patriot* and
Vertical Limit, prompting a lawsuit from two Californian
film-goers who brought a class action on behalf of all those
who had been duped into watching bad movies via the
'international and systematic deception of consumers'.
'We're horrified,' said Susan Tick, spokeswoman for
Columbia's parent company Sony, whose damage-limitation
exercise reportedly involved agreeing to refund dissatisfied
customers to the tune of $1.5 million. In a rare moment
of humour Joe Roth, whose Revolution studios had
produced *The Animal*, got the last laugh by balefully telling
reporters, 'If [Manning] doesn't exist, he should at least
have given us a better quote!'

The Manning affair opened up a whole can of worms about
the ways in which critics' 'quotes' are used by film companies

to (mis-)sell their product. 'The real question,' observed Horn astutely, 'is why Sony had to conceive the counterfeit critic to begin with, given the world of movie junkets, where normal reporting standards don't apply.' Horn went on to describe an 'all-expenses-paid gravy train where the studios give journalists free rooms and meals at posh hotels and the reporters return the favor with puffy celebrity profiles and enthusiastic review blurbs. No one complains, and bad movies end up with great quotes . . . Reading the glowing news-paper-ad recommendations for even the lamest movie, you might wonder if those quoted critics are real. Unlike Manning, they are.'

Certainly the writer who was so impressed by *Run, Fatboy, Run* was real, with a real website on which he described himself as a 'presenter, journalist, gossip guru, and global showbiz king' – although crucially *not* a critic, an important factor when assessing his description of the film as 'simply perfect'. Perfect? *Citizen Kane* is perfect. *Some Like It Hot* is perfect. *Toy Story* is perfect. David Cronenberg's *Crash* is perfect. But *Run, Fatboy, Run*? In what universe is that perfect? I guarantee you that even the people who made the movie would concede that it is at best patchy. But taken at face value, that quote attests that *Run, Fatboy, Run* could not be improved upon in any way whatsoever (the definition of 'perfect'); it was not only the best laugh-fest of the year but the very Platonic ideal of an immaculate comedy film, putting actor-turned-director David Schwimmer (the horse-faced one from *Friends*) up there with Billy Wilder, Charlie Chaplin and Woody Allen.

This is, of course, symptomatic of the key difference

between film criticism and showbiz reporting. A showbiz reporter can call a film as average as *Run, Fatboy, Run* 'perfect' since it is part of their job is to be a 'friend of the stars' and to be enthusiastic about the wonderful 'world of show'. The problem occurs when the line between critic and 'gossip guru' becomes blurred, as I believe it did on that poster. To be clear, this is not the fault of the gossip guru, who may indeed be at the very forefront of their profession, but of the marketing department who were clearly trying to pass his words off as some form of bona fide critical endorsement.

Of course, critics can be every bit as unreasonably gushing as gossip gurus. Chris Tookey, long-standing film critic for the *Daily Mail*, runs a jolly website that ranks the critical community's Top 30 'Quote Whores', measured by a peculiar 'flying pig' count which awards airborne porkers for reviews that (in Tookey's opinion) 'grossly exaggerate a film's merits [in] a shameless bid to be on the poster'. Thus a review describing *Pearl Harbor* as 'Fantastic! More gripping than *Gladiator,* more tear-jerking than *Titanic* and, unlike a lot of recent historical epics, honest and accurate' earns a maximum three flying pigs.

But, as ever, let he who is without sin cast the first stone. Even the most cynical critic will have experienced the strange thrill of championing a movie they really love and then somehow basking in the reflected glory of a publicity campaign that uses their words of praise for promotional purposes. On the comparatively few occasions that my name has appeared on ads for movies I really like, I confess to feeling pathetically proud, and never more so than when posters for the 25th-anniversary re-release of *The Exorcist* appeared in 1998, bearing the legend 'The Greatest Movie Ever Made – Mark Kermode, Radio 1'. This may seem to you like an abject act of quote-whoredom that puts all others in the shade and should send me immediately to the top of Tookey's list. The difference (in my opinion at least) is that I really meant it. I really do think *The Exorcist* is the very best thing produced by the first century of cinema, and it is an opinion I have been proudly espousing not just for years, but for decades. If you know anything about me at all, you'll know that I'm the guy who's seen *The Exorcist* over 200 times and won't stop going on about how great it really is. Plus, there's a deliberate act of belligerent militancy about my claim that it is the greatest movie ever made as opposed to merely the greatest *horror* movie ever made, a reaction to the dreary assumption that no horror movie could possibly be that 'great' in the first place. It doesn't matter whether you agree with me about this (and very few do); what matters is whether *I* agree with me – and believe me, I do. Wholeheartedly. So when that quote appeared on the poster and everyone laughed, it bothered me not one jot. It's something I believe to be true, and I would be happy for it to be carved on my tombstone.

Would the same be true of those quotes for *Pearl Harbor* or *Run, Fatboy, Run*? Well, maybe. As I said before, all judgements are subjective and it is entirely possible that both those movies have defenders as staunch as those of any other canonised classic. I know people who were ridiculed for giving an enthusiastic thumbs-up to *Caddyshack* when it first came out and who, with hindsight, now look like the smartest kids in class. I have already fessed up to an abiding love of *Breathless* which few could countenance back in the mid-eighties, but which contrary view I now discover (to my shame) that I share with Quentin Tarantino. One of my very favourite critics of all time, Philip French, is among the many who have argued passionately for the wholescale reassessment of Cimino's *Heaven's Gate* which he considers to be a wrongly maligned classic, something which gives me pause for thought every time I casually malign it once again. After all, if someone as well versed in the history of the Western as Philip thinks there's merit in Cimino's lavish folly, then am I not missing something?

The question, as always, is the context in which such praise is offered. Does the writer have anything to gain by being overly positive about movies – or anything to lose by being honestly critical of them? Are their reactions based upon a hard-earned bedrock of film knowledge that may cause one to reassess one's own personal responses, or are they merely the burblings of an easily pleased dilettante whose senses have been dulled by the lowered expectations we encountered in Chapter Two?

Or are they just trying to get their name on the poster?

These are questions that you should ask yourself every time you see a critic (or indeed a gossip guru) quoted on an advertisement for a forthcoming movie. Who said this? Why did they say it? What are the grounds upon which they said it? Did they *really* say it? (Clue: the more '. . .'s in any given

quote, the more likely it is that they *didn't*.) And, most importantly, have they said the same thing before in relation to
other movies that really didn't deserve it?

As for film-makers, their professed disdain for critics
may be understandable but it is also utterly self-serving.
Reading Kevin Smith's 'power to the people' declaration
that he'd had it with critics and would, in future, let the
ticket-buying punters judge his work reminded me of
producer Jerry Weintraub's bold announcement in the mid-
1990s that he was refusing to press-screen his abysmal reboot
of *The Avengers* because he believed, from the very bottom
of his heart, that the 'fans' had a right to see it first. Weintraub
is an entertaining showman (he promoted Elvis concerts back
in the day) who had somehow wound up backing William
Friedkin's much-picketed eighties thriller *Cruising*. Friedkin
tells a terrific story about Weintraub inviting Richard Heffner,
then chairman of the American ratings board, to an early
screening of *Cruising*, in which Al Pacino plays a cop who
goes undercover in the heady world of New York's gay S&M
scene and discovers his own dormant (and possibly
murderous) sexuality. A forerunner of *Basic Instinct* (which
provoked similarly overcooked responses from the politi-
cally correct community), *Cruising* boasted *cinéma-vérité*
scenes shot in clubs around the Christopher Street district
of Greenwich Village to which Friedkin had gained access
dressed only in a jockstrap. It was here that he witnessed
(and filmed) scenes of fisting, golden showers and other
variants of young men in leather chaps getting along
famously in the vibrant days before the spectre of AIDS

reared its hideous head. The resulting movie, which offers an eye-opening account of a largely secretive world, was one of Friedkin's finest – although he admits that his wife hates it and can't understand why the hell he made it in the first place. Certainly it brought him nothing but trouble, expressed nowhere more clearly than during that first screening for Richard Heffner.

According to all reports, Heffner was in a state of anxiety from the get-go, sweating bullets during the opening scene in which cop Joe Spinell and his police partner enjoy each other's company with truncheons whilst spreadeagled upon the bonnet of a squad car and singing 'I'm going to *Ka-a-a-a-a*-nsas City!' During the club scenes, Heffner was horrified: repeatedly loosening his collar, unhitching his tie and all but gasping for breath. By the time the screening finished, he was a man barely alive.

And then the lights went up . . .

'So?' said Weintraub, ever the optimist. 'Whaddya think?'

'What do I think?' replied Heffner, aghast. 'What do I *think*?'

'Yeah,' said Weintraub, still defiantly upbeat. 'Whaddya think of the movie?'

Heffner was speechless. 'Jerry, I just don't know where to begin,' he conceded. 'I thought it was . . . *awful.*'

'Yeah, yeah,' shot back Weintraub, unfazed, 'but what about the *rating*? What rating will it get?'

'*Rating*?!' cried Heffner, incredulous. 'Jerry, there aren't enough Xs in the *world* to rate this movie . . .'

And so the cutting began, starting with the removal of that now-legendary 'Kansas City' sequence. And when the reviews of *Cruising* started to come in, claiming that the movie made no sense, audiences were subtly directed toward the censorious carnage that followed after that first fateful screening (and the further cutting that ensued at the hands of the BBFC in Britain), suggesting that the baffling ellipses and ambiguities that were always present in the script (of which I have a copy) were somehow the result of censorious fiddling, and not the fault of the film-makers at all.

If only the fans had got to see the movie *first* . . .

Which brings us back to *The Avengers*. Word that the movie was a stinker had leaked out months in advance, with those who had toiled to pull it together in the editing room unanimous in their utter disdain for the project. But Weintraub was a pro, and predictably his interviews turned out to be infinitely more entertaining than his solidly uninteresting movie, which (as promised) the public got to see *first*. The fact that they all hated it when they finally saw it mattered not a bit – everyone knew the film sucked, most of all Weintraub surely, which was precisely why he had refused to let the press set eyes on the damned thing. But, credit where it's due, he had somehow turned adversity to his advantage – at least for the opening weekend, which is, sadly, all that matters nowadays.

As for Kevin Smith, he has duly recovered from the debacle of *Cop Out* and returned to his creative roots with the potentially more interesting *Red State*, a low-budget horror thriller which he has chosen to finance and distribute independently. This is a bold move, which arguably vindicates his claim to be turning his back on 'the whole system' and reminds us of the punky forthrightness that first made *Clerks* such a foul-mouthed treat. More power to him. But for an awkward moment surrounding the release of *Cop Out*, he was just another coasting film-maker blaming critics for the poor reviews of work which he (like Jerry Weintraub) should have known full well to be unworthy of his talents. And like so much comparable trash, *Cop Out* would later become a best-seller on DVD, where (as we have previously noted) even the most abysmal theatrical flops can recoup their losses if they feature an A-list star. This doesn't mean they're good films – it just means that DVD renters tend to have a more completist attitude toward star vehicles than their big-screen counterparts. For a film featuring an A-list actor to die on DVD would be almost unthinkable in the current marketplace – even a film as lousy as *Cop Out*. But the DVD success did at least give Smith the opportunity to claim once again that the critics didn't know what they were talking about, so to be fair he got the last laugh.

Meanwhile, film-makers and distributors continue to use the press to sell their product to the public, and (much as we may hate to admit it) film criticism is as much a part of that process as the puff pieces, promos and pathetic personality profiles that some of us profess to despise. And like those gluttonous 'celebrities' who court tabloid attention whilst whoring their sorry arses around town to flog stuff, and then complain about 'invasion of privacy' when they get papped in circumstances beyond their media-savvy control, film-makers can only legitimately complain about negative film criticism if they have *never* used a critic's words to endorse their product. In which case, I'll make the following deal with any film-maker willing to take it: I will agree to pay to see every one of your movies from hereon in, as long as you respect my right to say whatever the hell I like about them and you don't use my words – positive *or* negative – to endorse whatever product you're hawking at the time. That means that if I say your next film is 'The Greatest Movie Ever Made – Yes, Even *Better* Than *The Exorcist*!' you agree never to repeat that comment in print, in broadcast, in conversation – in fact, in *any* situation in which it might conceivably encourage the passingly curious to go see for themselves what all the fuss is about. It's a 'no pain, no gain' solution: you don't suffer the pain of dishing out free tickets to a disrespectful freeloader like me; nor do you enjoy the possible gain of quoting me if I really like your movie; nor even (as we have seen) if I really *don't* like your movie, but your publicists want to quote me in a way which gives the entirely false impression that I really like your movie.

Deal?

Thought not.

Which brings us back to square one and the as yet un-answered question – what the hell are critics for?

Some deluded souls still believe that critics, with their sniping highbrow opinions (or, increasingly, with their babbling lowbrow lack of opinions) can actually damage a movie's box-office takings, a view that is frankly laughable.

As we have already seen, critical opinion plays almost no role in the marketability of blockbuster movies, as demonstrated by the fact that the top end of the blockbuster charts is regularly dominated by movies which critics (or at least 'proper' critics) have canned. Take, for example, the case of *Sex and the City 2*, a movie which goes some way toward justifying the global resentment against America and the English-speaking world. If you haven't seen it (and if you're reading this book I sincerely hope that you haven't), *SATC2* follows the adventures of four staggeringly wealthy Americans who go on an all-expenses-paid jolly to Abu Dhabi – where they assert their right to buy shoes, patronise the impoverished locals and have sex in public places – under the guise of offering two hours of frothy women's-lib-lite entertainment. Imagine *Carry On Up the Khyber* minus the sparkling wit and understated observational humour, but with a cranked-up budget, glistening marketing campaign, and jaw-droppingly over-stretched (and under-edited) running time. Got that? Good. Now hit yourself hard and repeatedly about the face and neck with a wooden rolling pin, and carry on doing so for a couple of hours. By the time you're finished you'll still be nowhere near imagining the dark-hearted Kurtzian horror of *SATC2*.

A spin-off from the hugely popular (and, I am reliably informed, engagingly empowering) TV series, *SATC2* began life as a complicated financial transaction predicated upon a series of professional prenuptial agreements between Hollywood agents who were only in it for the money.

Nothing wrong with that – many great Hollywood movies have been made by people with little or no interest in art but an obsessive–compulsive desire to be paid obscene amounts of cash for doing absolutely zip. Yet few Hollywood movies have managed quite so perfectly to crystallize what's wrong with processed, mainstream multiplex fodder, and to demonstrate so thoroughly the foul financial imperative that turns undiscerning ticket-buying into an act of casual cultural vandalism. As I said when the first *Sex and the City* movie was released, if you pay to watch this ugly corporate drivel, then don't come crying to me when they make an even-worse sequel with the money *you gave them* the first time round. In essence, anyone who bought a ticket for *SATC1* is in some small way to blame for the crimes of *SATC2* – and if you're one of those people, then on some level this is your fault.

It's hard to know where to begin in describing the putrescence of *SATC2* – there's just so much to hate. With a bum-numbing running time of 146 minutes, this piece of corporate consumerist pornography is about the same length as Kubrick's *2001*, a film which traces the evolution of humans from crawling apes to space travellers, from the birth of man to the dawn of a new star child. As I have frequently said, *2001* is the yardstick of cinematic economy by which all movie lengths should be judged, and if you can't tell your story in less time than it took Kubrick to map out the evolution of mankind then frankly you're not trying. *SATC2* is trying (it's *very* trying – boom boom!) and yet, sadly, despite its bloated running time, the group of shoe-shopping caricatures depicted in the opening reel have evolved into nothing more than a group of marginally more suntanned shoe-shopping caricatures by the time the end credits finally roll. If aliens had indeed been observing our earth (as The Carpenters so convincingly sang) and caught a glimpse of this lot, they wouldn't have bothered leaving a weird monolith that taught us how to make tools and fly to the moon; they would have nuked us out of the galaxy and moved on forthwith.

When *SATC2* first opened in cinemas, several female critics wrote breathtakingly scathing articles about the movie's monstrous reduction of women's emancipation to the right to have sex and buy expensive footwear. Fair enough – but as both a man and an old-school Trot I'd like to move the argument on from gender politics to class war. Here's my ideological problem with *SATC2*: it is, in essence, a film that requires its audience to sympathise with the plight of drippingly wealthy Americans, whose opulent ownership of stuff leads only to self-pitying whingeing and the ownership of more stuff. The lead character, Carrie, is a writer (allegedly) who lives in an uptown New York apartment with her husband who, I have been forced to conclude, is an international arms dealer – how else could they afford this gaff? The seething marital tension between these two supposedly loveable folk explodes when he buys her a massive flat-screen TV and she complains that she actually wanted jewellery. Boo hoo. This materialist misunderstanding precipitates a crisis so profound that Carrie decides to leave the aircraft-hanger-sized apartment in which hubby insulted her with the $10,000 TV and flee back to the safety of her *other* apartment, which she appears to have been keeping on the off-chance that just such a present-buying cock-up would arise. Even though the first apartment had a walk-in wardrobe so large she could have set up a second home in there, Carrie apparently has enough disposable cash to leave apartments lying all around town without ever worrying about the bills. But she's still unhappy, and decides that what she really needs is to get away from it all.

To get away from her two apartments, giant flat-screen TV and arms-dealing husband.

At which point, I cease to care what happens to her.

The film-makers, however, are just getting started. Having established that poor Carrie needs a break, they send her and her chums off to stay in a hotel which, we are informed, would cost $22,000 a night if they were actually paying for it (although, as Richard E. Grant observes of Uncle Monty's country cottage in *Withnail & I*, such things are 'free to those who can afford it, very expensive to those who can't'). On arrival, each of our heroines is presented with their very own exotic flunky to do with as they wish – to wait on them hand and foot, and be ready to make hot chocolate at any time of day or night if the pain of being an obscenely rich American suddenly becomes too much to bear. At a key moment of emotional dawning, the flunky who has been assigned to Carrie reveals that, rather than just being a boot-licking slave, he actually has a wife whom he is only able to visit every other month because the airfare home is far too expensive for someone of his lowly standing. Clearly this is the moment at which Carrie will realise that her gargantuan wealth has consequences in the 'real world' – that in order for her to bathe in opulence others must suffer and perish. But no! What looks like the movie's revelatory scene of economic and emotional saving grace (Carrie realises that there are *other people in the world*) actually turns out to be yet another vomit bag of 'me time' as Carrie is struck by the similarity of this poor waif's predicament to her own heartache. Just like this foreign flunky slave, she too is spending time away from her beloved. She too is suffering, just like him! In a genuinely awe-inspiring moment of capitalist propaganda, *SATC2* conspires to make us feel that there is a common bond of pain being shared between an impoverished Middle Eastern doormat and an overpaid Yankee sloth. The message of this scene is *not* about the staggering inequality of wealth and opportunity between the rich and the poor, but about the universality of the pain of love. Or, to put it another way: 'Don't worry about eating the world alive in material terms; just enjoy your own emotional pain – because you're worth it!'

I am reminded here of Billy Bragg's wonderful anthem of the disillusioned left, 'Waiting for the Great Leap Forwards', which opens with the following lines:

It may have been Camelot for Jack and Jacqueline
But on the Che Guevara highway filling up with
   gasoline
Fidel Castro's brother spies a rich lady who's crying

Over luxury's disappointment
So he walks over and he's trying
To sympathise with her but he thinks that he should
   warn her
That the Third World is just around the corner.

Somehow, I doubt Billy Bragg is on Carrie's iPod.

Other *SATC2* characters include a lawyer who is treated badly at work and so quits her job with apparently no financial repercussions (perhaps she was working pro bono on lowly human rights cases – or perhaps not). Another is a mother who has a full-time nanny tending to her sprogs but who still finds time to go cry in a cupboard because she is so oppressed by the pressures of motherhood, which include getting jammy handprints on her expensive vintage skirt. 'How on earth do people who don't have help cope?' she asks rhetorically, giving a metaphorical wink to the audience. Clearly the writers think this sort of thing acknowledges a common experience but, without wishing to state the bleeding obvious, if any of *us* were in *Sex and the City*, we wouldn't be proper characters – we'd be the help. We'd be the serfs, the doormen, the flunkies, the elevator operators. In this world of wonder, even those of us on way-above-average wages wouldn't get a look in.

And there's just so much more to rail against: the inherent racism of a script which sends Americans to a Middle Eastern country so they can throw condoms at foreigners with self-righteous anger; the sub-Paul Raymond conceit of women in burkas hiding racy designerwear under their religious robes, just *dying* for the opportunity to swap fashion tips with the Western women whose heathen life-styles they absolutely *adore*. All in all, it adds up to a vile and pernicious slice of imperialist propaganda which cele-brates misogyny, belittles non-Americans, insults audiences, and wallows in greed, avarice and bulimic vomit. At great length.

It is, to be clear, not good.

And I felt the need to say so. As did pretty much every other film critic in the country, nay the world.

According to the official studio line, *SATC2* 'underper-formed' at the box office thanks to almost universally nega-tive reviews, which briefly put the kibosh on the development of any further plans for *SATC3* (although a 'prequel' is now in the works). It's a convenient argument: 'bad reviews killed our movie'. But let's look at the harsh economic realities. *SATC2* cost $100 million and took $280 million worldwide, meaning that it more than balanced its box-office budget sheets whilst racking up further profits on home-viewing sales, TV tie-ins and countless other promotional opportunities. The studio and its enfranchised distribution partners would have been laughing all the way to the bank (as would the exhibitors and DVD outlets), even if the profits that poured in were not quite the engorged river of cash they might have expected. The writers, directors, production designers, advertising exec-utives and PR companies who worked on the movie would have had a multimillion-dollar money-making machine on their hands that paid their salaries and looked good on their

CVs. And, of course, the four leading players were handsomely rewarded and lavished with worldwide press attention, thereby increasing their immediate media-market
value and helping them sell more stuff (of their own
choosing) in the future. Because they're worth it!

Fact: lousy reviews did not kill *SATC2* (although having
to watch lousy *SATC2* came close to killing this reviewer).
The film still did far better at the box office than anything
so despicably dismal ever deserves to do. And the awful
truth is that, no matter how vitriolic, even the negative
reviews almost certainly drew some punters to see the
movie. In the weeks after the film's widespread critical
savaging an entirely predictable press backlash began to
emerge, with columnists, cartoonists, letter writers et al.
proudly defending the movie, which had (inevitably) gone
straight to number one in the box office. Even though
received critical opinion was that the film was not just bad
but world-beatingly terrible, audiences were still flocking
in, making it incumbent upon editors to mollify their potentially alienated readers and viewers by hastily putting forth
the 'alternative' view. This is standard practice – any
extreme critical reaction not only justifies, but positively
demands, an equal and opposite right of reply. If you really
want to rubbish a movie, the most effective thing to do is
give it a two-star review which says the film is not terribly
good and generally a bit boring and unremarkable. Or,
better still, don't review it at all – why give multiplex
terrorists the oxygen of publicity? Leading your weekly
reviews with an attention-grabbing tour de force trashing

of *SATC2* (as did so many British critics – myself included) will simply increase the film's talking-point potential, ensuring that none of your listeners/readers/viewers are unaware of the film's existence and, perversely, making some of them want to go see what all the fuss is about. And as we have seen, thanks to the miracle of 'lowered expectations' it is entirely possible that some of them may actually enjoy the film, all the more so because they were half-expecting to see the worst film ever made and were surprised when the film actually ran through the projector without the auditorium exploding in a conflagration of crap. Hell, if they even so much as smile, smirk, giggle or titter in the first 30 minutes they'll start to feel they're watching a different movie to the one you reviewed; or (more likely), that you're just a stuck-up critic who's entirely out of step with popular taste and doesn't know what real multiplex popcorn punters want from their Friday night blah blah blah blah blah.

The difference is that the critic (hopefully) went into the movie wishing for the best and was genuinely shocked and appalled when it was worse than they could have imagined. But after reading/hearing/watching the reviews, the punters went in expecting the worst and were shocked and appalled to discover that the movie didn't live *down* to the vitriolic critical trashing. Or maybe it did, and they just wanted to demonstrate that critics don't know nothing.

A popular view, apparently.

In fact, no matter what anyone tells you, audiences

generally don't trust critics one jot. And if you're in any doubt about that fact then go online and check out the aforementioned YouGov poll, which puts paid once and for all to the idea that critics can make or break a movie. If that were true, how come so many of you went to see *Transformers*, *Bride Wars* or *Paranormal Activity 2* after I specifically advised you not to?

It doesn't surprise me that my reviews hold so little sway with the movie-going public, although it may surprise you to learn that those of others hold even *less*. But the reality is that critics cannot kill a movie – only distributors can do that. And of course multiplex-cinema chains who are sucking the very life out of interesting, offbeat (and often indigenous) films by glutting the market with over-produced franchise fare, turning mainstream film exhibition in the UK into a dumping ground for Hollywood's most poisonous refuse (more of which in Chapter Six). We critics can say what we like about the latest Iranian masterpiece from Abbas Kiarostami. We can give it a rave review and urge all our readers/listeners/viewers to go and see it at their earliest possible convenience. But unless those readers/listeners/viewers live within striking distance of a thriving independent cinema, they won't be *able* to see until it comes out on DVD. Why not? Because every multiplex screen in the country is taken up with showing *Sex and the City 2*, *Transformers 3* and *Pirates of the Caribbean 4* (in 3-D) for the foreseeable future. No wonder the box-office figures 'reveal' that everyone *loves* blockbusters and wants to see nothing *but* blockbusters for evermore. The fact is that most people simply don't have a choice. For most cinema-goers in the UK, it's blockbusters or nothing.

And if that's the case, who the hell needs critics?

Chapter Five

'THE BRITISH AREN'T COMING . . . OR GOING'

'Is it a "British" picture?'
Ken Russell's mum

Two significant events occurred during the writing of this book. The first was the announcement in July 2010 of the closure of the UK Film Council, which, it was declared in some quarters, would mark the 'end of the British film industry'. The second was the Oscar-winning success of *The King's Speech*, which, it was declared in some quarters, would mark 'the rebirth of the British film industry'.

Neither of these statements is true. Let's see why . . .

To begin with, the idea that the Oscars can be seen as a serious indicator of the state of cinema, whether national or international, is risible. Look, for example, at this list of movies from the past 15 years: *Crash*; *Boogie Nights*; *Eternal Sunshine of the Spotless Mind*; *A History of Violence*; *Pan's Labyrinth*; *The Assassination of Jesse James by the Coward Robert Ford*; *Of Time and the City*; and *Let the Right One In*. What do these movies have in common? Firstly, they were all the best

217

picture of the year when they were first released. Secondly, none of them won the coveted Oscar for 'Best Picture'. Thirdly (and most damningly), none of them were even nominated in that category. Oh, and before you go complaining that *Crash* beat *Brokeback Mountain* to the top prize, I'm referring to David Cronenberg's adaptation of J.G. Ballard's novel – the film which prompted the *Daily Mail* to launch a 'Boycott Sony' campaign and which remains banned in Westminster to this day – rather than the Paul Haggis *Magnolia*-lite confection that bucked the odds when it trumped Ang Lee's *Brokeback Mountain* in 2006. I rather liked Haggis's movie, and indeed predicted its Oscar triumph simply on the basis that its message ('Hey, we're all interconnected in strange ways, aren't we?') was more Oscar-friendly than that of Ang Lee's challenging love story which, as writer Larry McMurty explained, 'is not a gay cowboy film . . . they're gay *shepherds*'.

Sadly, gay shepherds don't win Best Picture Oscars.

All you really need to know about the Oscars is that they're the awards that didn't give a Best Picture gong to *Citizen Kane*, but *did* give one to *Driving Miss Daisy*. Just think about that for a moment, and try to imagine a world in which *Driving Miss Daisy* really was the best film you were going to see all year. Be honest. You'd throw yourself off a bridge, wouldn't you? Or, at the very least, you'd give up going to the cinema and instead develop an interest in violent video games. In fact, when it first opened in the US in December 1989, not only was it not the best film of the year, it wasn't even the best Morgan Freeman film of the week. When I interviewed Freeman for the *New Musical Express* he had two new films coming out back-to-back: the anodyne *Driving Miss Daisy* and the rather more forthright *Glory*, a film from director Ed Zwick about the US Civil War's first all-black volunteer company. Frankly, I was far more interested in the latter and was delighted to discover that Freeman felt exactly the same way, dismissing *Miss Daisy* as a harmless piece of fluff before turning the conversation back toward more substantial matters. Yet, according to the Oscar voters, things in 1989 didn't get any better than a stagey adaptation of Alfred Uhry's play about a rich white woman and a sage black chauffeur sharing quality time together in a big old car. (By far the most entertaining thing about *Driving Miss Daisy* was the fact that it inspired a porn spoof entitled *Driving Miss Daisy Crazy*, a parodic title which ranks up there with *Saturday Night Beaver*, *The Sperminator* and *Shaving Ryan's Privates,* the last of which is actually a documentary about comedy porn titles – apparently.)

Or ask yourself this: What is Martin Scorsese's greatest film? Many would go for one of the seventies classics like *Mean Streets* or *Taxi Driver*, although the monochrome wallop of *Raging Bull* probably packs more of a punch. The hyper-kinetic *Goodfellas* has stood the test of time, too (without it we wouldn't have *Boogie Nights*), and even *Casino* has gained stature over the years. For sheer mischief-making controversy you could argue that *The Last Temptation of Christ* was Marty's finest hour – clearly it's his most personal and passionate work. My vote would be for *The King of Comedy*, a note-perfect dissection of psychopathic celebrity culture in which De Niro channels the ghost of Travis Bickle for darkly satirical ends. But according to Oscar history, the defining pinnacle of Scorsese's screen career to date is . . . *The Departed*. Yup, that's right – as far as Oscar voters are concerned, maestro Marty's greatest film is the remake of a Hong Kong actioner which had a far more memorable English language title (*Infernal Affairs*) than Scorsese's Oscar winner, the name of which no one can ever remember. How's that for a killer pub-quiz question?

Other howlers in the 'Oscar, Schmoscar' hall of historical infamy include the fact that no animated feature has ever been judged the best film of the year, despite the fact that animation has remained the single most diverse, popular and adventurous of all cinema genres for more than a century. These are also the awards which didn't give the top prize to a horror film until *The Silence of the Lambs* broke that duck in 1992, and even then they only did so because the distributors managed to persuade Oscar voters that it wasn't really a horror film at all. Rather, it was an 'intense psychological thriller' that just happened to feature some scary bits (including the sight of a serial killer attempting to get his victim to rub lotion on to her body so that her skin would be smoother when he cut it off and wore it as a dress. So, nothing at all like *The Texas Chain Saw Massacre* then . . .).

To understand why the Oscars are quite so bland, you simply have to look at the industry that spawned them. Part of the problem is the name – the 'Academy Awards' – a misleading title, which has been used to foster the lie that the Oscars are some form of independent celebration of the wonders of international cinema. They're not (in the same way that the 'World Series' is not a sporting event which involves any part of the world other than North America). They are an insider party at which the American motion picture industry slaps itself on the back for being brilliant and for raking in billions of dollars worldwide, while the rest of the world gawps and wonders why the US so often comes out on top. This is not a matter of opinion – it is cold, hard fact. The Oscars are run by the American-based 'Academy of Motion Picture Arts and Sciences' (AMPAS, which was initially founded to 'mediate labor disputes and improve the industry's image'), and voted for by members of that institution, who are (for obvious reasons) overwhelmingly American. Just as the BAFTAs are repeatedly accused of having a 'British bias' because they're voted for by members of the British Academy of Film and Television Arts, so the Oscars should rightly be referred to as the 'American Academy Awards', and recognised as a showcase for US-based productions to which the occasional foreigner will be invited to add exotic spice.

But how do Oscar winners and nominees actually get chosen? Well, as far as the Best Picture category is concerned, what's meant to happen is that the massed ranks of the American Academy membership cast their learned eyes over all the movies released in the US in the past year, and then coolly and dispassionately select their favourites for possible nomination. Inevitably, most of them can't actually be bothered to wade through all those boring movies, most of which they imagine are probably utter crap. I get that same feeling sometimes, but the difference is that I have to watch the movies anyway because, hey, that's my job. And, invariably, some of the very best films of the year turn out to be the ones for which you had the lowest expectations. That's why it's necessary to watch *all* the eligible movies, or at least to watch as many of them as you possibly can, before you cast your vote for an awards ceremony which has such ludicrous significance in the worldwide marketplace.

Yet somehow the American Academy voters (whose average age is something like 107) have become increasingly content to allow the initial selection process for Oscar consideration to be conducted on their behalf by a bunch of unaccountable drunken bozos whose reputation for corruptibility is second to none. I am speaking, of course, of the members of the self-styled Hollywood Foreign Press Association, organisers of the Golden Globes awards – which have unofficially become Round One of the Oscars selection process. Unlike the Academy, whose members are real film-makers, the HFPA is a group of 90-odd Pharisaic hacks who get together once a year to draw up a list of famous people they really want to meet and hang out with. They then proceed to invite these famous people to what is essentially their annual work knees-up, by nominating their crap films for Golden Globe awards. You may think this sounds harsh, but how else do you explain the fact that, despite being a critical and commercial flop, *Burlesque* was mysteriously nominated for a Golden Globe for 'Best

Motion Picture – Musical or Comedy' after members of the HFPA were flown on an all-expenses-paid jolly to Las Vegas to watch Cher perform in live concert? Do you think those two events might possibly be connected? They also gave a similar nomination to *The Tourist*, despite the fact that it was neither a musical nor a comedy, thus ensuring that Johnny Depp came to their party.

The venality of the HFPA membership is legendary and should have made the Golden Globes the laughing stock of the world; after all, these are the people who gave a New Star of the Year award to Pia Zadora, an actress so lousy that, as the popular gag goes, an ill-judged title role in the stage play of *The Diary of Anne Frank* prompted an audience member to shout 'She's in the attic!' when the Nazis turned up. When Globes host Ricky Gervais 'joked' in 2011 that HFPA members hadn't only nominated *The Tourist* because they wanted to meet Johnny Depp but that 'they also accepted bribes', the laughter that filled the room was as hollow as Worzel Gummidge's head.

The Globes would be nothing but a horrible joke were it not for the fact that their position in the so-called 'awards calendar' means that they have an unhealthy power over Oscar voting. Since American Academy members don't have time to watch all the eligible releases, they tend to wait until the Golden Globes shortlist is announced and then make their selection from that random field. Thus a group of toadying numbskulls effectively get to control the first stage of Oscar voting, thereby elevating their otherwise utterly irrelevant standing in the world and (more importantly) skewing the results of the most prestigious entertainment awards ceremony in the world. If you don't believe me, take a look at the list of Golden Globe nominees for the past ten years and then compare it to the list of Oscar contenders for the same period. You'll be astonished how closely they match up.

The other thing you should be astonished by is how often one name turns up in connection with Oscar winners – that of American movie mogul Harvey Weinstein. Along with his brother Bob, Harvey was a founding member of Miramax, which started life as a punchy American independent studio with a talent for distributing niche-market movies but ended up becoming part of Disney's 'House of Mouse' empire. Between 1992 and 2003, Miramax had at least one film nominated for Oscar's Best Picture category every year, sometimes more. In 1999, the company had a whopping 23 nominations in one ceremony. After leaving Miramax the brothers moved on to form The Weinstein Company, where they continued to work their strange awards-courting magic. If you want to win an Oscar, then there is no greater ally in the world than Harvey Weinstein; nor is there any greater adversary. His Oscar campaigns are infamous: they make headlines; they make enemies; they get results. Jack Mathews, film critic for the *New York Daily News*, once wrote an open letter to Harvey claiming: 'Your campaigns are obnoxious. They're tainting the Oscar process.' As if such a thing were possible! But so notorious are Harvey's strategies for awards season that whenever mud starts being thrown around come Oscar time, all eyes turn to him. Many believed, for example, that he was responsible for the press stories about John Nash's alleged anti-Semitism that surfaced when *A Beautiful Mind* did battle with Miramax's *In the Bedroom* for Best Picture in 2002. And when the British movie *Slumdog Millionaire* was hit with allegations of child-labour exploitation in 2009, Weinstein (who was backing rival Best Picture bid *The Reader*) told the press: 'What can I say? When you're Billy the Kid and people around you die of natural causes, everyone thinks you shot them . . .'

His battles (or non-battles?) with *Slumdog* aside, Weinstein has long held the key to Oscar glory for Brits. It was Harvey and The Weinstein Company who backed the comparatively low-budget drama *The King's Speech*, turning it into a Best Picture-winning blockbuster with worldwide takings in excess of $368 million. Looking back at the list of (allegedly) British movies that have scored big at the Oscars over the past 25 years, it's hard to find one with which he was not somehow involved – be it *The Crying Game*, *The English Patient* or *Shakespeare in Love*. Indeed, on the basis of the Oscars' scoresheet, you could be forgiven for concluding that native New Yorker Harvey Weinstein *is* the British film industry. No wonder Colin Firth thanked him.

Weinstein is certainly a divisive figure, and anyone who's been on the wrong side of him (myself included) knows that his conduct can be what Dougal the dog would call 'not at all British'. But without him there would have been far less opportunity for the sort of nationalist flag-waving that happens every time an (apparently) British movie wins Best Picture at the Oscars, allowing everyone to quote Colin

Welland's 'The British are coming!' battle cry from 1982, when *Chariots of Fire* stormed the American Academy Awards. And if you're going to judge the state of a nation's cinema by the size of its Oscar cabinet, then the awful truth is that Weinstein offers a rare ray of sunshine amidst a prevailing climate of doom, despondency and despair. Because if there's one thing the Brits love more than a winner, it's a *loser* – hence the endless stories about the 'end of the British film industry' that have become such a staple of our national press.

The idea that the British film industry is in terminal decline is as old as the hills, with the French leading the charge in terms of cheap put-downs and pompous jokes (*quelle surprise!*). It was François Truffaut who complained of 'a certain incompatibility between the terms "cinema" and "Britain"', while Jean-Luc Godard quipped sardonically that 'To despair of British cinema would be to admit that it exists.' (Oh, that world famous French sense of humour.) One may retort that this is pretty rich coming from a nation which thinks that Jerry Lewis is a comic genius, and whose own major contribution to world cinema has been the image of Jacques Tati riding a bicycle while smoking a pipe. But that would be petty and cheap.

Yet, despite claims to the contrary, Britain continues to produce world-beating film-makers and actors upon whose talents a large section of the international cinema market depends. In 2011, all eyes may have been on *The King's Speech* but for my money the most significant British presence at the Oscars that year was the Best Picture nomination for

Inception, from home-grown writer/director Christopher Nolan. It's well known that many of the biggest and best Hollywood blockbusters have been built on the backbone of British craftsmanship, with our writers, directors, actors, musicians and technicians earning a worldwide reputation that is second to none. This has long been a sore point for our transatlantic cousins. In the eighties, Ridley Scott got himself into hot water whilst filming *Blade Runner* in Hollywood when he complained to the British newspaper the *Observer* that American crews weren't up to the standards of their UK counterparts. Frustrated by the levels of red tape that abound on stateside sets, Scott commented that if he asked a British crew to do something, they were much more likely to say, 'Yes Guv'nor', and just get on with it. The next day, Scott arrived on set in Hollywood to find his American crew dressed in T-shirts emblazoned with the logo 'Yes Guv'nor <u>MY ASS!</u>' (Scott and his British cohorts responded with T-shirts which read 'Xenophobia Sucks'.)

Incidentally, when was the last time you read an interview with a director saying they'd really love to work with more French crews?

In truth, the movie industries of Britain and America are inextricably intertwined: British film-makers cross the pond to work on American movies, while Hollywood studios base their most prestigious productions at UK studios such as Shepperton, Pinewood and Leavesden. Sadly, there's little that's newsworthy about this long-standing arrangement, so no one pulls out 'The British are coming!' headlines when *Inception* or *The Dark Knight* strikes it big in the Oscar nominations. But when a movie which *looks* quintessentially 'British', such as *The King's Speech*, achieves equivalent success, everyone suddenly starts writing articles about the state of our national cinema as if it somehow exists in isolation. And, we are all told, the Oscar triumphs of movies like *The King's Speech* can only serve to enhance the international standing of our indigenous industry, and make it easier to get home-grown films made in the future. But is that really true? And is the portrait of 'successful' British movies as painted by the Oscars really reflective of the diversity of UK film-making? Or is it, in fact, merely a picture-postcard of cabbages and kings?

To answer this question one need look back no further than January 2007, when Stephen Frears's TV movie *The Queen* became national news after picking up six Oscar nomi-nations, including a Best Actress nod for Dame Helen Mirren. In the UK all eyes were on *The Queen*, although arguably the most important British nominee at the Oscars that year was Paul Greengrass in the Best Director category, for his stunning docu-drama *United 93*. It is perhaps signifi-cant that, in terms of mainstream cinema, it took a British film-maker to interpret and mediate the terrible events of 9/11, an American tragedy which somewhat wrong-footed the great stateside auteur Oliver Stone. When trailers for *United 93* first played in New York, audiences famously balked, shouting 'Too soon!' at the screen, clearly fearing the worst. Yet when *United 93* finally opened (with the co-operation of many who had lost relatives in the tragedy), it was clear that not only had Greengrass been respectful, but also that he had managed to forge a genuine work of art from the rubble of a horrendous tragedy. In stark contrast to Stone's more melodramatic *World Trade Center*, which seemed almost overawed by its subject matter, Greengrass's rigorous film overcame initial audience anxieties to find solid support in the US, where the wounds it addresses still run deep. If there was any justice, it would have been *United 93* (a UK/French/US co-production), rather than *The Queen*, battling it out in the Best Picture category and showing the world what the cream of British cinema really looks like. Yet it was *The Queen* that ticked the royal boxes and found itself competing for the big prize.

Why? The simple answer is that the Americans love a good crown. Just look at the evidence . . .

In the year that Mirren won Best Actress for playing Elizabeth II in *The Queen*, her strongest competition came from Dame Judi Dench, who had previously won a Best Supporting Actress Oscar for playing Elizabeth I in *Shakespeare in Love*. No matter that Dench had been on-screen for less than ten minutes (making hers one of the shortest winning performances in Oscar history) – for several of those minutes she was wearing a crown, and that was enough for Oscar voters. Dench had previously picked up an Oscar nomination playing Queen Victoria in *Mrs. Brown*, directed by *Shakespeare in Love* helmsman John Madden. Like *The Queen*, *Mrs. Brown* began life as a low-key UK television project, but went on to garner an Oscar-nominated theatrical release after the US distributors played up its royal subject by retitling it *Her Majesty, Mrs. Brown*.

Are you starting to see a trend here?

By coincidence, the year that Dench won her Oscar for playing Queen Elizabeth I, Cate Blanchett picked up a Best Actress nomination for playing a younger version of the same character in the British movie *Elizabeth*. By the time Mirren made her way on to the Oscars stage in 2007, she had already won two royally appointed Golden Globes for her portrayals of Queen Elizabeths I and II in *Elizabeth I*, a TV production, and *The Queen*. Accepting the second award, Mirren declared that the honour rightly belonged to Her Actual Majesty, claiming that it was the real Elizabeth with whom the audience had fallen in love. Watching her Oscar acceptance speech, in which she invited the duly star-struck audience to toast HRH, it was hard to shake the image of 'Brenda' herself fondling the statuette and waving graciously to her loyal (former) subjects.

But while Oscar loved Mirren's regal turn, it's significant that the American Academy found no space to recognise and acknowledge Michael Sheen's role in *The Queen*. So prominent was his spot-on portrayal of Prime Minister Tony Blair that the film could quite justifiably have been called *Her Majesty, Mrs. Blair*. Sadly, Oscar voters seem to have confused fiction with reality and decided that Teflon Tony was unworthy of their vote.

The message here is clear: when it comes to British movies the Americans love royalty. Moreover, Oscar voters have a particular weakness for British period dramas in which a palace dweller forges a lasting friendship with a commoner, preferably overcoming a disability en route. You want proof?

OK, try this. In the nineties, *Her Majesty, Mrs. Brown* took around $10 million in US theatres and became an Oscar contender by telling the heart-warming story of a frosty queen who overcomes crippling bereavement by befriending and taking the advice of a beardy 'gillie' whom no one else likes; in the noughties, *The Queen* took $56 million in US theatres and became an Oscar-winning hit by telling the heart-warming story of a frosty queen who overcomes crippling unpopularity (as a result of her apparent inability to display bereavement) by taking the advice of an upstart politician whom no one else trusts; and in 2010, *The King's Speech* took $138 million in US theatres and became an Oscar sensation after telling the heart-warming story of a frosty king who overcomes a crippling speech impediment by befriending and taking the advice of an upstart speech therapist of whom no one else has heard . . . from the colonies!

Now, I really liked *The King's Speech*, not least because its central role of a man wracked by inner torment allowed Colin Firth to make good on the edgy promise he first displayed in Welsh director Marc Evans's sadly little-seen psychological thriller *Trauma*, for which he should rightly have been garlanded with awards years ago. Firth was a worthy Best Actor winner at the 2011 Oscars (although he did a better acceptance speech at the BAFTAs) but the fact remains that if you asked a computer to devise a mathematical equation for a British movie that was entirely tailored to meet Oscar's expectations, it would probably come up with something very similar to (if nothing like as good as) *The King's Speech*.

The downside of Oscar's infatuation with royalty is the blind spot it causes for so many other British movies. In the same year that *The Queen* was finding such favour with Oscar voters, Ken Loach's far superior Palme d'Or winner *The Wind that Shakes the Barley* was passing entirely under the American Academy's radar. Why? Well, perhaps Loach's famous lack of respect for the Crown ('the Royal Family is an absurd anachronism that encourages the worst things') offers some explanation. Indeed, so unlikely did an Oscar nod for Loach seem that the US distributors of *The Wind that Shakes the Barley* didn't even bother to release the film in time for American Academy consideration. Instead, producer Rebecca O'Brien was quoted as saying: 'We've already won the only prize that European and world film-makers truly covet [the Palme d'Or], so why try and compete with the majors at something they are much better at?'

Loach's absence from the Oscars' hall of fame (at the age of 74 he has yet to receive a single nomination) tells us something depressing about the transatlantic tunnel vision that ensures that the American Academy regularly overlooks our most potent home-grown fare. Everyone knows that Alfred Hitchcock never actually won an Oscar, but who remembers that Derek Jarman, that great rebellious artist of British cinema, went to his grave without even being nominated for an Academy Award? (Maybe Oscar took against him for directing the Smiths' video for 'The Queen Is Dead'.) My own list of post-war British classics would include Powell and Pressburger's *A Matter of Life and Death*, the Boulting brothers' *Brighton Rock*, Ken Loach's *Kes*, Ken

Russell's *The Devils*, Nic Roeg's *Don't Look Now*, Alan Clarke's *Scum*, Lynne Ramsay's *Ratcatcher*, Danny Boyle's *Shallow Grave*, and Shane Meadows's *This is England*. Take a wild guess at how many Oscar nominations that splendid group of very British pictures garnered between them. Answer: none. Pitiful.

As for film production in the UK, there is actually very little evidence that the statuettes garnered by *The King's Speech* have done anything to improve the lot of the struggling British film-maker. Instead, it has provided an opportunity for everyone to bemoan the demise of the UK Film Council, which for years administered the distribution of public money (from the National Lottery) amongst home-grown productions and which, of course, backed *The King's Speech*. The UKFC was a fraught organisation which, at its best, supported British stalwarts like Ken Loach and Mike Leigh (along with Boyle, Meadows, Ramsay and Andrea Arnold) and put their weight behind a catalogue of great British movies of which we can rightly be proud. At its worst, it invested in *Sex Lives of the Potato Men*, an unforgiveable crime against our national culture for which the UKFC should have been burned to the ground forthwith. I once had an excitingly heated on-air altercation with one of the heads of the UKFC about the funding of *Sex Lives*, a film which, he assured me, had been 'really good' at script level. I assured him that this was horseshit; if one single word of the screenplay matched the dialogue of the finished film, there was no possibility that the script had ever been anything other than utterly vile and repugnant.

Understandably, *Sex Lives of the Potato Men* was used as a stick with which to beat the still-warm corpse of the UKFC when its demise prompted headlines about the 'end of British cinema'. Yet, as anyone who knows anything about UK film production understands, the real problem here in Britain is not so much funding as distribution. With or without the UKFC, loads of movies get made in the UK every year – some of them good, many of them terrible. Yet only a scant few secure the width of distribution that allows an extensive audience to judge the film's relative merits for themselves. You can whinge all you like about how hard it is to raise the money needed to make movies in Blighty, but plenty of people still do it, and many of them do it without the assistance of the sort of public funding that causes MPs to ask embarrassing questions about how the hell we all ended up paying for grot like *Sex Lives of the Potato Men*.

Personally, I think the greatest boon to young British film-makers would be the resurgence of a thriving exploitation market, producing bankable low-budget titles on which aspiring cineastes could learn both the artistic and the financial tools of the trade without recourse to the public purse. David Puttnam, who produced *Chariots of Fire* ('the British are coming!'), once told me that the best advice he could give to a first-time film-maker would be to fund and film an inexpensive horror movie that made its money back – an exercise that teaches the film-maker both to understand the industry and to respect the habits and desires of their intended audience. This is, in fact, a formula which has been proven to work in the US, where exploitation maestros such as Roger Corman effectively nurtured new generations of American cinema throughout the sixties, seventies and eighties through just such a market paradigm. Directors as diverse as Francis Ford Coppola, Martin Scorsese, Oliver Stone, Katt Shea and James Cameron all learned their trade working for Corman, whose ground rules were simple:

1) No, you can't have any more money.

2) No, the movie doesn't need to be that long.

3) Yes, you do have to have either an exploding helicopter or at least one scene in a strip club.

4) After that, you're on your own – knock yourself out.

Corman believed that the best way to encourage new film-making talent was to find people who loved avant garde international cinema and were desperate to be the next Ozu, Fellini or Antonioni, and then set them to work making *Carnosaur 2*. Jonathan Demme may have won the Best Director Oscar for *The Silence of the Lambs*, but he started out making the women-in-prisons exploiter *Caged Heat* for Corman (and getting dropped from the British sex comedy *Naughty Wives*, aka *Secrets of a Door-to-Door Salesman*, due to 'artistic differences').

One of my great heroes is the American cinematographer Wally Pfister, who won an Oscar for lensing *Inception* in 2011 and who is living proof of the artistic validity of the 'trickle up' theory. Pfister, who has become Christopher Nolan's right-hand man, is regarded as one the best DPs working in cinema today, and has a reputation for achieving extraordinary results with the minimum of fuss. Crucially, although he now shoots movies budgeted at over $150 million, he learned his trade on exploitation fare such as *Body Chemistry* and *The Unborn*, which were both made for peanuts for Corman's Concorde-New Horizons stable. In the early nineties, Pfister shot a string of straight-to-video erotic thrillers for former porn king Gregory Dark (aka Gregory Alexander Hippolyte, aka Gregory H. Brown) which were notable for looking fantastically classy, coming to define the 'suspense in suspenders' genre that melded thriller plots with soft-core sex in a surprisingly successful bid to crack the home-viewing market for couples. Back then I used to write the video column for the British Film Institute's esteemed *Sight & Sound* magazine (which prided itself on covering everything that was released on VHS) and I remember clocking Pfister's name, knowing that if he featured in the credits then there was going to be *something* worth watching – no matter how trashy a particular title seemed to be. Take *Night Rhythms*, in many ways the *ne plus ultra* of the straight-to-video erotic thriller genre. The plot goes something like this: when late-night disc jockey Martin Hewitt is apparently heard murdering one of his listeners live on air, he hides out and has sex with an assortment of glamorously attired women until eventually Delia Sheppard gives up and admits that she did it because she is a lesbian. The End. Sounds awful? Well, whatever else you want to say about it, it looks *brilliant* – because it was shot by the man who would go on to shoot *Memento, Inception, The Prestige, Batman Begins, The Dark Knight* and, of course, *The*

Dark Knight Rises. How's that for a career trajectory? From lensing soft-core murder-mystery cheapies (with added lingerie) to shooting massive productions about a man with a role-playing fetish who wanders the streets dressed from head to foot in rubber!

The point is that, despite its sneering critics, self-financing exploitation cinema has a proven track record of providing entry to the industry for genuinely talented film-makers who have then gone on to excel in the more 'upmarket' arena. But this is not the kind of thing people want to hear when they talk about the 'British film industry' – because this is not the kind of material that attracts Oscar attention. Everyone conveniently forgets that back in the sixties and seventies, when Hammer won the Queen's Award for Industry, the two genres of movies for which the UK had become internationally known were comedies and horror flicks. In terms of our export market we were world beaters with these brands, and our 'national cinema' thrived upon their crowd-pleasing success. But then in the eighties the concept of British cinema was somehow hijacked by the Laura Ashley school of film-making, which was epitomised by the Merchant Ivory stable – a fantastically successful film-making partnership that produced such Oscar-bait as *A Room with a View* and *Howards End*. Many of these productions are fine movies indeed (and, as Kim Newman points out, as 'British' as only films produced by an Indian, directed by an American, and written by a Pole can be). I am particularly fond of *The Remains of the Day*, which is a surprisingly forthright adaptation of Kazuo Ishiguro's novel. But, like

The Queen and *The King's Speech*, Merchant Ivory movies represented only a tiny fragment of UK film production, and one that was not necessarily any more valid or authentically 'British' than its 'downmarket' counterparts. Yes, these were the kinds of movies that won Oscars, cut from the same tourist-friendly cloth that Harvey Weinstein would later make his own. But were they really the very best of Britain? And, in the end, does it really matter what the membership of American Academy think of the output of 'British Cinema'?

In 1997, Mike Leigh's *Secrets & Lies*, a terrific 'Brit pic' worthy of the home-grown seal of approval (despite technically being a UK/France co-production) achieved the staggering feat of getting nominated for *five* Oscars, including Best Picture – a real coup for a low-key gem which focused on recognisable English working-class characters with nary a crown in sight. Had Weinstein been involved the film might actually have won something, but Harvey was backing *The English Patient* that year (which Miramax had cannily picked up after funding failed just before shooting started) and nothing was going to come between him and a fistful of Oscars.

In the UK, there was plenty of 'The British are coming!' brouhaha that year, with Leigh and Anthony Minghella going head-to-head in the Best Director category, both praising the other's work in very gentlemanly (and very 'British') fashion. Yet while *The English Patient* wound up taking $78 million in the US, *Secrets & Lies* struggled to hit $14 million despite its multiple Oscar nods. And the reason given by the US media for its comparative failure to set the American box office alight was simply that it was 'too British' – whatever that meant.

I remember being sent to Hollywood to cover the Oscars for Radio 1 that year, and being told to walk down Sunset Boulevard with a microphone in order to find out 'what the average American really thinks of *Secrets & Lies*'. Thus the BBC's Hollywood reporter Peter Bowes and I headed out on to the street, where we singularly failed to find: a) any 'average' Americans; or b) anyone who had seen *Secrets & Lies*. Eventually, after much unbroadcastable trudging, we spied a cosmopolitan young man lounging photogenically outside an upmarket burger bar, wearing an ostentatious pair of Ray-Bans and looking for all the world like someone who really wanted to be interviewed by the BBC.

So we interviewed him.

'Hello,' I said. 'I wonder if you'd mind talking to us. We're from the BBC and we're trying to find some Americans who've seen the British movie *Secrets & Lies*, which, as you may know, is up for a Best Picture Oscar. Have *you* seen *Secrets & Lies*?'

The man hesitated, then smiled a big showbizzy smile, and replied, 'Well, as you know, I'm English.'

I didn't know this.

'Erm, sorry,' I replied. 'I didn't know you were English. I thought you were American. *Are* you English?' His accent was somewhat non-specific.

'Oh, you *know* I am,' he laughed again, to the bemusement of both Peter and me. 'You *know* who I am.'

Did I?

'I'm really sorry,' I said, somewhat sheepishly, 'but . . . have we met before?'

'Nah!' said the man, who clearly thought I was just playing out some elaborate charade. 'We haven't met before. But it's *me* . . .'

As he said this, he raised his hand theatrically to his face, and then very slowly pulled off his huge black Ray-Bans to reveal a pair of fabulously twinkly eyes glittering away in his fantastically famous face.

A face which I had never seen before.

Ever.

Honestly.

I looked to Peter (who'd done his fair share of celebrity reportage) for support. He stared back at me, blankly, and shrugged. We both turned back toward the 'famous person' who had, as yet, failed to register on either of our celebrity radars.

'Um, sorry,' I said again. 'I really don't know who you are.'

'Yes, you do,' he said assertively, turning up the smile to maximum, angling his head a little as if to give us a better view.

Still nothing.

'Nope,' I said. 'I really don't . . .'

'Oh, *come on!*' he said with a hint of irritation. 'It's me. *Me.*'

'Right,' I said. 'I can see that it's you. And the fault is surely mine. I'm terrible with faces. But I still don't know who you are. Maybe if you told me your name . . .'

'You're kidding?' he said, taken aback. 'You *really* don't know my name?'

'No,' I replied with a hint of desperation.

'But you recognise my face, right?'

'Well, not really, but . . .'

'From the telly? From *EastEnders*?'

'Ah,' I said with a sigh of relief. 'You're from *EastEnders*.'

'NO!' he shot back, now actually angry. 'I am *not* from *EastEnders*. I'm working here in Hollywood.'

'But you just said you were from *EastEnders* . . .'

'I said I *was* from *EastEnders*. I *used to be* from *EastEnders*. But now I've quit all that and I've come here to America. To work in Hollywood.'

'Oh, that's great,' I said, trying to make amends for my previous ignorance of his undoubtedly stellar work in Albert Square.

'Yeah, because in Britain I was getting typecast,' he explained. 'Because, of course, everyone knew me from *EastEnders*.'

'Oh, right, I see.'

'Which is why I came here. To Hollywood. You know, to escape the typecasting. Of *EastEnders*.'

'Yes, of course. Escape the typecasting. Good for you. And how's that working out?'

'Oh great, really great,' he beamed, replacing his sunglasses to hide his famous eyes once more. 'Cos here, no one knows me . . .'

'No, I see.'

'. . . you know, from *EastEnders* . . .'

'Right.'

'. . . so there's none of that "typecasting" trouble.'

'No, of course not. Well, that's terrific. And what sort of parts are you being offered here in Hollywood? Presumably nothing like *EastEnders* . . . a ha ha ha . . .'

'A ha ha ha.'

'So . . .?'

There was an awkward silence.

'Well . . . nothing right now. Not as yet. I'm just, you know, waiting for things to happen. Early days.'

'Oh right, of course, "early days". So how long *have* you been here?'

Another awkward silence.

'About a year.'

'About a year? Right. So, not *that* early days really . . .'

'Well, you know, *comparatively* early . . .'

'Oh, sure, "comparatively early". But . . .'

'What?'

'Well, you know . . . nothing's actually come up yet?'

'No.'

'OK. Anything on the horizon?'

'Not just now.'

'OK, I see.'

There was yet another awkward pause.

'I don't suppose you've seen *Secrets & Lies* . . .?' I ventured.

'No.'

'OK, never mind. Well, must be going. Thanks for your time. Good luck with everything. In Hollywood.'

As we walked away, I turned to Peter Bowes, a man who

makes his living knowing who famous people are and what they are doing, and said, 'Sorry, who the fuck *was* that?'

'No idea,' replied Peter. 'But whoever he was, he hadn't seen *Secrets & Lies* either . . .'

Chapter Six

AMERICAN WITHOUT TEARS

'You say the darndest things, Marina . . .'
Local Hero

'And the BAFTA goes to . . . *The Girl with the Dragon Tattoo.*'
There has been much heated discussion on the internet about the exact meaning of the expression that flitted across my face during that '. . .' when I presented the 2011 British Academy Award for 'Film Not in the English Language'. According to some viewers and Twitterers, I was 'making no attempt to conceal my annoyance' at the way the votes had fallen. This was an easy assumption to make – apparently my face looks annoyed most of the time, an unfortunate truth which keeps getting me into trouble. No matter how happy I may be with any given situation, my features naturally fall into a jowly scowl which makes everyone think that I'm: a) angry; b) smug; or c) both. Face it, no matter how much I try to look like James Dean the sad fact is that the person I most resemble is Richard Nixon. And Nixon *always* looked cross. And smug. It didn't matter whether he was smiling or

raving, opening a hospital or sending in planes to napalm women and children in Vietnam – something about his face just never looked happy. As his opponents famously asked: 'Would you buy a used car from this man?' The same could be asked of me. Apparently.

So, as I stood there on stage doing my best impression of Tricky Dicky reading the front page of the *Washington Post* in June 1971, it's easy to see why someone could have imagined that I was less than thrilled at the outcome of the award I was about to present. In fact I was delighted, not only because I really like *The Girl with the Dragon Tattoo* (a tough adaptation of Stieg Larsson's novel, boasting a stand-out performance from Best Actress nominee Noomi Rapace), but also because the film's BAFTA win tied in nicely with an ever-so-slightly embittered joke I had made onstage only a couple of moments earlier. Want to hear it? No? Well, never mind, because I'm going to tell you anyway . . .

'This award,' I had quipped, 'honours movies which take us deep within another culture, movies from around the world which can be understood by anyone thanks to the universal language of cinema and the miracle of subtitles . . . but which Hollywood will nevertheless feel the need to remake in English.'

Well, *I* thought it was funny . . .

This admittedly unremarkable aside drew a few polite chuckles and the very faintest suggestion of applause from the auditorium of the Royal Opera House in London's Covent Garden, along with some notable silences from the assembled Hollywood bigwigs, none of whom knew who the hell I was and many of whom had made large amounts of money remaking foreign language films for audiences who are too stupid to read subtitles. Indeed, later on in the ceremony Best Director winner David Fincher was unable to receive in person his prestigious BAFTA for helming *The Social Network* because he was too busy working on his new movie – an English language remake of *The Girl with the Dragon Tattoo*.

Poetic, huh?

The real reason I looked so sour up there on stage was that I had spent quite a lot of time prior to the ceremony learning how to pronounce the names of all the various creators of the five films nominated for the Not in the English Language (NITEL) award – a total of 13 names, many of them featuring crossed-out 'o's, underlying squiggles, acute accents, conjoined vowels, and dots. Foreign languages have never been my strong point, but as someone whose name when mispronounced (as it almost invariably is) sounds like a portable toilet, I hated the idea of screwing up someone else's moment of BAFTA glory by bending their name out of shape with my stumbling English tongue. So, having tracked down a list of phonetic interpretations, I had attempted to commit to memory the correct pronunciation of each film-maker's name, be it Juan José Campanella (Argentina, for *The Secret in their Eyes*), Luca Guadagnino (Italy, for *I Am Love*), or Etienne Comar (France, for *Of Gods and Men*). I already knew how to pronounce Alejandro González Iñárritu (Mexico, for *Biutiful*) because I'd interviewed him years earlier when *Amores Perros* became a controversial hit at the Edinburgh Film Festival and I had made such a balls-up of his name that he felt justifiably compelled to correct me on air. Any of these names could have come out of the envelope – the contents of which are kept secret from everyone, including the presenters, until they're actually read out up there on stage. Earlier on, whilst dashing to the men's room for a last-minute pee, I ran into British actor Dev Patel, who was also presenting an award, and when I asked him what category he was doing he blithely replied, 'Who knows – as long as it's not foreign language film with all those unpronounceable names!'

Thanks, Dev.

My biggest difficulty on the pronunciation front had been getting my head around 'Søren Stærmose', the producer of *The Girl with the Dragon Tattoo*, whose name featured a couple of terrifyingly alien-looking/-sounding vowels, only one of which I recognised. Sadly, the place from which I recognised it was the opening sequence to *Monty Python and the Holy Grail*, which famously features humorous cod-Swedish subtitling under the otherwise boring title credits. 'Wi nøt trei a holiday in Sweden this yër?' ask the subtitles, as the various set designers and lighting riggers get their moment of glory. 'See the løveli lakes, the wøndërful telephøne system, and mäni interesting furry animals, including the majestik møøse . . .'

The image of the 'majestik møøse' which 'once bit my sister' ('No realli! She was Karving her initials øn the møøse with the sharpened end of an interspace tøøthbrush given her by Svenge – her brother-in-law – an Oslo dentist . . .')

has stayed with me since I first saw *Holy Grail* at the Barnet Odeon back in 1975, and I have believed ever since that the Swedish language was packed full of 'ø's. It isn't. In fact, it is packed full of 'ö's, which are an entirely different matter. If you want to find an 'ø' you need to go to Denmark, where they speak Danish. I know this because I asked my trusted colleague, Hedda, who is from Holland and speaks both Dutchish *and* Swedish, and she assures me that there aren't any 'ø's in either alphabet. I also checked with a Norwegian ('Norvege Nul Points'), whose language has lots of 'ø's, and they said the same thing. At least I think that's what they said, although since they said it in Norwegian I can't be 100 per cent sure. Hedda says she doesn't speak Norwegian, but is pretty good at French and German, which is impressive but doesn't really help here. On balance, I think it's safe to assume that the collective Pythons made a humorous but linguistically inaccurate goof, and the subtitler's sister was actually bitten by a mööse rather than a møøse. Which is relevant because, although *The Girl with the Dragon Tattoo* is a Swedish language film based on a Swedish language book and set largely in Sweden, its producers are actually Danish. And the Danish language sounds completely different from Swedish, apparently. Sadly, I don't know any Danish people (and on the basis of Lars von Trier's genital-slicing *Antichrist* I'm not in any hurry to change that) so I had to rely on the pronunciation advice of a Norwegian (who spoke Danish but not English) and a Nederlander (who spoke English, Swedish, French and German but not Danish). As for me, I passed my French O-level on the third attempt and can do a pretty good impression of the Swedish chef from the Muppets, but neither of those talents was going to cut the mustard in the Royal Opera House.

All of this (the Pythons, the moose, the Muppets) was running through my mind during that endless '. . .' as I stood there on the BAFTA stage gathering myself to have a run at the names Søren Stærmose and Niels Arden Oplev, and looking like Nixon trying to pass a kidney stone. Before walking out on stage, I had resolved to take my time: to say the names silently in my head first before allowing them out into the world, and then to deliver them clearly, proudly, and with a sense of international confidence. And you know what? It paid off! I got both the names bang-on, so note perfect that anyone listening would have thought that I was born and bred in Copenhagen. Don't believe me? Well tough – you'll never be able to prove otherwise because the only person who heard me utter those names was . . . me!

As was perhaps predictable, the moment I uttered the words '*The Girl* . . .' the crowd erupted into spontaneous applause and any subsequent uttering was duly drowned out by the well-earned whooping and cheering of the assembled Dano-Swedish alliance, who appeared to have turned out in force. Clearly their film was a popular win and its makers promptly rose to the occasion by bursting into tears on stage – the first tears of the evening.

But wait, I hear you say, weren't the BAFTAs televised? Surely those super-sensitive TV microphones will have picked up your moment of pronunciation triumph, allowing us all to experience the clarity of your diction as if we were up there onstage with you? Sadly not, since the version of the BAFTAs which went out on BBC1 that night did not include the Film Not in the English Language category, save for a final fleeting also-in-tonight's-show glimpse of yours truly saying '*The Girl . . .*' and a shot of Stærmose and Oplev looking really happy. Why? Partly, I suspect, because nobody wants to watch Richard Nixon passing a kidney stone at what is meant to be a fun, upbeat fiesta of film-makers and their frocks. I was prepared for this, having been similarly snipped from the broadcast version of the 'TV BAFTAs', at which I presented an award for best documentary in my customary undertaker-on-a-day-out fashion. But, more importantly, one may well conclude that the Film Not in the English Language category failed to make the main body of the BBC broadcast because it was just too marginal, too specialist, too niche for a mainstream television audience.

This is a shame, because had the award been televised, viewers would have been treated to a glimpse of some of the very best films of the year, including *Of Gods and Men*, an electrifying drama about French Cistercian monks facing life-or-death decisions in an Algerian monastery, which was my second-favourite film (after *Inception*) of 2010. Based on the true-life tale of missionaries who were kidnapped and executed by local militia, Xavier Beauvois's gem had picked up the Grand Prix at Cannes and was looking like a strong contender at the BAFTAs, and yet had failed even to make the shortlist for the Oscars' NITEL category. This was nothing new; whereas eligibility for the BAFTAs' NITEL prize requires merely that a film be (guess what?) not in the English language, the selection process for the American Academy's equivalent category is Byzantine balderdash of the highest order which requires each country to select and submit just *one* film for consideration. This leads to all manner of internal squabbling within said countries about which movie deserves their national seal of approval (France, for example, had to decide in 2008 whether the Czech/UK/US-affiliated *La Vie en Rose* or the Iranian-based *Persepolis* best represented 'French cinema' – ludicrous!) and propagates the popularly held American belief that no country in which people speak a funny language could possibly produce more than one decent movie a year.

As for the BAFTAs, ask yourself this: if the forthcoming English language remake of *The Girl with the Dragon Tattoo* wins an equally significant award early next year, do you think that the broadcasters and newspapers who cover the increasingly prestigious ceremony will relegate David Fincher's victory to the realms of the 'also rans' as they did with Søren Stærmose and Niels Arden Oplev? Of course not. Why not? Because Fincher is American (rather than Danish) and therefore more inherently 'mainstream' (in the English-speaking world) than his Scandinavian counterparts. Sad, but true.

No wonder Hollywood executives are so keen to devour and regurgitate 'world cinema', remaking versions of foreign language movies which could not possibly be improved upon by the process of translation. Take *Let Me In*, an utterly unnecessary Anglo-Americanisation of Tomas Alfredson's genre-redefining 2008 Swedish gem *Let the Right One In*. Based on a novel by John Ajvide Lindqvist (which in turn took its title from a lyric by Morrissey, pop's very own Moaning Myrtle), Alfredson's eighties-set chiller used a tentative vampire-story template to conjure a heartbreaking coming-of-age tale about a bullied schoolboy and a mysterious young girl who claims to have been 12 'for a long time'. As the odd couple's awkward friendship grows, so blood flows, seeping quietly into the virgin snow of the bleak Stockholm suburbs in which both the novel and the film are very specifically set.

'It's true that the Swedish suburbs are perfect for a vampire story,' Alfredson told me when I met him in 2009, prior to presenting him with the prestigious 'Kermode Award' for Best Film (the award taking the form of a golden statuette which looks oddly like Richard Nixon). 'It's a scary place, with twenty hours of darkness a day in January.' The fact that Sweden had precious little horror heritage – and certainly no major vampire tradition – merely added to the sense of strange isolation, with *Let the Right One In* seeming to have appeared *ex nihilo*, its arrival every bit as enigmatic and inexplicable as that of the mysterious Eli, brilliantly played by young actress Lina Leandersson. 'I think I saw *Dracula* and *Frankenstein* on television as a child,' said Alfredson, who claimed to be otherwise totally ignorant of the long-standing traditions of horror cinema. 'But I try not to study other films because there are too many people just "blueprinting" movies. I looked more to music, literature or painting for inspiration, particularly the beautiful work of Hans Holbein. The expressions he finds in faces are very creepy. But I don't even know if *Let the Right One In* is a horror film. I just want to make movies that make people laugh or cry. For me, this story is very much about the anger that this tormented boy is carrying. He's not able to do anything with it. He can't talk to his parents because he's shy and he's afraid of them interfering; he cannot talk to his teachers; he has no friends. So for him, the vampire in the story is the body of all this anger. I had similar experiences as a boy and that moved me when I read the book, the feeling of wanting revenge without having the ability to get it. The other day, I spoke to a 76-year-old man who told me that when he was twelve they nearly killed him at school, and he'd never been able to talk about it until seeing the movie. After seeing the film, he'd been crying for two weeks and he wanted to say thank you. It made me cry too.'

Reading back the text of that interview, it seems clear to me that Alfredson was astutely identifying several key qualities, all of which contributed in strange and wonderful ways to the intangible success of *Let the Right One In*. In no particular order, these contributing factors were: the fact that the film, like the source novel, was set in Stockholm; that it was made by someone with no track record in the horror genre; that it was not essentially a vampire movie, but a movie about kids which just happened to feature vampires; that it was primarily intended to make the audience cry rather than scream. Now try to imagine what would happen if you systematically inverted every single one of those unique and exceptional elements that had alchemically created what was for me the very best film of 2009. Taking that list in order, you should be imagining something that was: *not* set in Stockholm; made by film-makers firmly ensconced within the horror genre; essentially a vampire movie which just happened to feature kids; intended to make the audience scream rather than cry.

Et voilà! You are now imagining *Let Me In*, the 2010 English language remake of *Let the Right One In* which is: set in modern-day America; made by the reborn Hammer studio, arguably the oldest horror factory in town; essentially a vampire movie which just happens to feature kids; marketed with the prominently featured endorsement 'The Best American Horror Film in the Last 20 Years: Stephen King' and 'The Scariest Vampire Movie I've Seen in Years! *New York Post*'.

Does that make you want to scream? It should do.

You wanna hear the really bad news?

When *Let Me In* tanked at the box office (it took around $12 million in the US – which is still $11.5 million more than *Let the Right One In* could ever have made in that subtitle-phobic marketplace) its failure was widely blamed on the (erroneous) claim that it had stuck *too closely* to the original, and wasn't dumb enough for English language audiences! This despite the fact that *Let Me In* entirely ditches the spine-tingling ambiguity of Alfredson's original in favour of by-numbers horror clichés (glowing eyeballs, shrieking sound cues) and ill-fitting CGI effects, which see Chloe Moretz transform from a young girl into a spider-walking bat-creature before our very eyes. Infuriatingly, director Matt Reeves (who previously helmed the effects-heavy sci-fi horror *Cloverfield*) seems to have understood just enough of what was great about *Let the Right One In* (whole set pieces are restaged) to mimic and desecrate it at the same time, leaving you wondering just who the hell this damned movie was made for. Surely no one smart enough to appreciate the brilliance of *Låt den rätte komma in* would have a problem with subtitles in the first place? And, by the same token, surely no one dumb enough to have a problem with subtitles would have any interest in a movie as intelligent as *Let the Right One In*, even if it had been remade in English with silly special effects and crowd-friendly horror clichés?

Yet despite the fact that *Let Me In* flopped, the comparative box office for 'Subtitles vs. Remakes' figures tell a sorry tale indeed. Time and again, regardless of quality, English language remakes of foreign language films have outperformed their predecessors financially, even if the remakes stink to high heaven and horribly mutilate (or even obliterate) the memory of the original. When Gore Verbinski (who helmed the first three *Pirates of the Caribbean* movies – go Gore!) took an English-language hatchet to Hideo Nakata's genre-defining Japanese horror *Ringu*, he scared up $128 million in the US and a total of $230 million worldwide with *The Ring*, ludicrously outstripping the success of the Japanese version, which was cheaper, cleverer, and (crucially) scarier. Shamefully, Nakata's epochal original (which followed a Japanese TV movie and had already been remade as a feature in Korea) was subsequently re-marketed on DVD as 'the original movie which inspired *The Ring*', as if the naff American version had now become some form of Platonic ideal in relation to which all other versions of this Japanese tale now existed. Ask someone if they've seen *The Ring* nowadays, and the chances are they'll think you're asking them about the Verbinski schlocker. If you mean the Nakata version, you actually have to say, 'Have you seen *Ringu*, you know, the *original* Japanese version?'

To which the answer is usually, 'No, but I did see *The Ring* . . .'

The remaking of *Ringu* was just the tip of an iceberg that saw Hollywood attempting to translate a slew of 'new wave' Asian hits for the mainstream English-speaking market in the ideas-strapped noughties. Titles included Takashi Shimizu's Japanese frightener *Ju-on* (2002), which was remade (by its original director) as *The Grudge* (2004), with money and sequel-spinning results; Hideo Nakata's *Honogurai mizu no soko kara* (2002), which was remade by Walter Salles as *Dark Water* (2005), more of which in a moment; and Danny and Oxide Pang's Hong Kong shocker *Gin gwai* (2002), which was remade as *The Eye* (2008), featuring rising star Jessica Alba. Central to this transnational trend were canny entrepreneurs Roy Lee and Doug Davison who, spying a lucrative hole in the market, set up Vertigo Entertainment to sell the remake rights of Asian movies to American studios. At its most successful, this policy resulted in the aforementioned Best Picture and Best Director Oscar wins for Martin Scorsese, whose Boston-set thriller *The Departed* was a Vertigo-brokered remake of the Hong Kong *Infernal Affairs* trilogy (aka *Mou gaan dou I–III*, 2002/3). At its worst, it gave us *The Lake House* (2006), an English language remake of the South Korean romantic fantasy *Siworae* (aka *Il Mare*, 2000) which re-teamed Sandra Bullock with her *Speed* co-star Keanu Reeves, who plays a talented-but-troubled architect (stop laughing at the back). Sandra and Keanu share the eponymous lake house, although due to a Doctor Who-style warp in the time–space continuum, they are separated by a two-year ellipsis, which can only be breached by placing notes in a mailbox that acts as a portal between dimensions. (Time-travelling note to Sandra: 'Dear Ms Bullock. If you are reading this letter in the past, please save the future by not making this lousy movie.') Sandra and Keanu are in love, or would be if they'd met. Actually, they have met – and talked and kissed. But she has a convenient habit of forgetting what her old boyfriends look like and he can't remember her because, hey, he hasn't met her yet! But he *can* plant trees outside her apartment that spring up overnight without anyone noticing, and she can send books and scarves back into the past without precipitating the sort of 'butterfly effect' catastrophes with which sci-fi writers have wrestled for years.

Costing around 16 times as much as its South Korean source, and boasting star names both in front of and behind the cameras (the screenplay is by feted *Proof* playwright David Auburn), this syrup-drenched supernatural whimsy achieves stupidity at a genuinely international level; it really is one of the dumbest films ever made.

Now, it is possible (but not, as Lieutenant Kinderman would say, 'probable') that all the idiocy of *The Lake House* is in fact present in *Siworae/Il Mare* and the Hollywood hogwash is simply an accurate translation of Korean crapness. I can't comment because (like most people in the Western world) I haven't seen *Siworae*, and nor am I ever likely to now, having been permanently put off the idea by the sheer mind-bending awfulness of *The Lake House*. And therein lies one of the great myths of the English language remake racket: that somehow the success of translated Hollywood knock-offs (which may well bear very little resemblance to their international pre-decessors) will draw attention to the other unseen originals. What nonsense! Just think about it: if a mainstream audience sees an English language remake of a foreign language film and finds the experience really satisfying, why would they bother seeking out the original – what would be the point? They've already enjoyed the movie in English, why should they watch it again with the subtitles that were precisely the reason they'd never bothered with the foreign language original in the first place? And if the English language version sucks, the situation is even worse. Can you honestly imagine someone paying good money to watch a really lousy movie in some overpriced multiplex, hating it, and then going home and getting straight on the internet to buy the original from Amazon in order to see whether it sucked even more? It's just not going to happen. For proof, ask yourself how many people you know who actually tracked down *Siworae* after enjoying or being appalled by *The Lake House*.

The answer is no one, right?

Quod erat demonstrandum.

It would be easy to use *The Lake House* as a touchstone

text that proves just how thick-headed Hollywood remakes of foreign language films tend to be. But the problems of translation are far more complex than Western film-makers simply doing a bad job of adapting Eastern texts, or English speakers having a tin-ear for European dialogue. There are underlying issues of cultural, linguistic and locational specificity which mean that no film can be lifted from the context of its creation and relocated to a foreign shore without fundamentally changing the original text to the point that it may cease to have any of the value which made it seem such a desirable commodity in the first place.

Or, to put it more simply, no matter how tactfully, artfully or respectfully an English language film-maker approaches the issue of translating a Japanese language film, a Japanese movie can *only* work in Japanese.

Let me give you an example.

In 2004, as part of Vertigo's efforts to bring so-called 'J-horror' hits to the West, acclaimed Brazilian director Walter Salles helmed a US-set remake of Hideo Nakata's masterpiece *Honogurai mizu no soko kara* (aka *Dark Water*). Like *Ringu*, *Dark Water* had its roots in the writings of Koji Suzuki ('the Japanese answer to Stephen King'), and told the haunting story of a recently separated single mother and her young daughter, who are forced to live in a run-down apartment block amidst increasingly acrimonious divorce and custody proceedings. Plagued by a mysterious dampness that seeps endlessly from the ceiling, and disturbed by the sounds of footsteps in the apparently abandoned rooms above, the mother starts to fear for her sanity as she imagines a mysterious lost girl coming back to haunt her and her daughter. Is the apartment, with its infernal plumbing, beset by the spirits of the undead? Or is the mother (who has wrestled with her own psychological demons) simply descending into madness?

For my money, Nakata's original *Dark Water* is one of the most underrated films of the noughties, and arguably one of the greatest screen ghost stories of all time. On a recent (and rare) trip to the theatre, I was particularly pleased to discover that the creators of the 'spooktacular' West End hit *Ghost Stories* (which has been causing audiences to shriek and jump like those scaredy-cats during the *Paranormal Activity* trailers) had cited *Dark Water* in their glossy programme as one of the Top Ten Scary Movies of All Time. It *is* scary. But more importantly, it's really sad. Like so many truly great horror movies, *Dark Water* is a film that uses supernatural themes to dramatise profoundly natural emotions, and at the heart of its spine-tingling spell is a profound sense of loss mingled with a protective acceptance of the burden of parental responsibility.

Is this selling the movie to you?

No? Thought not. That's why the front cover of the UK DVD says 'The most shocking film yet from the director of THE RING!' (which, incidentally, most people know from the English remake) rather than: 'A profound sense of loss mingled with the burden of PARENTAL RESPONSIBILITY!'

Such is sales talk.

Salles's *Dark Water* remake (which actively eschews any

sense of shock) is an interesting beast – the work of someone who clearly understands what's so great about Nakata's original, and as such it's in a completely different league to either Verbinski's dunderheaded translation of *Ringu* or Takashi Shimizu's enjoyably empty-headed retooling of his own endless *Ju-on* series. Having previously helmed the profoundly humanist Che Guevara biopic *The Motorcycle Diaries*, Salles was renowned for drawing outstanding performances from his casts and for almost wilfully addressing an audience more mature than the average multi-plex adolescents. Yet, like his predecessors in the Hollywood J-horror market, the Brazilian film-maker clearly faced a dilemma regarding how much – or how little – of his source material's cultural baggage to retain in the rush toward Americanisation. Because although both Suzuki and Nakata are clearly well-versed in the traditions of Western chillers (you can detect echoes in *Dark Water* of Nic Roeg's *Don't Look Now*, Polanski's *Repulsion* and Kubrick's *The Shining*), there are some elements of their storytelling that are so deeply rooted in the Japanese *kaidan eiga* (ghost-story film) tradition and its kabuki theatre ancestry as to seem utterly alien to American audiences.

For obvious reasons, the concept of ghostly spirits and their relationship to the 'real' world varies wildly from culture to culture. In Apichatpong Weerasethakul's wonderful Thai oddity *Uncle Boonmee Who Can Recall His Past Lives*, for example, a deceased wife materialises matter-of-factly at her dying husband's dinner table while his lost son reappears as a glowing-eyed apparition of a monkey – and no one (least of all the audience) registers the faintest degree of surprise, let alone alarm. When *Uncle Boonmee* became the unexpected winner of the Cannes Palme d'Or in 2010, several people (myself included) made lots of cheap jokes about how much we'd like to see Hollywood have a go at remaking *that* one. Just imagine the meeting: 'Yeah, we *rilly lurved* the Uncle Boonmee character, who we've "re-imagined" as an eighteen-year-old jock with a life-threatening sports injury named Boysie. But as for these ghosts and that undead monkey boy thing – dontcha think they should be a bit more . . . *scary?* After all, they are, like . . . *dead.*' On a conceptual level, the language barrier was the very least of *Uncle Boonmee*'s problems as far as Western multiplex acceptance was concerned; it was the ideas themselves that such an audience would struggle to understand.

Despite the apparent box-office appeal of English language J-horror remakes, a brief glance at the Japanese *kaidan eiga* cannon from which the source texts draw so much inspiration reveals a similarly unfamiliar attitude to the undead. Look, for example, at Satsuo Yamamoto's *Kaidan botan-doro* (aka *A Tale of Peonies and Lanterns*) or Masaki Kobayashi's prize-winning anthology *Kwaidan* (aka *Ghost Stories*) or, most significantly, Kenji Mizoguchi's *Ugetsu monogatari* (aka *Tales of a Pale and Mysterious Moon after the Rain*), all of which exhibit a distinctly un-Western acceptance of the supernatural that seems to be rooted in the animistic elements of Japan's Shinto heritage. 'Unlike ghost stories in the West,' wrote American critic Roger Ebert in his typically thoughtful review of *Ugetsu monogatari*, 'Mizoguchi's film does not try to startle or shock;

the discovery of the second ghost comes for us as a moment of quiet revelation, and we understand the gentle, forgiving spirit that inspired it.' Presenting its ghosts in a solidly human form that leaves both audiences and protagonists largely unaware of their otherworldly nature, *Ugetsu monogatari* had a profound influence on Nakata, both for its iconic lakeside set pieces (which are echoed throughout his waterlogged chillers), and for the neo-realist flavour of its 'supernatural' scenes. Significantly, Nakata also cites *Tokaido Yotsuya kaidan* (aka *Ghost Story of Yotsuya*) as indicative of the fundamental divide between Eastern and Western ghostly traditions; he told the Japanese arts and culture magazine *Kateigaho* that 'the difference between Japanese and Western horror can be traced back to the difference in religious beliefs. When making horror films, the methods of describing the spirit world and the expression of horror are totally different between Japan and the West.' While Suzuki points to writers such as Junichiro Tanizaki, Naoya Shiga and Natsume Soseki as evidence that 'Japanese literature is full of ghosts', film fans need look no further than the runaway domestic success of Hayao Miyazaki's *Spirited Away* (a childhood fantasy in which a young girl finds employment in a bathhouse for spirits) for proof of the ease with which Japanese audiences of all ages embrace such concepts. 'The supernatural [is] such a large part of the Japanese culture,' agrees Salles, 'in the way they don't question it in the way we question it. It's much more a part of their world – not something they visit every now and then, as we do.'

This is not to say that Japanese audiences are never scared

by ghosts – clearly teenage fans of the original *Ringu* movies were completely creeped out by the vengeful apparition of the lank-haired Sadako, an incarnation of an iconic *kaidan eiga* figure whose heritage can be traced back through the chilling 'Black Hair' segment of *Kwaidan* and beyond, and who represents a genuinely threatening presence. Yet in a culture in which everyday spirits exist within the most mundane settings, even within household objects (the distressed spirit of a broken clock, for example), the mere presence of ghosts is neither unnatural nor alarming. Indeed, the *absence* of such spirits would be unusual in certain contexts, most notably in relation to bodies of water, which in the East are commonly associated with the metaphysical. 'Walking along a body of water you sense ghosts being born,' Suzuki told the readers of Japanese magazine *Kateigaho*, as if this were the most natural thing in the world. Yet when being interviewed by a British magazine, Nakata felt the need to explain that 'Japanese ghosts are supposed to appear where water exists' and to clarify the 'strong connection between water and the supernatural' that has underwritten his most celebrated works. Elsewhere, he reminds us that 'water, scientifically speaking, is the mother of life, but it also takes an enormous amount of life. I think Japanese people all share that kind of fear . . .'

All of which is a rather long-winded way of saying that as soon as you 'translate' something that has its roots in one culture into the parlance of a foreign audience, more gets lost in translation than just the language. Nor is this a one way street: *Dark Water* screenwriter Rafael Yglesias (who had written for Polanski on *Death and the Maiden* and whose work Nakata had therefore almost certainly seen) made it quite clear that he felt there was something lacking from Ken'ichi Suzuki and Yoshihiro Nakamura's original script, most notably in the apparent passivity of the central mother character. In Yglesias's version, the supernatural elements that beset American actress Jennifer Connelly (inheriting her leading role from Japanese star Hitomi Kuroki) are made more explicitly psychological, filling the thematic void left by downplaying the foreign metaphysics and thereby realigning the piece as a cracked character study in which all the action is essentially driven by the film's star rather than her environment. According to producer Ashley Kramer, Yglesias effectively 'transformed the more passive Japanese heroine of the original into a very poignant and relatable American single mom trapped in a personal dilemma'. And in 'creating a very strong and memorable female character [who] . . . would make for a compelling core of the film' the US version also shifted the narrative away from the external ghosts, spirits and even locations of its Eastern source, drawing a more explicitly psychological veil over the otherworldly presences of *Honogurai mizu no soko kara* to create what Yglesias tellingly calls 'a very American ghost story'.

At first glance this shift may seem both sensible and inevitable: if an American audience won't understand or be familiar with the underlying themes of the original Japanese story, then surely there's no point in writing those themes into an English translation of the script. Better to abandon the foreign concepts altogether and come up with something more 'relatable' (a ghastly word in *any* language) to a Western audience, and more appropriate to a Western cast and setting. After all, an American single mom probably *wouldn't* react to the rising tide of portentous disturbances in the same way as a Japanese mother in similar circumstances. Changes *have* to be made, right?

Right.

But here's the rub. What if those changes only have to be made because of the very act of translation itself? What if the original Japanese story wouldn't make sense to a Western audience simply because it had been moved to the West? Would an American or English audience have intuitively understood the strangely alien metaphysics of the Japanese story had they watched it in (subtitled) Japanese? Doesn't the whole root of the problem come down to a fundamental misunderstanding of what it really means to be a stranger in a strange land?

I think the answer to this question is a resounding 'Yes', and I would like to offer myself as living, breathing proof of that truth. Firstly, I am at heart a terrible xenophobe: an Englishman with an overly developed attachment to his Manx heritage who lives, breathes and *thinks* like a 'little islander', and who is most at home in his *own home* or having a pint at his local pub. If you asked me to pick a character from literature who most embodies my own outlook on life, I would choose Arthur Dent from *The Hitchhiker's Guide to the Galaxy*, the dressing-gown-clad humbug who travels the galaxy and sees the wonders of the universe but still spends most of his time worrying about where he can get a decent cup of tea. Or Dougal from *The Magic Roundabout*, who reacts to every new crisis by threatening to write an angry letter to *The Times* (in the days before it was owned by Rupert Murdoch). I am not proud of this but I know it to be true that, left to my own devices, I would never stray more than a couple of miles from my own front door. Worse, I would not read any books that I had not already read, meet any people whom I had not already met, or allow any changes to be made to my immediate environment which would cause me, in any way, to have to re-evaluate the world as it already exists inside my own head.

To be clear: I do not like change.

And yet somehow I have managed to experience the world outside of North London first-hand – I have been to Tokyo and New Orleans and Disneyland Paris, and all those other places where they do things so differently. (Incidentally, the thing they do most differently in Disneyland Paris is smoke, with every parade and ride queue engulfed in a poisonous cloud of freshly exhaled Gitanes fumes.) And I have enjoyed the experience – immensely. I have been privileged to eat freshly caught tuna at a sun-scorched beachside bistro in Grenada; to promenade with young lovers in the cool evening air of Barcelona; to take a tram to the borders of three countries on one ticket in Basel; and to argue with a waiter about the meaning of the word 'vegetarian' ('Is not meat, is pork!') in Lisbon. None of this would I have done had I not been eternally bound to somebody (Linda) who really looks forward to 'going abroad on holiday', and who has often had to fight tooth and nail to drag me kicking and screaming on to a plane so that I might broaden my minuscule horizons and see the rest of the world for the wonderful thing that it is.

And it *is*.

Crucially, the minute I've actually got anywhere to which I had claimed I really didn't want to go, I've realised just what a fool I'd been to resist going in the first place, and found myself overwhelmed by the wonder of everything that just wasn't English. Now, I know what you're thinking, that I'm just some naff Shirley Valentine clone who's been seduced by the cod scenery of a summer holiday and intoxicated by the prospect of a naked swim and a quick shag with a moustachioed Tom Conti. And frankly, you'd be right. But what's important is not the authenticity of my experience of the 'world' as an economy-class tourist but rather the fact that, when forced to visit a foreign culture, I found that I both enjoyed and understood it a lot more than I had ever expected. Why? Simply because once there, I knew that I was in a foreign land where they 'do things differently' and, like every other two-bit tourist in town, I was able to watch and learn how things work outside of the M25, and generally get the hang of ordering a meal, or buying a beer, or renting a hire car that had at least four wheels. The fact that I was in a foreign country where everyone spoke a language I didn't understand (I remain spectacularly mono-lingual) actually *added* to my ability to adapt to unknown customs. If anyone spoke English, I simply assumed that they did things the same way I had always done, but the minute

I was faced with dialogue which was 'Not in the English Language' I became surprisingly open-minded (a first for me) and oddly receptive toward the rituals and peculiarities of otherwise alien cultures. In short, my lack of linguistic understanding made me more receptive to the difference of foreign cultures.

I am not alone in this. Everyone who has ever been on holiday to a country where the native language is anything but their own has experienced exactly the same thing. You board a plane at Heathrow looking like a recruitment poster for UKIP and you come back ten days later wearing a sombrero, drinking wine out of a pig's bladder, singing 'Torremolinos', and making plans to retire to the Costa del Sol. OK, so it's not a permanent state – it usually wears off somewhere between the horror of the baggage carousel and the dull thud of the delayed bus to the long-stay car park, which remind you that you are back in England. But for the time that you're away, and however 'inauthentic' your experience may actually be, the fact is that most of us, when faced with a 'foreign' culture, learn to adapt pretty damned fast.

And we love it.

The same is true of movies. In fact, doubly so. *Quadruply* so. Once you've got over the peculiarly Anglo-American grouch of having to watch a subtitled movie, which involves reading and looking at the same time (a problem which devotees of furtive European arthouse porn never seem to encounter, strangely), audiences of foreign language films tend to find themselves strangely receptive to the myriad different ways of doing things that make the world such a terrifically diverse source of pleasure and entertainment. And it seems to me that a key element of this new-found acceptance is the fact that our brains work differently when they know that they are outside their comfort zone. Throughout history even the most aggressively nationalistic invading armies (the Romans under Hadrian, the French under Napoleon) have reported that the mindset of their soldiers has been fundamentally altered by the landscape, the food, the architecture and (most significantly) the *language* of the cultures they have attempted to occupy and obliterate. (If you don't believe me, ask a Welshman why it's so important that their native language, long-outlawed under English rule, is now taught in schools as a matter of course.) Even if you need a translator, the very sound and cadence of a 'foreign language' has a profound affect upon the listener.

Or, to put it another way, if you watch a movie in which everyone is speaking a language other than your own, you know that things will be done differently in this world, and you become almost instinctively alert to the hidden signs of these differences. Thanks to the oft-cited 'international language of cinema', most of the key cultural signifiers will be built into the visual architecture of the piece – not just its physical setting, but the entire *mise-en-scène* – along with the rhythms of the editing, the composition of the soundtrack, and all the other non-linguistic elements at work in the playing of a movie anywhere in the world.

All of which brings me to the second reason why I am living proof that English-speaking audiences can, in fact, understand foreign language films even if they have no prior knowledge of the culture from whence they came. To return to the example of *Dark Water*, the creators of the Hollywood remake knew that an Anglicised adaptation of Suzuki and Nakata's haunting tale would have to take into account the differing customs of Western metaphysics and they re-ordered the story accordingly for American (and presumably English) audiences. Yet when I first saw *Honogurai mizu no soko kara* in Japanese it made perfect sense to me, despite the fact that what I knew about Japanese culture wouldn't have filled the back of a very small postage stamp. Oh, I'd seen a few contemporary J-horrors like *Ringu* and Takashi Miike's South Korean co-production *Ôdishon* (aka *Audition*), along with exported classics like *Ugetsu monogatari* and Kaneto Shindô's *Onibaba* (aka *The Hole*). But I was certainly no expert, having grown up thinking that *Merry Christmas Mr. Lawrence* was authentically exotic because it had a plinky-plonk soundtrack by Ryûichi Sakamoto, who used to play with the Yellow Magic Orchestra. So when I came to write an article for *Sight & Sound* magazine about the differences between Nakata's *Honogurai mizu no soko kara* and Salles's *Dark Water*, the first thing I did was to ring my good friend Tomoko Yabe to see whether my cockamamie conclusions about conflicting cultural traditions, which I had cooked up on the sole basis of watching the films, had any basis in reality. And, surprisingly enough, they did. Tomoko confirmed for me that the Japanese word '*rei*' (the definition of which encompasses the soul of a person, the souls of ancestors and the mysterious invisible powers that are perhaps closer to gods) had very different connotations to the English word 'ghost'; that water was indeed commonly viewed as a metaphysical gateway, something the Japanese movies I watched had made abundantly clear without ever having had to *explain* it; and that the epilogue to *Honogurai mizu no soko kara* (which Salles's *Dark Water* doesn't even attempt to recreate) was clearly intended to be poignant rather than terrifying, heartbreaking rather than horrific. Tomoko, who is an extremely generous soul, even went so far as to track down and send to me a selection of reading matter about Japan's Shinto and Buddhist heritage, all of which merely reconfirmed what the movies had already expressed so eloquently. It really was astonishing to discover just how much you can learn about a country by spending some time in their cinema.

The point is that if a xenophobic Luddite like me can understand a subtitled movie on both a linguistic and cultural level, then frankly anyone can. These movies don't need to be remade in English, because most of them make perfect sense in their original language, as would be immediately apparent to anyone who took the trouble to watch them in the first place. OK, so some people clearly have a deep-seated disdain for subtitles, a prejudice which American studios are entirely happy to reinforce, for obvious reasons. Yet throughout the rest of the non-English-speaking world, subtitles are accepted as a matter of course; indeed, in many Asian territories it is not unusual to find two separate sets of subtitles (Mandarin and Cantonese, for example) simultaneously running vertically and horizontally along the side and bottom of the picture. I remember being impressed by screenings at the Cannes film festival where a movie would be shown in one language, with French subtitles burned on to the picture and English subtitles being displayed on a second monitor strip beneath the screen. This seemed novel to me, but in many international territories it is simply business as usual. Only in the English-speaking world do audiences seem to have a problem with subtitles per se, and I am increasingly convinced that the root of the problem is nothing more than habitual. We are not in the habit of watching subtitled films. Why not? Because Hollywood keeps remaking them in English.

In the case of *Dark Water*, despite the best efforts of Jennifer Connelly and some genuinely impressive location work (most notably New York's haunting Roosevelt Island), Salles's remake disappoints on several levels. Yet with $25 million in US box-office takings, it still achieved a degree of financial success that would have been inconceivable for the subtitled Japanese original in the American marketplace. Since Salles's remake cost a reported $30 million, it was (unlike its predecessor) technically a 'flop' – proving once again that nothing loses money like a mid-priced movie with a whiff of the 'arthouse' about it – but that is a factor which only has relevance for the financiers. As far as the English-speaking movie-going public were concerned, Salles's version eclipsed Nakata's film in an instant, consigning the original to secondary 'source' status, to be known only by navel-gazing cinephiles and horror fans – or 'specialists', as the market-place now likes to call them . . .

Call us . . .

Call me.

Nakata ended up following the money to Hollywood and replaced Noam Murro as director of *The Ring Two*, which, despite the title, was actually *not* a remake of Nakata's own *Ringu 2* (nor indeed of Jôji Iida's *Rasen,* Norio Tsuruta's *Ringu 0: Bâsudei* or Dong-bin Kim's *The Ring Virus* – all of which followed *Ringu*). Even though it's probably the best that the ongoing American remake series is going to produce (*The Ring 3D* is due in 2012 – can't wait), *The Ring Two* did little to establish Nakata as a bankable director in the West, and his generic UK-based follow-up film, the overwritten cyber-thriller *Chatroom*, was disappointing fare indeed. But at least Nakata got *something* out of Hollywood's ambushing of his work, which is more than can be said for the creators of most subtitled films that suffer the remake treatment. As for Nakata's fellow countryman Takashi Shimizu, he opted to exploit the situation to the hilt and got himself locked into a seemingly endless cycle of Japanese originals and English language remakes after hitting the financial jackpot with *The Grudge*. So far, Shimizu has directed six versions of *Ju-on/ The Grudge*, including two straight-to-video originals, two Japanese feature films and two American-backed English language remakes (he's also been involved in a *Ju-on* computer game). To be honest, there's really very little difference between the Japanese feature *Ju-on* (2002) and the Americanised (but Japanese-set) remake *The Grudge* (2004), save for the presence of *Buffy* star Sarah Michelle Gellar and the use of English dialogue, both of which helped the remake take $110 million in the US as opposed to the $325,000 earned by the original in the same territory. Even in Japan, the Hollywood version gave its Japanese source a run for its money, offering depressing evidence of a horrible cultural imperialism that has made American the default language around the globe.

Other international directors who have opted to 're-inter-pret' their own work for English-speaking audiences have fared far worse. Top of the cautionary-tale pile is poor old Dutch maverick George Sluizer, whose CV includes the utterly awesome Euro-shocker *Spoorloos* and its unspeakably terrible American remake *The Vanishing*. When I first saw *Spoorloos* in a preview theatre on Wardour Street back in 1989, I was so freaked out by its claustrophobic finale that I almost fainted from fear. Watching Sluizer's American remake a few years later in the very same theatre, I almost died of embarrassment as the heaving stupidity of the final act caused the assembled critics to roar with laughter and groan with disbelief. What the hell happened?

In the original (PLOT SPOILERS AHOY), our bedrag-gled anti-hero is buried alive by the horribly ordinary Raymond Lemorne (played in terrifying everyday fashion by a deadpan Bernard-Pierre Donnadieu), discovering at last what happened to his long-lost love as he awaits his own imminent death. In the remake, our bedraggled anti-hero is buried alive by Barney Cousins (played in terrifying rent-a-mental fashion by a gurning Jeff Bridges), but then his new girlfriend digs him up and all three run around hitting each other over the head with shovels. Really. If someone else had done this to the original it would have been bad enough, but the fact that Sluizer did it *himself* (albeit under extreme duress and doubtless as a result of the tyranny of test-screenings, which leave all the most important artistic decisions to the lowest forms of multiplex pond life) was both horrifying and heartbreaking. Why would he *do* such a thing? For money, I presume; *The Vanishing* was unspeakably terrible on every level, but even with a miserable $14.5 million at the US box office, it still did way better than the Dutch/French language original and probably helped Sluizer pay a few bills in the process. OK, so (like *Dark Water*) the remake cost a load more to make, and was therefore comparatively less profitable than *Spoorloos* in real terms – whatever that means. But more English-speaking audiences saw the remake than the original, despite the fact that almost every single review of the film told them to avoid it like the plague and seek out *Spoorloos* on the arthouse revival circuit or on clunky old videotape (this was back in the days before DVD or VOD).

Fast-forward 14 years, and we find Austrian director Michael Haneke retooling his remarkable (if deeply unlikeable) German language torture-fest *Funny Games* for American audiences with similarly (if less spectacularly) flatulent results. Having made a stern name for himself with such gruellingly callous and intellectually cruel works as *Benny's Video*, Haneke's magnum opus on the evils of violent entertainment was unveiled at the Cannes Film Festival in 1997, where it played with both French and English subtitles. The story is simple: two apparently civilised young men, dressed in tennis whites and surgical gloves, arrive at the door of a rich couple's holiday home, ask to borrow some eggs and then proceed to humiliate, torture and kill the couple – and their child – for fun. The central (and somewhat simplistic) thesis of the movie is that the audience are distressingly complicit in the on-screen violence, much of which is actually *off*-screen, save for the sounds of death and dismemberment that creates the illusion of unwatchable visual horror. At key moments in the drama, the alpha psycho (brilliantly played by Arno Frisch, looking like Richard Gere's Nazi twin) turns to the camera and asks the audience why they are still there, why they haven't left the theatre. Some people did. As for me, I really wanted to walk out of the movie but couldn't, because professional etiquette required that I stick it out to the bitter end. Believe me, if I hadn't been compelled by my job description to see this thing through to the final reel I would happily have bailed. But you can't review movies you haven't watched in their entirety (a lesson I learned the hard way with *Blue Velvet* – see previous book) and having got into the screening in the first place (always a nightmare at Cannes) I wasn't about to abandon ship before the final credits. My persistence paid off: having watched *Funny Games* from beginning to end I was able to vent my righteous anger about it in the pages of *Sight & Sound* magazine, complaining that Haneke was merely reworking 'fourth wall' ideas better expressed in *Henry: Portrait of a Serial Killer*, and accusing him of preaching to the converted by making a film that would *never* be seen by its intended 'target' audience (i.e. the enthusiastic mainstream consumers of what would later be called 'torture porn'), who would never dream of watching a movie as archly academic as *Funny Games*.

A few years later, it transpired that Haneke himself had reached exactly the same conclusion. Having gone on to make far superior (and significantly less hectoring) films such as *The Piano Teacher* and *Caché* (aka *Hidden*), Haneke decided to revisit *Funny Games* which, he now claimed, had indeed failed to reach the audience who would benefit most from its traumatic power – namely the American masses who mindlessly lapped up the violent entertainment against which *Funny Games* railed. With peculiarly Teutonic logic, Haneke (who had previously told his producer that if *Funny Games* was a 'success' it would be because the audience had misunderstood it) concluded that there was nothing essentially alienating about the premise of his film per se, but that as a 'foreign language' venture the movie simply would never have the ear of a mainstream American audience. So he set about re-filming it, pretty much shot for shot but with an English-speaking cast headed up by Naomi Watts, who had scored such a big hit with the English language remake of *The Ring*. The result was *Funny Games U.S.*, a spectacularly misguided venture which ranks alongside Gus van Sant's shot-for-shot remake of Hitchcock's *Psycho* as a prime example of wanky navel-gazing by directors who seem to think they're above the lumpen multiplex masses but would still like to take some of their money, thank you very much. Having declared with a splendidly straight face that there was no need to change anything about *Funny Games* (other than the language) because the original was damn near perfect, Haneke must have been somewhat surprised when the Anglicised polemic of *Funny Games U.S.* failed to gain any substantial traction either. In both the US and the UK, *Funny Games U.S.* was seen by pretty much the same audience demographic who had watched the original *Funny Games* a decade earlier – upmarket arthouse-friendly audiences who don't mind being lectured about the evils of horror cinema, are up for a bit of a stern European telling-off (albeit with English dialogue), and who actually quite enjoy the purging experience of being made to feel really miserable and uncomfortable in the cinema. Of course, any of these liberal-minded souls who had already seen the original German language *Funny Games* would doubtless find themselves wondering what exactly the point was of doing it all again, particularly since the shot-for-shot nature of the remake suggested that Haneke hadn't actually advanced as a film-maker over the intervening years (which, on the evidence of his other work, he most definitely had). More significantly, Haneke himself was made to look rather foolish, because his rigorously planned and clinically executed experiment in entryist cinema had in fact proved exactly the opposite of what he had avowedly set out to demonstrate – that the problem with *Funny Games* was nothing to do with subtitles after all.

If you've seen either version of *Funny Games*, then you'll understand immediately what was apparently so incomprehensible to Haneke: the reason the film had a limited audience was because it is such a gruellingly unpleasant and upsetting experience which offers the audience almost none of the traditional pleasure of cinema but asks them instead to either walk out of something they've already paid to see or sit and suffer in shamefaced silence whilst being made to feel bad about paying to see the film in the first place. I refer you once again to my experience of watching the film for the first time in Cannes and feeling furious that I simply could not leave. It may work in a lecture hall or as part of an A-level media studies course, but as a work of cinema *Funny Games* is simply intolerable. This doesn't mean it's not a 'good' movie, or that it fails to do exactly what the director intended, albeit within a rather limited context. But very few audiences will tolerate being told off for that long without some sense of gratification or reward en route. Popular revenge movies, for example, can harp on endlessly about the destructive search for retribution and the self-generating cycle of vengeful violence, as long as we actually get to revel in some of that senseless carnage and morally problematic bloodlet-ting along the way. As for *Funny Games*, it's just no fun at all. In any language.

So where does all this bad news leave us? Looking at movies from countries as far apart as Sweden, Japan, Hong Kong, Holland, France and Austria, it seems fairly apparent that remaking these films in the English language is not a solution to the 'problem' of their comparative unpopularity in the UK and the US, and may even be the very cause of the problem. In fact, audiences are actually *more* able to understand foreign language films in their original foreign language versions than they are to understand the neces-sarily altered and compromised English language remakes. Yet, traditionally, English speakers have a problem with subtitles, a problem not shared by the rest of the world and which merely works to diminish our communal cinema-going experience.

Of course there is one significant area in which foreign language films *have* found a foothold in the UK multiplex market, but that success was largely achieved (at least initially) by virtue of them not being in a 'foreign language' to a significant proportion of their audience. For the past 25 years, the UK Box Office Top Ten has regularly featured Bollywood movies, in which the primary spoken languages are Hindi and Urdu (with odd blasts of English). These films pack out both multiplex screens and 'arthouse' cinemas, where they merrily outperform their domestic and international competitors. In 2002, the crossover hit *Devdas* capitalised on a high-profile unveiling at the Cannes Film Festival by taking £1.6 million at the UK box office – a very respectable sum. At around the same time *Kabhi Khushi Kabhie Gham. . .* took £2.5 million in the UK – a figure that would have put many mainstream Hollywood productions to shame.

Yet despite the huge popularity and financial success of movies such as *Kabhi Khushi Kabhie Gham. . .* and *Kal Ho Naa Ho* (which took £1.5 million in the UK), reviews and coverage of Bollywood movies have often been limited to specialist Asian publications such as *Eastern Eye*, *Stardust*, *Cine Blitz* and *Filmfare*, or to internet sites such as RadioSargam. com. The reason for this peculiar critical ellipsis is that, in the past, comparatively few Bollywood films were screened for the English-speaking press. Why? Because their distributors had long considered such outlets irrelevant to the films' performance. In essence, these movies were not viewed as 'foreign language' fare at all – rather, they were Hindi movies for Hindi speakers.

When writing a piece about this phenomenon for the *New Statesman* in 2004 I spoke to Tim Dams, news editor of the industry paper *Screen International*, who confirmed that 'companies like Eros and Yash Raj, which distribute these films in the UK, have developed a fantastically successful niche market which has in effect bypassed mainstream English-speaking audiences and reviewers'. As a result, many British reviewers (myself included) would only find out about Bollywood releases when they showed up in the *Screen International* chart. Significantly, many of the titles that racked up such healthy figures in the nineties and noughties did so without the aid of subtitles. Indeed, at an eagerly anticipated press show of the gritty thriller *Dev* in 2004, there was widespread Babel-like confusion when a subtitled print failed to materialise (to the dismay of the assembled English-speaking critics). I muddled through on the strength of physical language alone, and understood some of what was going on, but others simply gave up. This was a real shame, because that screening had come about as a direct result of Eros (which had achieved notable hits in the UK with *Chalte Chalte*, *Khakee*, *Baghban* and *Devdas*) becoming the first major Bollywood distributor to join the Film Distributors' Association, the UK-industry body that coordinates the national press shows at which (largely English-speaking) critics view each week's releases.

When I asked Eros's managing director Kishore Lulla why

his company was signing up to the FDA now, having achieved such extraordinary success without its assistance in the past, he told me that they wanted to become more involved in industry forums on piracy (a particular problem for Bollywood movies) and also to 'take advantage of the national press show schedule'. This was significant because it meant that for the first time a UK Bollywood distributor was actively targeting English-speaking audiences, something that had never concerned them in the past. According to Rana Johal, key examiner of South Asian movies at the BBFC, the reason for this shift was two-fold: on the one hand, Eros clearly wanted to expand its market to non-Asian audiences, particularly since Bollywood movies were fast gaining international critical respect; more significantly, they needed to hang on to the increasing number of second-generation Asian immigrants for whom English was now their first (and perhaps only) language. 'We've started to see a marked rise in subtitling in the past few years,' Johal confirmed in 2004. 'Bollywood movies are a great transmitter of culture, and the kids want to see them to make that cultural connection. But many of them do not necessarily speak the language of their grandparents.' By coincidence, at almost exactly the same time, the Channel 4 reality show *Bollywood Star* was reaching its tear-jerking conclusion, during which much was made of the contestants' ability to act with their eyes rather than their voices – a relief to one of the contestants, who had made it to the final despite being unable to speak a word of Hindi.

Intriguingly, as subtitling has become more commonplace for Bollywood movies (meaning that more and more of their viewers are not primarily Hindi speakers), their extraordinary success in the UK has continued. Apparently, Eros's attempts to hang on to the next generation of core-audience viewers (for whom Bollywood movies *are* effectively 'foreign language' fare) are working, and the company continues to go from strength to strength. More importantly, here is evidence that a large section of the UK market, who have been raised on movies spoken in a language other than their own, are entirely at home with subtitles. Which can only be a good thing.

If only the rest of us could become equally comfortable with the concept of subtitled movies as part of mainstream entertainment. If only we'd *all* been raised on the fruits of international cinema. Wouldn't that be great? And wouldn't a good way of achieving that goal be to introduce a quota system, whereby multiplexes were required to show one foreign language film for every four or five English language offerings? After all, wasn't the whole point of the multiplexes in the first place to offer us more choice?

In a word – no.

As far as choice is concerned, multiplexes have *never* been a positive force for change, nor will they ever be. In the same way that the proliferation of satellite-TV stations has merely led (in the words of Bruce Springsteen) to '57 Channels (And Nothin' On)', so the explosion of the multiplexes that now dominate the UK's film-going landscape has simply offered cinema-goers a greater number of screens showing the same thing. Bollywood movies only found a foothold in the multiplexes because they came with a large and devoted audience and they reliably make money – lots of it. No one in the multiplex planning rooms is program-ming those films through any desire to be 'diverse'. If you want diversity for diversity's sake, you have to look outside of the multiplex system, to the independently programmed cinemas whose cultural roots are buried deep in the soil of the once-flourishing repertory circuit. It is these cinemas that have consistently provided an alternative to the domi-nance of Hollywood blockbusters for UK audiences, catering to audiences who want something other than the movie they last saw adorning the front cover of *Empire* magazine. There's nothing intrinsically wrong with those movies – *Inception* was one of them, for heaven's sake. But take a look back at the covers of the UK's most popular movie magazine and you'll notice a distinct absence of foreign language fare. (Indeed, I struggle to think of a single issue of *Empire* that has run with a foreign language film on the cover, although there must be a few . . . musn't there?) This is neither a coinci-dence nor a conspiracy. As the UK's biggest-selling movie mag, *Empire* is simply reflecting the predominant interests of the mainstream movie market, in which foreign language films have always been essentially marginal.

But what if multiplexes were required to show more of them? Wouldn't that improve the situation? Strangely, no – in fact, it might well make the situation worse. Indeed, there is an argument (which I first heard passionately espoused late one night in the bar of the Bristol Watershed, after one too many pints of the old Johnny-Knock-Me-Down) which says that multiplexes should be expressly forbidden from ever showing foreign language films, and be restricted solely to the exhibition of formulaic Hollywood fare. You want to hear the argument? Well, I'm going to tell you anyway. It goes something like this . . .

Unlike multiplexes, independent cinemas in the UK struggle from year to year to maintain a balance between showing a wide selection of movies from around the world that reflects the enormous artistic diversity of international film, and getting enough bums on seats to be able to continue showing that enormous diversity of film in the future. As we all know, the cutting-edge movies that represent the very best that cinema has to offer as an art form are very rarely the same movies that constitute the top-grossing products of the year. This may change in the future – blockbusters may indeed become better (see Chapter Two). In the meantime we have a marketplace in which, for whatever reason, artistic merit has little or no relationship to financial success, and in which foreign language movies, no matter how brilliant they may be, will always be a harder sell than their English language equivalents. Thus it falls to independent cinemas to provide a counter-programming service which offers an alternative to the homogeneity of the mainstream, showcasing movies (often 'Not in the English Language') which are never going to do the kind of business upon which multiplexes depend. But every now and then you get a 'breakout' movie: a film typically destined for the independent cinema circuit which somehow captures the popular imagination and causes cinema-goers to break the habits of a lifetime. The classic examples of this strange phenomenon are French movies like *Jean de Florette* and its sequel *Manon des*

Sources; or Italian language oddities such as *Cinema Paradiso* or *Il Postino* (the latter of which is technically a British movie); or even – to play devil's advocate – Mel Gibson's insanely violent religious epic *The Passion of the Christ*, the dialogue of which was entirely in Latin and Aramaic, and which proved that everyone can deal with subtitles if you give them enough gratuitous gore and theological guilt.

All of these movies broke out of the subtitled ghetto and into the mainstream market, reaping healthy profits in the process. And by rights, such rich rewards should be shared by the independent cinemas that have supported subtitled movies all year round – with little or no financial reward – and who rely on this kind of irregular windfall to balance the books. Yet as soon as the multiplexes get a whiff that a foreign language film might be a money-maker after all they go in like sharks in a feeding frenzy, and their attentions are understandably hard to ignore. Think about it: if you're the distributor of a foreign language film that suddenly starts to attract interest from the multiplexes, you're immediately going to start wondering whether a wider audience awaits you in Screen Six of the local enormodrome than in Screen One of that bijou arthouse venue which has been stoically showing your niche movies to small or moderately sized audiences for as long as you can remember. And should you decide to place your movie in the multiplex, where it may or may not hold its own against 14 screens of competing Hollywood fodder, then you will inevitably be knocking a sizeable dent in the profits of the independent cinema, which really needs these breakout hits to survive.

By way of comparison, think of the NHS spending all its time and money teaching doctors and nurses to do their jobs so brilliantly in public hospitals and GP surgeries, and then the private sector (which has invested no time or money in their training whatsoever) coming along and stealing the cream of the crop with offers of bigger pay cheques to provide services for paying customers only, using skills that were funded by the taxpayer in the first place. Just as private medicine could not survive without public healthcare, so the few foreign language hits that flourish in the multiplexes only do so because they have their roots in the soil of the arthouse circuit. If you allow the multiplexes to cream off the hits, you will, in fact, strangle the lifeline of foreign language cinema in the UK.

OK, so it's only an argument and, as I said, one espoused in a state of advanced refreshment by someone who was on the verge of becoming the armed-wing of independent cinema programming. But you must admit there *is* a kernel of truth in there somewhere. And peculiarly, the evidence of this truth is offered most starkly by a genre of films whose greatest problem is the very fact that they *don't* qualify for 'foreign language' status. I am talking of course of the always embattled 'British Picture' of which I spoke in the previous chapter. As we know, the biggest obstacle for the indigenous UK film industry is not production but distribution, and the more one looks at the sea of Hollywood product filling UK screens, the more it becomes apparent exactly why that is the case. Thanks to the export success of American cinema – a cinema which apparently 'speaks our language' – British film-makers have effectively become foreigners in their own country. Whereas subtitled imports have a hard time finding screening space in the mainstream market because they require subtitles, the insurmountable hurdle facing British movies made in English is the fact that 'American' is, to all intents and purposes, not a foreign language and therefore does *not* require subtitles. Would that it did. When George Bernard Shaw (or possibly Oscar Wilde, or maybe even Winston Churchill) joked that England and America were 'two nations divided by a common language', he had no idea just how divisive that common language would prove in terms of the British film industry.

It is no coincidence that countries in which English is not the mother tongue have imposed far more severe quota systems to 'protect and preserve' their national cinema than we ever have here in the UK. In France, for example, a quota system was introduced in 1928 — in response to the welter of cheap American product flooding the market — requiring distributors to offer one French film for every seven imported films. In May 1946, the Blum—Byrnes agreement opened France up to American movies (in return for erasing part of the national debt) but established a new quota of four weeks of French films per quarter, which was later increased to five. In June 2004, Argentina ratified a quota system that required all exhibitors to show at least one local film in each quarter for each screen — meaning that a 16-screen multiplex would have to show 64 Argentinean films a year! Similar quota systems have been enforced over the years in countries as diverse as Italy, Brazil, Korea, Malaysia, Portugal and Spain, all of which have in some way helped stimulate or preserve domestic production in the face of overwhelmingly American competition. In 1930, as part of his First Five-Year Plan, Stalin took the ultimate sanction of banning the import of all American films into the USSR outright, thereby boosting Soviet production by freeing up more screens to show home-grown films of the 'Boy Meets Tractor' variety. And, as recently as March 2011, the World Trade Organization was still trying to strong-arm China into allowing more than a mere 20 foreign language films to be shown in its cinemas each year, a government-imposed limit that generates a staggering boost for home-grown productions in a marketplace where annual box-office receipts have long exceeded the $1 billion mark. No wonder Hollywood is lobbying so hard for a larger slice of the action.

Now, as anyone with an ounce of common sense will tell you, quotas are effectively unenforceable in an age in which DVDs and internet downloads can easily traverse national boundaries – it's no surprise to discover, for example, that the black market for Hollywood films in China is massive (as we noted earlier, restrictive distribution practices are a breeding ground for piracy). But when faced with the behemoth that is the American film industry it's equally easy to understand why governments resort to such quotas, particularly if their national cinema is in a language not catered for by Hollywood. While many people instinctively see trade barriers as a restriction of their freedom of choice, many more understand the need to preserve the production of entertainment that speaks to them in their own language.

Imagine how postal American audiences would go if six out of seven movies showing in *their* local multiplexes were in a foreign language and required either redubbing or subtitling. No matter how convoluted quota systems may seem, there will always be a home market for movies made in the mother tongue.

Which is great, unless your mother tongue is American, which as far as the British film industry is concerned, it is. In the typically prescient words of Elvis Costello, our indigenous film industry now struggles for survival in a country in which we 'don't speak any English, just American without tears'. For UK films, there is simply no language barrier to separate our cash-strapped home-grown productions from being eaten alive by bloated Hollywood fodder. Linguistically they exist on an even playing field, which is no help at all when everything else (production weight, distribution muscle, promotional clout) is loaded so heavily in favour of our American friends. In the *one* area in which non-English-speaking nations have some say in the 'Undeclared War' (to use David Puttnam's phrase) with Hollywood – the persistence of their national language – the UK has been rendered horribly mute. If the Americans are already making movies *in our language*, why the hell do we need to make our own? What's the point?

The upside of this equation, we are constantly told, is that our own movies enjoy the privilege of being able to be exported to America, where they can play in the multiplexes because, although they're technically 'foreign', they don't need to be subtitled (unless they're *Trainspotting*). Yet if you look at the

British movies that do indeed reap such rewards in the US (and which tend to be the same movies that do so well at the Oscars – see previous chapter), you'll find that very few of them are actually as British as you may think. Take *The King's Speech*, which, despite being an English language production (obviously), is actually a Weinstein-backed Anglo-Australian affair considered Down Under to be *their* first ever Best Picture winner. (Blimey, next thing they'll be wanting independence . . .) Or what about *The English Patient*, another Oscar winner whose very name screams home-grown credentials but which, as previously noted, was actually rescued by Miramax when funding floundered and which is correctly listed on the Internet Movie Database as being a US/UK co-production (rather than the other way round)? Or *Braveheart*, which was set in Scotland, filmed in Ireland, directed by an Australian and financed by Americans? Or *The Full Monty*, whose stripping Sheffielders owed so much of their success to the support of LA-based Fox Searchlight? Or *Four Weddings and a Funeral*, which was produced by the British arm of PolyGram who are, in fact, Dutch? Ironically, the biggest recent British hit was *Slumdog Millionaire*, which is set in Mumbai, and a large proportion of which is in subtitled Hindi.

I could go on. The point is that most (if not all) of the allegedly British movies which apparently benefit from sharing a common language with their American competitors are, in fact, more accurately viewed as international co-productions that constitute only a very small and strangely exportable segment of the 'home-grown' market. The relative merits of each of these movies, which range from the drab to the delightful, are less important than the fact that for every British movie that benefits from the attentions of American audiences, there are hundreds whose chances of capturing a UK audience are entirely scuppered by the market predominance of American movies.

So, to recap:

1) Foreign language films from around the world can't crack the UK multiplex market because they use subtitles, with which mainstream English-speaking audiences have a problem, apparently.

2) English language films from Britain can't crack the UK multiplex market because the screens are already full of Hollywood movies (which don't use subtitles), many of which are English language remakes of the foreign language films which couldn't get in there in the first place (because they use subtitles).

3) If British movies are to succeed in the mainstream UK marketplace, they must first and foremost appeal to Americans.

This is a pretty grim situation, both for our indigenous film production and for the distribution and exhibition of foreign language films in the UK.

So what's the solution?

The answer most regularly offered in response to the first part of this question is 'more public funding for British movies', although frankly what's the point of funding movies people either don't want to see or (more importantly) *can't* see? As I keep saying, the problem in the UK is not film production but film distribution, and we're not going to solve anything by simply helping people make more dismal movies like *Sex Lives of the Potato Men*. As for quota systems in order to artificially boost the presence of British and foreign language films in the multiplexes, all the evidence suggests that such restrictive trade practices merely encourage piracy – a situation from which no one benefits, least of all the film-makers.

No, the solution is far simpler, and it is this . . .

Stop worrying so much about film production, and start worrying a bit more about the support and upkeep of independent UK cinemas that show the kinds of movies (British, foreign language, arthouse, etc.) in which the multiplexes have little or no interest. This is where public funding will have the most impact: fostering and maintaining an exhibition circuit that can help home production to thrive, encourage audience interest in non-English language fare and prevent Hollywood from steamrollering all other cultures into cinematic oblivion. Spend money supporting the cinemas that show movies *other* than the American blockbusters; help them rebuild their often crumbling old buildings, some of which have stood for over a century; invest in their role as centres of local culture, places where people can go to watch and talk about movies in terms other than their box-office clout. Help them to pay for ushers to monitor their screenings and ensure that patrons are properly respectful of each other and of the movies, and for projectionists who actually care whether a movie is shown in the right order, and in the correct ratio, and are able to give each individual performance their undivided attention. You don't need to dictate the programmes of these cinemas, or set up quotas to ensure that they partake in the contractual exhibition of films no one wants to see. On the contrary, you give them the freedom to decide for themselves what to show, to build a relationship with an audience who are fed up with being fed visual junk food, and to nurture cineliterate film-goers who want something to look forward to other than *The Ring 3D*.

In short, you invest in cinemas that speak the language of film – a language which knows no national boundaries, which has no fear of subtitles, and upon the continued existence of which the very future of cinema (in *whatever* language) depends.

Epilogue

THE END OF CELLULOID

*'Your scientists were so preoccupied with whether
or not they could, they didn't stop to think
if they* should.*'*
Jurassic Park

One evening in the spring of 2009, I found myself at the Hyde Park Picture House in Leeds, introducing a screening of one of my favourite films of all time, *Silent Running*. The cinema is a beauty; a proper old-fashioned picture palace with a sweeping balcony, theatrical curtains, sensible ticket prices, and a projection booth that smells of celluloid and sweat – in a good way. The clientele (many of whom are students from the local university) are enthusiastic, attentive and apparently more interested in films than in their mobile phones – at least while they're in the cinema.

All looked set for a wonderful occasion – a lonely journey to the farthest reaches of the galaxy with Bruce Dern and a couple of walking dustbins, accompanied by the heart-breaking warblings of Joan Baez (see previous book). The only problem was that the print of *Silent Running* was old and scratchy and had started to turn a peculiar shade of pink – a common problem with films from that era. Watching the opening credits, in which a pink snail crawled over a pink plant in the middle of a pink forest in pinky-black outer space, I started to wonder whether the audience would be able to appreciate the full melancholic majesty of the movie. Wouldn't this new candyfloss colouring somewhat undercut the sense of awe and wonder that director Doug Trumbull had worked so hard to achieve?

Fortunately, the projectionist at the Hyde Park Picture House was an old-school type who had taken the trouble to test-run the print the evening before the screening and discovered that the chemical degeneration of the past 30 years eased up significantly during the second reel. Thus we were able to warn viewers in advance that while the credits sequence looked a little unusual, if they could just bear with it things would improve dramatically long before the second act kicked in. After all, we explained, the print they were watching was probably the same print that had done the rounds when the movie was first released in the early seventies, and if any of them had seen it on its first run (as I had) then they were about to be reunited with an old friend who (like them, probably) had become a little greyer and more crumpled round the edges since their last encounter.

I really liked this idea that the film had aged along with its audience, and for all the imperfections of the picture I was thrilled that we were projecting from celluloid rather than digital because somehow it made the experience seem more special, more magical, more . . . *real*. I am not alone in this. In the 25 years since I first started working as a film critic (rather than living a fantasy life as one), it's amazing how many directors have waxed lyrical to me about apparently obsolete celluloid. In 2006, on the occasion of his 60th birthday, Steven Spielberg (arguably the most successful director of the 20th century) described to me the 'extreme exhilaration and fear of this new medium' that had been provoked by his first visit to the cinema, to watch *The Greatest Show on Earth* – an experience which left him addicted to the terrifying thrill of celluloid. An anxious child who never recovered from his parents' separation, Spielberg described himself as 'afraid of everything: of the dark; of small enclosures; of people talking too loud; and of my own imagination'. To such a person, a cinema – essentially a small darkened enclosure with amplified sound in which the imagination runs riot – should have been hell on earth. And yet the young Spielberg who sat there aghast as 'these images washed over me, frightening me, overwhelming me' was immediately addicted, desperate to break into the projection box and delve into the mystery of film. Having once been 'afraid of everything', Spielberg – who went on to scare the shit out of a generation with *Jaws* – crucially described his obsession with cinema as being not a way of exorcising his fears but of 'freezing them, of collecting them, and keeping them for my whole life'. It was as if he were the cinematic equivalent of a butterfly collector, capturing the primal fears that flitted around him every night and pinning them to a board, to be marvelled and wondered at by the watching world.

A key part of this clearly transgressive process was the inhalation of the vaporous fumes that had first given cinema its explosive reputation. Just as lepidopterists use chloroform to capture the form of a flitting creature, wings open as if in flight, so cinema captured its images on celluloid via the administration of chemicals which, if inhaled too deeply, could send one off into the rapturous sleep of dreams. And unlike so many of his contemporaries who had already succumbed to the sterile precision of digital information, Spielberg at 60 still clung to that heady whiff of celluloid, greedily inhaling the scent of vagrant history which wafted in its wake like the trailing embers of an opium pipe. 'An editing room with film,' he told me with nostril-filling relish, 'smells like . . . well, it's the same smell that King Vidor smelled, and D.W. Griffith smelled, and Cecil B. DeMille smelled, and John Ford smelled. It's the same smell that Kurosawa smells, and Truffaut smells and Antonioni smells. It is the smell of our medium.'

This is something I have heard a thousand times before: from film-makers who have no interest in drugs but who seem to achieve an artistic high simply by inhaling the air of an editing room; and from projectionists who handle the sacred prints that pass through their hands with the care and attention of bomb disposal experts dealing with the most sensitive high explosives. And the smell that causes so much comment is on some level the 'smell of fear' (as the subtitle of *Naked Gun 2 1/2* would have it), a sanitised relative of the nitrate reek that had once turned the air into an atmospheric tinderbox in search of a naked flame.

No wonder the Cinematograph Act of 1909 viewed the emergent medium of cinema with such sulphurous distrust, as anxieties about what was *on* the films (basically gunpowder – or, as silent film expert Bryony Dixon more accurately says, 'gun *cotton*') became inextricably intertwined with what was *in* them (spectacle, excitement, moral depravity, etc.). The earliest critics of the peep-show arcades and picture palaces that followed (those who had sniffed the future and recoiled from its pungent power) had been particularly incensed about the effects of film on women, children and servants (underlings all), complaining about crinolines catching fire, kids fainting and being abducted in the dark, and workers spontaneously combusting with unregulated revolutionary delight. Soon the critics' attentions turned to the activities of courting couples who, drunk on the darkness of the cinema auditorium, would cavort while the movies played. Indeed, this concern led to the introduction of 'daylight projection', through which films were shown in a darkened alcove above the audience, who remained respectably illuminated below. It didn't catch on: 'I have tried the light and dark halls,' one showman complained, as quoted in Tom Dewe Mathews's terrifically lively work *Censored: The Story of Film Censorship in Britain*, 'and find the public prefer the latter, especially the young couples, who like to see the pictures and have a canoodle at the same time. I found that I lost nearly all the courters – the biggest portion of my patrons – by adopting the lighting principle, and soon went back the old principle.'

On the front cover of Dewe Mathews's book, which I have in front of me now, is an image that is striking in ways which the author surely never intended – a pair of scissors, the blades opened to form an 'X' shape (like the BBFC rating that had once excitingly denoted 'adults only' entertainment), ready to cut and slice celluloid. For decades, scissors were the universally acknowledged visual shorthand for censorship, with every piece published on the subject requiring an accompanying picture of a sturdy pair of stainless steel blades. Such articles would invariably include umpteen alliterative references to 'the censor's scissors', which would be used to 'snip' and 'cut' key scenes from controversial movies. I should know: I wrote enough of those pieces myself, and eventually had to put an embargo on the overuse of my favourite hackneyed phrases – an embargo which invariably was broken by the end of the second paragraph. Indeed, looking back through my ramshackle collection of press cuttings, I find an early article I wrote about the BBFC for *Time Out* magazine back in 1989, the masthead of which uses that trusty scissors-variant 'rusty knife' (why would a censor's knife be rusty?), while the opening paragraph features two 'cuts', one 'snipped', and a fleeting 'trimmed'. *Plus ça change.*

What's interesting about this habitual slicing vernacular, with its constant references to scissors, knives, cuts, trims and so on, is that it makes no sense whatsoever in the modern digital era. You try editing a digital movie with some form of physical blade and see how far you get. The very idea of anyone merrily setting about a movie with a pair of scissors is rooted in the age-old physicality of celluloid, and harks back to a time when 'film' was a physical entity rather than a conceptual conundrum. Nowadays, movies aren't 'cut'; they are modified, reformatted and adjusted to fit your screen. If you've been to the cinema in the past few months, chances are that what you were watching wasn't even a 'film' at all. More likely it was a stream of electronic information, uploaded on to a server and then beamed on to the screen by a digital projector without ever having passed through the translucent celluloid that once gave the medium of 'film' its very name.

This change was inevitable, and perhaps in the long run it will also be seen as liberating. Much has been gained, no doubt – indeed many of the independent cinemas I love so much have benefitted greatly from the installation of digital projectors, which now stand side by side with their celluloid counterparts, allowing an even greater diversity of programming (under the watchful eye of a trained projectionist). Digital movies are downloadable and therefore don't need to be shipped around the country (and indeed the world) in bulky containers, which are expensive to transport and clumsy to handle. They don't catch fire, turn to vinegar or generally degenerate in the manner of celluloid (although DVDs and hard-drive storage systems *do* appear to have a finite shelf-life, which means that back-up clones are a constant necessity). And, perhaps most importantly, the quality of a digital image is more consistently controllable than that of physical prints, each of which will be subtly different from its siblings – particularly after it's done the rounds of a few mishandled projectors. I remember very clearly listening with amazement to David Fincher on the DVD extras for his stylish serial-killer thriller *Se7en*, wherein he claimed that only on this carefully corrected digital imprint would we be guaranteed to see the movie the way he had intended. Apparently the post-production process on *Se7en* had involved striking some very expensive prints that used a 'silver retention' process called CCE, a way of rebonding silver to the celluloid which created a greater contrast between the chasmic darkness and shimmering luminescence of the image. Due to cost restrictions, only some of the prints distributed in the UK were created using this process, meaning that the film you saw in any particular cinema may have been only a pale reflection of Fincher's original vision. This became the subject of much heated debate in the letters page of *Sight & Sound* magazine, with cineastes arguing over the definitive authenticity (or other-wise) of particular screenings of the movie. On digital DVD, however, Fincher was able to assure the viewer that every frame had been colour-corrected to within an inch of its life and the frame ratio correctly locked to his exact spec-ifications.

For cineastes, this is clearly a significant development, and there are similar artistic arguments for digitally projected movies being more controllable than their celluloid ances-tors. Yet for me, and for several generations of film-makers and movie-goers, there is still something irresistible about the act of light shining through celluloid, an almost intangible quintessence of cinema that harks back to the superstitions and shadowplays of our forefathers. In his 2010 movie *Cave of Forgotten Dreams* (which, as I may have mentioned, is clearer, brighter and better in 2-D) Werner Herzog talks about paintings etched onto rock walls being the earliest form of cinema, the drawings of animals animated by the flickering light of a fire which lent the illusion of movement to the static images. There's an echo of that primitivism buried within every frame of a celluloid film-print, the scars and scratches of which tell the story of its life and travels. I recall an old friend, Ronan O'Casey, who played the murder victim in Antonioni's endlessly enigmatic sixties classic *Blow-Up*, telling me that by the end of the film's first run in Britain every print had been snipped of a single explicit frame in which an actress's nethers were fleetingly exposed during a playful romp. The cut wasn't made by censors (who missed it) but by projectionists who, knowing their way intimately around the prints that passed through their hands, had all kept a little something for themselves. And I still get a thrill thinking of the look on editor Mike Bradsell's face when I first showed him a reel of film that had been missing from Ken Russell's *The Devils* for 30 years, and hearing him exclaim, 'My God, I recognise the edits!' Not the edited visuals up there on the screen, you understand, but the *physical* edits on the reel of film itself. This was something Mike had handled and crafted and pored over for months on end, and now his own cuts and splices were running through the Steenbeck for the first time in three decades, scurrying over the spools to greet him like lively animals released from a cage.

All of these memories are tied up with the physicality of film – with the tangibility of celluloid and the lusty mechanics of projection. British film-maker Michael Powell understood this addictive appeal when he made *Peeping Tom*, the film that outraged critics by suggesting that there was something dangerously perverse about a passionate devotion to the cinema. 'It's interesting because the fetish ideas are all there in *Peeping Tom*,' Martin Scorsese told me on the eve of a 40th-anniversary re-release of Powell's much-maligned masterpiece. 'All the elements are there: the projector is correct; the lenses are right; the sprockets are correct. Even the *sounds* of the sprockets are correct. And there is a point in time, many times over the years . . . where I've loved to hear the sound of film going through a projector. And I could tell you if it's 35mm or 16mm, you know. It's like going into a trance almost, or I should say a "meditation" of some kind. And now, of course, that's gone . . .'

For Scorsese, this meditative or trance-like state that even the sound of celluloid passing over sprockets can induce is part of what he calls 'the pathology, the obsession, the compulsion of cinema'. It's a compulsion that Scorsese recognises as an intrinsic element of the cinematic urge, summed up in one blackly comic line from Leo Marks's script for *Peeping Tom*, in which one of the killer's acquaintances mutters ominously: 'All this filming isn't healthy . . .'

'A friend of mine sent me that line on a note when we were making *Raging Bull!*' Scorsese told me. 'I think it was one of the cinematographers who'd just seen *Peeping Tom*. And there is no doubt that [film-making] is aggressive and it could be something that is not very healthy. When you make a film . . . there are times in your life when you're burning with a passion and it's very, very strong. It's almost like a pathology of cinema where you want to possess the people on film. You want to live through them. You want to possess their spirits, their souls, in a way.'

This idea of the possession of the soul being tied up with the alchemical process of light on celluloid is as old as photography itself. Some cultures still regard the taking of photographs as being an inherently weakening experience, with the subject spiritually compromised by the capture of their image. Others believe that it is possible to take 'soul photographs' – a peculiar branch of ectoplasmic entrapment which suggests that the camera can see what the eye cannot. Kenneth Anger thought his experimental films were 'spells' rather than 'movies', while the evangelist Billy Graham declared that there was 'evil' embodied in the very celluloid of *The Exorcist*. No wonder the amiable seventies shlocker *The Omen* used the popular fear of photography as a key plot device, with shadowy shapes bisecting the forms of Satan's future victims showing up on a shutterbug's prints: look, there's the nanny who hangs herself with the suggestion of a rope around her neck; there's Patrick Troughton's bedraggled priest with a dark line running from shoulder to thigh, alluding to the church-tower spike that will skewer him like a kebab; and (most memorably) there's David Warner with a thick black line that prefigures him losing his head after an unfortunate encounter with a truck laden with plate glass.

This sense that the soul and celluloid are somehow intertwined remains as powerful for some of today's leading film-
makers as it was for the photographic pioneers who first
captured the moving image over 100 years ago. Despite the
ubiquitous rise of digital projection, Quentin Tarantino insisted
as recently as 2010 that his sprawling Second World War epic
Inglourious Basterds (in which explosive nitrate stock is used as
a weapon against Hitler) be distributed on 35mm film, clearly
believing that the message of his movie was somehow embedded
in the medium – in the magic of celluloid. Such affection for
celluloid, with all its attendant dangers and degenerative shortcomings, is surprisingly common among directors of a certain
age, even those who understand that the battle with digital
has already been lost. As Spielberg told me with an almost
heartbreaking sense of melancholy: 'I will rue the day when I
too will be forced to conform, when theatres convert to digital
projection and I'll have to convert as well. And I'll be the last
to convert. But my company won't. My company will be at
the forefront of the conversion because I can't stop progress.
But as a film-maker when I still have final cut and I still have
the final choice of mediums with which to make my movies,
I'll always select film.'

'I've had the chance to make up some amazing old films,'
projectionist Sam Clements told *Time Out* magazine in their
piece about the inevitable decline of celluloid. 'Recently I
had original prints of Tarkovsky's *The Mirror* and *Stalker*. They
had frames missing where something may have gone wrong
during playback or a projectionist had nabbed a still for their
collection. For me, it's amazing to hold the print and think

that it was being screened before I was born. These films have their own history, and that's something you can never replicate with digital . . .'

Clements works at the Brixton Ritzy (another fine cinema) and reading his words reminded me of a peculiar encounter I'd had in the foyer of the Hendon Odeon several decades earlier, during the interval of a *Ben-Hur* re-run. I was watching the film for the second time because, in terms of pence-per-minute entertainment, this was the best-value ticket I had ever bought. The film had *everything*: action, romance, intrigue, wild animals, stunning vistas, religion, big men in loincloths, gladiator fights, Charlton Heston's chest, revolutionary political speeches, a harrumphing score, and a chariot race during the filming of which someone had actually died. Really. That's dangerous cinema for you. For sheer thunderous spectacle that film was pretty hard to top, and frankly I was glad of the mid-way toilet break that the word 'Intermission' once signalled. Films don't have intermissions anymore because, thanks to ever more automated projection, the films themselves don't need them – although my bladder still does. But apparently multiplex cinemas are thoroughly against intermissions since they require an usher on hand to allow people in and out of the screening, and (as we know) ushers are now rarer than decent Michael Bay films. Although surely the extra popcorn sales would more than cover their salaries . . .?

Anyway, making sure to leave a jacket on my left-side aisle seat to prevent any person with evil intentions from slipping in there whilst I was away, I headed off to the restrooms (or 'gents' as they were known back then) and thence to the foyer to peruse the cardboard boxes of chocolate-coated stale nuts and raisins we encountered in Chapter Four. As I loitered by the counter (I had no money and was merely window shopping) a somewhat older gentleman sidled up to me and attempted to engage me in conversation in a manner that today would be probably be viewed as rather creepy. Everyone of my age remembers hanging around outside A-certificate films waiting for strange men to 'accompany' them to the ticket office in order to gain admittance to films that required 'a responsible adult'. Anyway, this particular grown-up seemed harmless enough, and only wanted to talk about the movie. Clearly he was desperate to find someone with whom to share his thoughts and, as luck would have it, he found me. And so we talked a little about the movie – about William Wyler's direction and Heston's chest, and the stories of on-set deaths that always accompanied a genuine epic. And we talked about the first time he had seen the movie, back in 1959 in a cinema in Leicester to which he had gone with his wife, who was sadly no longer with us. Apparently she had been a big fan of 'Chuck' Heston (I had never heard anyone call him 'Chuck' before), and in particular his chest. I asked if she'd ever seen *Planet of the Apes*, in which his chest was equally prominent, and the man replied that she hadn't but that she did like *The Ten Commandments* even though he mostly kept his shirt on in that one. (Writing this conversation down now, it sounds a lot creepier than it did back in 1972; I think something is getting lost in the translation.)

After a while an announcement came over the Tannoy telling us all to gather up our chocolate-coated stale nuts and raisins and make our way back to the auditorium, where the second half of the main feature was about to commence. I worried briefly that the gentleman whose wife had liked Charlton Heston's chest would wish to accompany me to my seat, but no; he was right at the back on the right-hand side of the auditorium, and I was on a middle aisle seat on the left and so we went our separate ways. But as we parted he said something that has stayed with me ever since:

'He looks so young.'

'Who?'

'Heston. Chuck Heston. He looks so young.'

'Well,' I said, thinking myself very cineliterate and quite the film connoisseur. 'He *was* young when he made *Ben-Hur*. Comparatively. I mean, he was in his thirties back then. I think he's pushing fifty now. He looked a lot older in *Planet of the Apes*. Although his teeth looked the same.'

The man, whose name I can't remember (if indeed he ever told me), looked a little cross and disgruntled, as if I'd somehow blown the otherwise pleasantly nerdy conversation we seemed to have been having up until that point.

'Well of *course* he was younger then,' he said with a hint of exasperation. 'But that's not what I meant. I meant that my wife and I saw this film when it first came out, back before you were born, young man. And since then I've gotten older and she's passed on, and the film has clearly had a few too many birthdays of its own. But Chuck looks just the same. He hasn't aged a bit.'

And with that he headed back off into the auditorium to take his seat and (I imagine) resume a date with the dearly departed love of his life, who had been waiting patiently for him to return with chocolate raisins.

I thought about this a lot as the second half of the movie played – about the way that film had captured a moment in time but had continued to age itself. And I started to wonder whether the print of the movie we were watching there in the Hendon Odeon in the early seventies was the same print he and his wife had seen projected 15 years before in a cinema in Leicester. It almost certainly wasn't; *Ben-Hur* had enjoyed a widespread tenth-anniversary re-release in 1969, and the print we were watching was very likely newly struck for re-run distribution. But this print was definitely far from perfect (it did indeed look like it had celebrated 'a few too many birthdays'), and with every scratch and flicker that played upon the screen I wondered about the glamorous life it had led prior to winding up here for a Sunday matinee at the Hendon Odeon. Even in the relatively few years that I had been going to the cinema, I had become familiar with the jumps and bumps of films I'd seen more than once, in the same way that one becomes intimately acquainted with the scratches and needle skips on a well-worn vinyl LP. After a while I would come to recognise and cherish those defining marks, in the same way that one cherishes the lines on the face of a loved one who becomes more beautiful with age precisely because such lines tell the story of their life.

Today, films have discovered a form of cinematic Botox

that prevents such ageing. But, just as the timelessness of Dorian Gray's outer beauty led to the casual destruction of his inner soul, so the advent of ageless digital information has also allowed cinemas to throw off the last shackles of their responsibility to the audience, and indeed to the movies themselves. Compare the experience of watching that fragile and faded 30-year-old print of *Silent Running* as it was painstakingly escorted through the projector in Leeds to the experience of watching a perfectly colour-corrected and all-but-indestructible digital print of some family-friendly blockbuster which is misaligned on the screen from the outset but which the projectionist is never able to correct because he or she is too busy tending to the on–off switch in the next screen.

This is the engine of the modern multiplex: a computer programme with no memory of the past, no human interaction, no history, no soul. We did away with celluloid because it needed too much care and replaced it with a stream of digital information about which no one cares. We handed the control of our ticket purchases over to speak-your-weight machines only to discover that they were actually running the whole cinema. And while we were all so busy squinting at pointy digital images through smudgy 3-D glasses we didn't notice the lights going off in the projection box behind us . . .

'There's something magical,' the 60-year-old Steven Spielberg had wistfully told me in that 2006 interview, 'about having something as primitive-sounding today as twenty-four pictures a second moving past a shutter gate with a light beam projecting on a big silver or white screen. It's magic. And it's our forefathers. The films we love the most were made in this process. It was good enough for them, why isn't it still good enough for us?'

Why indeed?

THE END

ACKNOWLEDGEMENTS

During the writing of this book, I called regularly upon the expertise and assistance of others whose detailed knowledge of cinema is far greater than mine. Each of them contributed immeasurably to the finished book, and I would like to thank:

Linda Ruth Williams, my partner, friend and inspiration whose original ideas I continue to pass off as my own, and without whom I could not write a single coherent sentence. Ever.

Hedda Archbold at Hidden Flack, my trusted friend and colleague who speaks both Dutchish and Swedish, but who doesn't know how to say 'No, that can't be done' in any language.

Nigel Wilcockson at Random, who helped me find the book I was trying to write, and without whose excellent editing I would have come a real cropper on several occasions.

Gemma Wain at Random, for her meticulous proofing, and for using the phrase 'I love doing corrections!' in such a deadpan manner that I still can't tell if she's being ironic.

Tim Clifford, whose extensive Index is a thing of beauty, and is also arguably a better read – punchier, pithier, more elegant – than the book itself (read it and see . . .).

Bryony Dixon, Curator of Silent Film at the BFI, for explaining the difference between 'gun powder' and 'gun cotton', and for handling my manuscript with as much care and attention as a can of nitrate film.

Boyd Hilton, editor at *Heat* and one half of my favourite critical double bill (Floyd and Boyd), for leading me through the maze of box-office figures, and for knowing far more about screen ratios than I ever expected.

Kim Newman, for running his encyclopaedic eye over the manuscript and picking up several embarrassing errors en route, and for knowing the correct title(s) for *Saw 3-D*.

David Norris, the 'last projectionist standing', for his invaluable insights into a magical world of cogs, pulleys and dowsers that continues to mystify and amaze me.

Tomoke Yabe, for being my guide through a foreign culture, for introducing me to the joys of 'Engrish', and for making cakes that appear to have their own gravitational field.

And finally to Georgia and Gabriel Willams, for going to the cinema with their dad, and for being a credit to their mum.

INDEX

INDEX

British Academy of Film and Television Arts (BAFTA) 150, 221, 242
British Board of Film Classification (BBFC) 35, 203, 283, 301
British Film Institute 128, 183, 236
Brixton Ritzy, London 308
Brokeback Mountain (2005) 218
Bronfman Jr, Edgar 88
Brooks, Louise 147–8
Brooks, Mel 170, 177
Brown, Gregory H. 236
Brown, Ralph 24
Bruckheimer, Jerry 71, 73–4
Brynner, Yul 12
Bubble, The (1966) 139
Buffy the Vampire Slayer (TV series) 274
Bullock, Sandra 257
Burlesque (2010) 222
Burr, Ty 160
Burton, Richard 78
Burton, Tim 128, 156
Bwana Devil (1952) 134, 139, 154

Caché aka *Hidden* (2005) 278
Caddyshack (1980) 200
Caged Heat (1974) 235
Cameron, James 95–6, 99, 113, 126, 154–6, 162, 165, 235
Campanella, Juan José 246
Campbell, Alastair 181
Cannes Film Festival 42, 152, 250, 262, 273, 276–7, 280–1
　　Grand Prix 250
　　Palme d'Or 232, 262
Carnosaur 2 (1995) 235
Carousel (1956) 10
Carpenters, The 208
Carrizo Gorge, California 148
Carry on Cleo (1964) 78
Carry On Up the Khyber (1968) 206
Casino (1995) 219
Cave of Forgotten Dreams (2010) 165, 304
CCE, silver retention process 303
celluloid 1, 7, 9–10, 13, 57, 62, 69, 160, 194, 296–313
Censored: The Story of Film Censorship in Britain (book) 300
Chalte Chalte (2003) 282
Channel 4 117, 283
Chaplin, Charlie 86, 197
Chariots of Fire (1981) 226, 234

Chatroom (2010) 274
Cher 223
Churchill, Winston 289
Cimino, Michael 81–3, 85–6, 88, 90, 200
Cine Blitz (magazine) 281
Cine City Cinema, Withington, Manchester 143
Cinema Exhibitors' Association 9
Cinema Paradiso (1988) 287
cinemas
　　AMC Loews Boston Common 160
　　Astor Theatre, New York 132
　　Brixton Ritzy, London 308
　　Cine City Cinema, Withington, Manchester 143
　　Classic Cinema, Hendon, London 83, 174–6
　　Empire Leicester Square, London 122
　　Hyde Park Picture House, Leeds 296–7
　　Odeon, Barnet, London 248
　　Odeon, Hendon, London 308, 311
　　Odeon Leicester Square, London 103
　　Phoenix, East Finchley, London 43
　　Prince Charles Theatre, Leicester Square, London 7, 93
　　Regal Fenway, Boston 160
　　Scott Cinemas, Bridgewater, Somerset 10
　　Screen 1–5, Manchester 144
　　Vue Cinema, Shepherds Bush, London 192
CinemaScope 137–8, 153–4
Cinematograph Act of 1909 2, 4, 300
Cinématographe 132
Cinerama 138, 159
Citizen Kane (1941) 193, 197, 218
Clapp, Phil 9
Clarke, Alan 233
Clash of the Titans (1981) 154
Clash of the Titans (2010) 126, 154–8
Classic Cinema, Hendon, London 83, 174–6
Clements, Sam 307
Cleopatra (1963) 69, 77–81, 84, 86, 89, 94
Clerks (1994) 204
Clifford, Max 156
Cloverfield (2008) 255
Coen, Joel and Ethan 148
Color of Night (1994) 194
Comar, Etienne 246
Comin' At Ya! (1981) 140
Condon, Chris J. 141–2
Connelly, Jennifer 265, 273
Connery, Sean 172
Constantine (2005) 184
Conti, Tom 268

INDEX

INDEX

INDEX

INDEX